ANYONE'S SON

Anyone's Son

Roberta Roesch
with

Harry De La Roche, Jr.

ANDREWS AND McMEEL, INC.
A Universal Press Syndicate Company
KANSAS CITY

Portions of the song "Love Them Now" have been used by permission of Proclamation Productions, Inc. Orange Square, Port Jervis, NY 12771. Copyright 1970 by Richard K. Avery and Donald S. Marsh. From THE AVERY & MARSH SONGBOOK. Portions of letters to and from Harry De La Roche, Jr., have been published with the permission of Harry De La Roche, Jr. Family pictures used throughout the book have been published through the courtesy and permission of John and Arden Greer.

Library of Congress Cataloging in Publication Data

Roesch, Roberta Fleming.
   Anyone's son.

   1. De La Roche, Harry, 1958-   2. Crime and criminals—New Jersey—Biography.   3. Murder—New Jersey—Case studies. 4. Parricide—New Jersey—Case studies. I. De La Roche, Harry, 1958-   joint author. II. Title.
HV6248.D36R63   364.1'523'0924 [B] 79-11355
ISBN 0-8362-6608-0

CONTENTS

PREFACE

On a gray November Sunday in 1976 I was writing complacently at my desk when my husband came to my office and said, "I just heard on the radio that a family has been murdered in Montvale." Since Montvale is only a stone's throw from my home, that statement affected my life.

Soon, as I read newspaper reports and watched TV accounts, I knew, as a journalist and parent, that I had to get behind the scenes and try to understand what happened to the De La Roche family—and their young son, Harry, Jr. I had to find the answers as completely as I could to such timeless but timely questions as: Why do families go awry? What causes intrafamily breakdowns? How did this human tragedy start? And where is it going to end?

Most of us say (and really believe): "These things can't happen here!" But unfortunately figures are rising on homicides among families, and the problem is more widespread than we care to believe. To cite a few examples, in Louisiana two teenagers were accused of killing their father, stepmother, half-brother, and half-sister. In Kansas a fifteen-year-old boy was charged with killing his parents and younger brother. In New Jersey another fifteen-year-old killed his parents with an axe. On Long Island a twenty-three-year-old systematically shot his mother, father, and four brothers and sisters in their backs with a rifle. And in Texas a "model" sixteen-year-old—and a member of the Texas Girls Choir—knifed her mother to death.

In Montvale this human disaster happened to the kind of people who might have been the family next door, facing the crises and problems millions of families face. And given the same situation Harry, Jr.—the sole survivor—could have been the son of any of us, except for the grace of God.

As a first-hand narrative account (rather than a psychological or sociological study) much of this book is written from Harry, Jr.'s, viewpoint. Other sections are documented by a wide cross-section of people who knew Harry, Jr., and his family. Every fact and every event has been verified by more than one person.

In order to get the full story of this human tragedy, I've drawn on my direct involvement and personal observations—plus an exclusive agreement with Harry De La Roche, Jr., permitting me to be the only book author to talk with him in prison. I have obtained his personal story through hundreds of hours of interviews. During part of the time the jury was out deciding on its verdict, I was allowed to sit with him in his suicide watch cell.

In addition to hundreds of hours of jail interviews, I also spent a great deal of time researching private family papers and letters, unpublished and confidential files, lawyers' briefs, police records and official documents, court and judicial proceedings, and trial transcripts. I attended the trial from start to finish and drew from my own notes on that. And to gain objective insights I made every possible effort to talk to individuals on every side of this case.

Those interviews included extensive and in-depth sessions with relatives, family friends and acquaintances, neighbors, peers and classmates, teachers, clergymen, lawyers, jury members, law enforcement officers, the Bergen County Medical Examiner (and other physicians involved with the case), jail and prison inmates who associated with Harry, Jr., and staff members and students at The Citadel. In scattered instances a few individuals would not comment on the court case while an appeal was pending. In other situations persons who knew the De La Roches were reluctant to discuss the family because the topic had become controversial in the town where the family lived. Occasionally people requested anonymity or fictitious names.

Except for these few instances, literally hundreds of people reached out to give me help, so that now that my work is finished it would be an impossible task to name each one of them here— though often their names are obvious in the pages of this book.

For their special help along the way—and at every step of the way—I say "thank you" to them all.

ROBERTA ROESCH

Westwood, New Jersey
December 1978

We are parents, we are children
   and we're living here together,
But the way we treat each other is bizarre.
We must learn to see each other
   with the eyes of understanding,
As the hungry, needing people that we are.
   Love them now.
Don't wait till they've gone away.
Love them now, while they're around.
Touch them, hold them, laugh and cry with them.
Show them, tell them, don't deny with them.
   Love them now
Before they're just a guilty memory.
   Love them now, love them now.

Richard K. Avery and
Donald S. Marsh
From the Avery & Marsh Songbook

I

The Unbelievable Tragedy

1

It was Thanksgiving as usual in the Harry De La Roche home—and no one at the holiday feast that November 25 could have imagined in the wildest sense that in a matter of days Montvale, New Jersey, where the family lived, would experience the most unbelievable tragedy the town had ever known.

Nor could their neighbors possibly foresee that what looked like an ideal family in the Norman Rockwell tradition would be the center of a bone-chilling crime that would shake the foundation of the community and make people say for miles around, "This couldn't have happened here!"

A town of almost eight thousand in population, residential Montvale was justifiably proud of its consistently low crime rate in 1976. A suburb of New York City, the Bergen County community is bordered by Rockland County to the north, affluent Upper Saddle River to the west, and historic Old Tappan and River Vale to the east and south. Farther south is Hackensack, the county seat of Bergen, and a city that goes back in history to 1647 when Dutch settlers from Manhattan established a trading post there. Montvale's newer $100,000-plus houses are built away from the town's center, while the older, smaller homes congregate close to the village green.

The De La Roches' $50,000 home at 23 East Grand Avenue—a two-and-a-half-story red clapboard house with a tall stone chimney—was two blocks from the green. Tall maple trees that were losing their leaves shaded the corner lot, while a bas-

The De La Roche home in Montvale, New Jersey, after the murders.

PHOTO BY PETER KARAS, *THE RECORD*, HACKENSACK, NEW JERSEY.

ketball hoop and backboard lined the driveway behind the house. The totem pole in the backyard had been a Cub Scout project, and a broken slide and sandbox were abandoned nearby. Similar homes were scattered up and down the tree-lined street.

It was a special holiday that November 1976 as Harry, Jr., the eighteen-year-old son, was home for his first vacation since leaving nearly three months ago to start college at The Citadel in Charleston, South Carolina. In two days he'd be returning to the military school. But for the moment it was family and food—and talk of the high school football games—around the dining room table. Two other sons sat at the table, Ronnie, age fifteen, a high school sophomore, who'd been an all-star third baseman on a baseball team his father had coached, and Eric, twelve, a seventh grade student, who had played third base on a Little League team and who was now playing football with the local Mustang League. Some people called Ronnie "Chipmunk" because of his baby fat cheeks while Eric was often called "Dimples" since he had a contagious grin.

At the opposite ends of the table Harry, Sr., and his wife, Mary Jane, felt the sense of fulfillment most parents experience on a holiday when the first child to leave for school returns to the family circle. Even Lucky and Muffins, the family dog and cat, had found their way to the dining room and were lying at young Harry's feet.

Guests for the turkey and trimmings were Johanna and Ernest Ebneter, Harry, Sr.'s, mother and stepfather (Grandma and Pop Pop to the boys). Ernie, a tall, slim, gray-haired man, now retired from a job in the hardware department of a local Korvettes, spent most of his time in his Lodi home reading a wide variety of books and magazines. Ernie was also an avid coin collector, and nobody knew at the time that later there would be much debate about the fate of his coins. Johanna, whom everyone called Honey, was a sweet pliable person who'd had little formal education. She had thin brown hair with straggly bangs and her face looked noticeably careworn from the difficult life she'd led while working — and sometimes, doing laundry as a cleaning woman—to bring up Harry, Sr. Now, into her seventies, she still cleaned doctors' offices. But she didn't regret her life of hard work because Harry, Sr., and his family made everything worthwhile. Though Harry, Sr., was forty-four, she still thought of him as "her baby."

For Harry, Sr., the master of the house, life had been upward mobility since his early days in Weehawken, New Jersey, when he'd lived with his mother and grandmother. As soon as he was able, he worked at a variety of jobs until, at this point in his life, he was an administrator employed in the export department of Ford Motor Company in Newark. Six years younger than his wife—and also a few inches shorter—he was the unquestionable head of the house and a father who appeared to be close to his sons and something of a youth leader in sports. Away from his job he had won kudoes for his community work with the Boy Scouts, Masons, American Legion, Christ Lutheran Church, and Montvale Athletic League. A gun-oriented man, he spent many hours at a nearby rifle range where his three sons learned to shoot. In fact, exactly a week ago, Eric had received a certificate from the National Rifle Association for successfully completing basic rifle training. Harry, Sr., was proud of that since he wanted his boys to achieve. He ran a tight ship to encourage this and often disciplined them sharply. As Steven Madreperla, his boyhood friend, often pointed out, "He thought the way to love the most was to discipline your children."

Mary Jane, age fifty, a still pretty red-headed woman and a former model, now worked part-time as a district newspaper distributor a few hours every week. She subjugated herself to her husband and usually deferred to his wishes, while she found her personal identity in working for the town. Because of her dedication she was extremely well liked for the many hours she contributed to the Athletic League Auxiliary, Welfare Board, Chamber of Commerce, ACTION Committee, and local Republican Club. Just a few feet away from the table was a plaque which bore the inscription "April 25, 1976: In Recognition of Mary Jane De La Roche for many years of devoted service to the Montvale Athletic League."

That plaque summed up the family and the image they projected. But the image would soon be shattered and before

Thanksgiving weekend was over the half-carved turkey that was left after dinner would be a grim reminder of a holiday celebration they'd never have again. Not knowing, they talked of many things as they dined on the ecru lace cloth to the glow of an orange candle surrounded by fall flowers. But mostly their favorite topic was tall, lanky Harry, Jr., and their pride at having their oldest son a student at The Citadel.

Though Harry, Jr., was wearing his jeans while munching on a turkey leg, he'd been the faithful grandson and, after the high school football games, obediently put on his dress uniform to show his grandparents how he looked as a military cadet. Now they wanted to see him in his full dress garb, so later he'd phone a fellow cadet to see if that local student, who had driven home by car, had remembered to bring the uniform as Harry had asked him to.

"We brag about you to everyone," Harry, Sr., said, beaming, as he sliced more servings of turkey. "Somebody asked in church last week how you were coping with school and I told him you were doing great. I said, 'He's making out fine.' You're certainly proving everyone wrong who said you wouldn't last."

"You've always been a fine boy," Honey quickly put in. "And you know how much we love you and want you to make good."

From the other end of the table Mary Jane declared, "Everyone thinks it's wonderful that you're at The Citadel. Wherever I go people envy us because we have you there."

While the talk went on around him, Harry, Jr., had nothing to say since he had written from college that he wanted a real vacation and wouldn't talk about life at school until Thanksgiving night. Now he was thinking to himself that maybe he'd wait until Sunday. Or possibly he could put it off until his Christmas vacation, which was only two and a half weeks away.

It wasn't unusual for young Harry to keep his thoughts to himself because he was known to be a closed person who seldom showed his feelings. In fact, the entire family was not the kind of family in which the various members unburdened themselves to each other. Instead they were fairly rigid, and the atmosphere was never quite right for talking about the anxieties they sometimes felt inside. Harry, Jr., particularly kept a wall around himself, and when he had a problem he worked it out alone. His nails were chewed and bitten, and often he twisted his reddish brown hair and nervously rested his chin in his hands or fingered his ear when he talked.

At eighteen, Harry was six foot three inches and wore glasses with gold metal frames. In person he was far better looking than his picture on the living room mantel. He was also extremely well spoken for a person of his age, and though he'd earned average grades in school his intelligence was above average. People saw different sides of him, depending on what he showed, and while he was liked by some of his peers he was disliked by others. "Everybody can't love you," he'd say, "and you can't love everyone either." He was always looking for people, though, and after he bought his car it seemed he was constantly driving around searching for friends or peers.

As the conversation continued Harry, Jr., in teenage fashion, wanted to be excused. As soon as he could he left the group and headed for one of the loves of his life—his 1965 Ford Mustang.

"I decided to go out and look for someone," Harry, Jr., would say later on. "But I guess everybody was home that day. I couldn't find anyone."

When Harry, Jr., went out to his car there was no way to foretell that as he'd left the table he'd had his last Thanksgiving with the traditional family circle. And as he drove over the railroad tracks by Montvale's village green he had no way of anticipating that before his vacation ended he'd jump from a car on November 28 and yell to a cop by that green, "I just found my parents and my younger brother dead and my middle brother missing."

But according to Patrolman Carl Olsen, a heavy set cop with sandy hair, who was making checks on businesses, Harry was observed at 4:10 A.M. on November 28 going through a stop sign at a Grand Avenue intersection. As Olsen watched him through the fog, the car Harry was driving, which was Mary Jane's, made a right turn to Park Avenue and headed toward Park Ridge, a town just south of Montvale.

"As I was about to pull the car over," Olsen stated, "Harry stopped and jumped from his car in front of Davy Jones Locker, a local tavern and hangout."

"Quick, come up to my house," he hollered. "I've just found my parents and younger brother dead and my middle brother missing."

Later Harry would challenge the report that Olsen pulled him over and insist that as soon as he saw the cop he cut around the police car and spun his tires to stop him. He did this to gain attention, he said, since the horn in the 1970 Falcon didn't work. This was the first of several conflicting statements and claims.

On their encounter, however, Olsen tried to calm Harry down. But before he could get the full story Harry jumped back into his car and called for Olsen to follow him for the three blocks to his home. Quickly the cars sped around the green and up the hill to the house, while Olsen radioed for Patrolman Fred Parodi to respond as a backup unit.

Harry and Olsen arrived at the house before Parodi came and entered through a side door that had a porch light outside. Then Harry led Olsen through the living room halfway up the stairs.

"They're up there," he said, pointing to the bedrooms. Then he returned to the living room and slumped down on the couch, while Olsen continued up the stairs.

Olsen entered the master bedroom first. But the horror of the scene he saw was sufficient to turn the stomach of even the toughest cop. He took a quick look at another room, then telephoned for more help.

"When I entered the first bedroom on the left I noted a bed with a large amount of blood on the pillow," he reported. "Mrs. De La Roche was lying there, apparently dead. I noted the other half of the bed also had some blood stains."

"As I looked down the hall into the other bedroom I could see a twin bed and two human legs. Harry, Sr., was dead on the bed. He was lying face down. Eric was face down on the floor by another twin bed."

Next Olsen ran down the rubber-padded steps and confronted Harry, Jr., with, "What the hell happened here?"

"I was out till four o'clock on my last night home," Harry

replied, "and when I returned I noticed the porch light by the side door—the door that we always use—wasn't lighted as usual. That gave me a very strange feeling that something might be wrong. My premonition grew stronger when Lucky, our dog, didn't come to meet me as soon as I entered the house. When I started to go upstairs to my room, I found my parents and brother."

"And what did you do after that?" Olsen asked.

"I left the house immediately and got into my mother's car to go to Montvale Police Headquarters to report what I had found. No one was there, so I tried to use the emergency call box by the door. When I couldn't get any connection I left to go to the Park Ridge Headquarters to the triboro radio dispatch room. That's where I was going when I saw your car."

"But who would commit this crime?" Olsen queried. "Who would do this terrible thing? What would the motive be?"

"I don't know," Harry responded as he chain-smoked cigarettes. "All I can say is my father learned that my brother used drugs. They had a big fight about it and Ronnie told my father he'd bury him under his bed."

By then Patrolman Parodi, who had answered the backup call, was also at the house, so while Olsen checked for Ronnie, Parodi sat with Harry. When the search for Ronnie was unsuccessful Olsen alerted Chief George Hecker and Detective Michael O'Donovan of the Montvale Police and brought them up to date on what was going on. The officers also notified the Bergen County Prosecutor's Office and Dr. Lawrence Denson, the county medical examiner.

"Next we'll send out a teletype to pick up Ronnie and hold him," Olsen assured Harry. "In the meantime come out to the kitchen so I can ask you more questions."

At the kitchen table beneath a plaque saying "What little boys are made of—frogs, and snails and puppy dog tails" (and by a telephone sticker that read "In Case Of Emergency Call ————") Olsen questioned Harry.

"You're not a suspect," he explained. "But we need information you can give us."

At 4:30 A.M., when this questioning began, Harry seemed

relatively calm as he told how he'd last seen Ronnie between 6:30 and 7:00 on the previous night when he'd dropped Ronnie off at the Nottingham Apartments to make collections for his paper route.

"After that I went all over," Harry related to Olsen.

As other officers began to arrive they filed, one by one, through the cluttered living room with Mary Jane's wedding portrait hanging by the fireplace. An embroidered sampler on a wall said "After the Rain Comes the Sunshine." The maple and slipcovered furniture was strewn with sneakers and books, and pendants in the upstairs hall boosted Pascack Hills High School, Seton Hall University, The Citadel—and the Mets, Jets, and Knicks. In the kitchen Olsen told Harry it was routine procedure to ask him to empty his pockets. Harry, wearing blue jeans, combat boots, long johns, an Army field jacket, and a blue tee shirt saying "El Cid," complied immediately. As he emptied his front jacket pocket he removed a pipe and plastic bag containing an ounce of marijuana.

"I guess I'm in trouble now," he said. "I could be kicked out of The Citadel for having marijuana."

Next Harry pulled out $78.76 in bills and change from one pants pocket—and $501.00 from another.

"That's lots of money," Olsen declared. "Do you always carry this much?"

"Last Monday I cashed in my coin collection and got sixteen hundred dollars," Harry revealed. "I needed the money for tires for my Mustang and I also bought a new watch. The money I'm carrying is what I have left."

"We found Ronnie's wallet on his night table," Olsen pointed out. "It had ten dollars in it and his glasses were on top of it. Isn't it strange if he ran away that he didn't take his glasses and money?"

"Not really," Harry answered. "Ronnie only needed his glasses to read, and he would have ample money because he was selling drugs."

While Harry was being questioned, Det. Michael O'Donovan, a well-spoken officer who'd been with the Montvale police ten years, was placed in charge of the town's investigation. Inv. Frank Del Prete, a Bergen County officer whose face was distinguished by a large brown mustache, took charge for the county. Det. Sgt. Louis Parisi of the New Jersey State Police handled things for the State. When he looked at a person his penetrating eyes seemed to see right through you. The yard was roped off, and a sign went up. It said CRIME SCENE—KEEP OUT.

At 4:30 A.M. it was still too early for neighbors to be up and out. But soon the curious would gather outside while law officers on the inside tried without very much success to put together the incongruous pieces of this human puzzle. Before onlookers assembled the Bergen County medical examiner arrived to do a scene investigation and pronounce the bodies dead.

Dr. Lawrence Denson, a graying and balding fairly slight man, had been a medical examiner since 1957. For the past ten years he'd been chief M.E. and, in this capacity, he did scene investigations of approximately twenty crime scenes a year. Upstairs in the pale blue master bedroom he found Mary Jane in yellow pajamas. She had been shot twice in the head. There were traces of blood on the floor leading to the hall and, in the hall, there were droppings of blood that led to Ronnie and Eric's room.

In the boys' room, with the football wallpaper and books on camping and crafts, Dr. Denson found Harry, Sr., surrounded by blood and shot twice in the head. As he lay in Ronnie's four-poster twin bed Harry, Sr.'s, body was clad in a white undershirt and tan plaid boxer shorts. Bruises and abrasions indicated he might have been dragged. On the floor beside the other twin bed Eric's body was lying in a pool of blood. A wastebasket with the "Happy Face" sign was directly back of his head. A sign on his desk read "Keep Out."

On further observation Dr. Denson noted that Eric's tee shirt was blood-soaked, and though Eric had been shot three times it appeared that he had put up a fight and was struck on the head with a blunt instrument. Despite the fact that he had been shot Dr. Denson said Eric had died from massive lacerations of the brain. The medical examiner ascertained that the time of all three deaths was approximately 3:00 A.M. and that the bullets fired came from a small caliber pistol. All of the bodies were warm. No rigor had set in.

For the rest of the day more officers continued to arrive. In addition to Olsen and Parodi—and O'Donovan, Del Prete, and Parisi—others who worked were Inv. Stephen Kunz, Lt. Joseph Dodd, Inv. Kenneth Nass, Det. John David, Det. Charles Lange, all of the Bergen County Prosecutor's Office; Det. Sgt. Paul Likus and Det. Leroy T. Smith of the New Jersey State Police; and Det. James Ewings, Lt. Anthony Scarangella, Officer Joseph Marigliana, Chief George Hecker, and Capt. John Hanna of the Montvale Police Department. As the officers were shown around the crime scene they were advised to search the house for the possible presence of persons in hiding. At 4:35 the officers set up an internal command post in the kitchen. Later a secondary command post was established at the Montvale Police Headquarters.

After Olsen asked Harry to empty his pockets, O'Donovan gave him a pat down search. All of his possessions were looked over again and his wallet and car keys were taken. An examination of his clothing and fingernails disclosed no visible presence of blood. Next, O'Donovan, Parodi, and Olsen checked the basement, ground floor, and second floor. They found no indications of ransacking or forced entry. Olsen asked Harry if the house had an attic so the officers could look there. He reported Harry answered "No." But Harry denied this answer.

"There was a door in the upstairs hallway that went to the attic," he explained later. "Two laundry baskets were kept by that door. You'd think the cops would open the door and see the attic steps. If you looked you could also see the stairs from my bedroom closet.

"While the cops were going through the house I saw my dog Lucky," Harry added. "At first he wouldn't leave my mother. Then when the cops finally got him away he acted terribly confused."

As darkness turned into daylight Olsen and Parodi canvassed the neighborhood to see if any of the residents had heard or seen anything. Other officers checked the garage and other exterior premises. They also looked through the shrubbery and leaves to determine whether Ronnie had committed suicide. Later in the day a neighbor said she'd heard a car idling loudly between 11:00 and 11:30 P.M. for half an hour or so. She stated it left squeaking its tires. But when she looked out of her window there was no sign of the car. As part of the search the three cars belonging to the family—Harry, Sr.'s, 1970 green Ford station wagon, Mary Jane's 1970 white Falcon, and Harry's 1965 Mustang were inspected. A mysterious note in Harry's car (which Harry had no knowledge of putting there) said "Call Grandma" and "Call Police." There was also a jacket with a fur hood on the seat of this car.

While different aspects of the search continued Harry was told that he was to have a routine paraffin test. The paraffin test is one that is used to determine whether a person has fired a gun in the recent past. While the test was being considered an officer brought in equipment. But before Harry took the test other officers declared it wouldn't be necessary.

By that time—a little before 6:00 A.M.—Capt. John Hanna, a friend of the family, who had been with the Montvale Police Department for a total of 21½ years, came to the house to talk to Harry and do what he could do. He'd last seen the De La Roches on the previous weekend when the De La Roches and Hannas attended a Montvale Athletic League game at Port Jervis, New York. After the captain talked to Harry he told him he would be taking him down to the Montvale Police Headquarters while the officers worked at the house.

"You're not a suspect," he emphasized, "and you're not under arrest. We'll make some calls to try to find Ronnie and you can give us some names."

The time was approximately 6:30 A.M. as Harry and Captain Hanna drove to the Montvale station, with Harry resting his chin in his hand and having little to say. They parked by the door of the building, and as they went inside Harry began the longest, most eventful day of his life. Only twelve hours later, Harry, who'd never been in court or trouble with the law, was arraigned before Judge Fred C. Galda of the Bergen County Superior Court and charged with four counts of murder. Following the shocking arraignment, he was quickly escorted from Montvale headquarters—past TV cameras and reporters and away from the waiting crowd—and driven to Hackensack to Bergen County Jail.

No one could believe what had happened. No one knew what lay ahead.

II

The Harry De La Roche Family

2

Exactly eighteen years, two months, and five days before Harry was led into Bergen County Jail, a five-story fortress-like building that looks like a medieval dungeon, he was born Harry William Frederick De La Roche, Jr. (later shortened to Hatchy). The date was September 23, 1958, and the place was Englewood (New Jersey) Hospital. He was three-and-a-half months premature, and since his mother's pregnancy had been threatened with miscarriages he wasn't expected to be born alive.

But Harry survived his early birth and eventually went home to Lodi, an industrial, melting-pot borough. When he was christened with his father's full name, Steve Madreperla, his father's boyhood friend, became his godfather—and "Uncle Steve." Harry's first home was on Avenue F, a few doors from the Ebneters' house. Then after six years at that address he moved with his family to Montvale and settled in the Grand Avenue home. Though Harry was too young to know it, prior to the move to Montvale, the paternal and maternal sides of his family were an intricate study in contrasts. In fact, as far back as three generations, the seeds of family conflicts began a slow growth into tangled roots.

On the maternal side, Harry's great grandfather, George Bronson Howard, had been a weaver of stories. He was a playwright—and playboy—and at various times he lived in Paris Nice, London, Baltimore, and New York. He traveled with a theatrical crowd, and the family liked to tell stories of how he'd

16

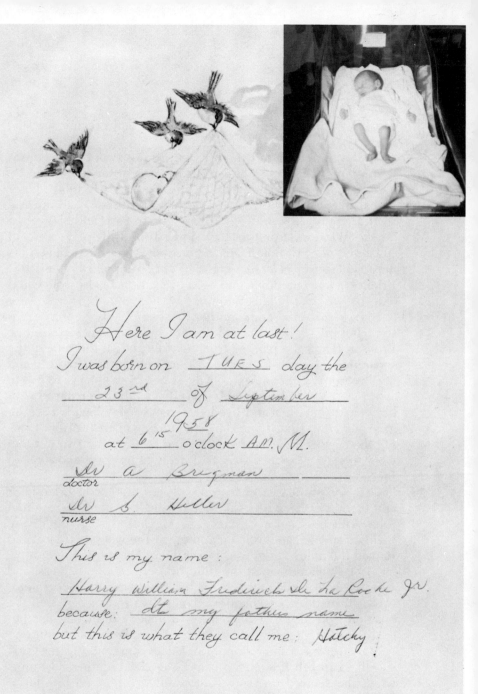

Here I am at last!
I was born on TUES *day the* 23rd *of* September
1958
at 6:15 *o'clock A.M. M.*

Dr. A. Bregman
doctor

Dr. S. Heller
nurse

This is my name:
Harry William Fredricks de La Roche Jr.
because: its my fathers name
but this is what they call me: Hatchy!

Harry De La Roche, Jr., at the Englewood Hospital, October 1958.

come home from parties and jump into the shower while wearing his top hat and tails.

By the time George Bronson Howard was twenty-one he was writing magazine stories about a secret agent for the State Department. This was a new type of hero for the early 1900s. Later he expanded to romances, essays, plays, criticism, and musical revues. He was a vaudeville impressario in Paris and a librettist for the Winter Garden in New York. Two of his plays were in collaboration with Booth Tarkington and David Belasco, and his most famous work *The Red Light of Mars* was published in 1913. Friends who remember him recall that he was also connected with the original Follies Bergere.

Harry's maternal grandmother, Margaret, was George Bronson Howard's daughter. While she was growing up George Bronson Howard separated from his wife and, at the time of the separation, Margaret's mother, Margaret Horan Howard, and her brother George moved to Edgewater, New Jersey, to live in an artists' colony along the Hudson River. Margaret stayed with her eccentric father and lived in Greenwich Village where he gave her a fine education. They spent many hours together reading the classics and poetry aloud, and because the two of them were so close Margaret absorbed many of his ways and took on theatrical mannerisms she never really lost.

Occasionally Margaret stayed with her mother in Edgewater and on one of her visits she met Ronald Francis Greer, son of John William Greer and Mary Jane McGrath Greer. Both were highly respected and well liked in town. But when Margaret and Ronald fell in love there was much discord about it. Edgewater, an old-fashioned town at the time, was critical of outsiders, and George Bronson Howard, with his cosmopolitan background, was disturbed by his daughter's small-town romance. When she married Ronald Greer her father ultimately disowned her because, according to his terms, she'd married beneath her status.

Margaret was a show-stopper in Edgewater, and in later years she liked to tell the story of how she shocked the old-timers when she showed up at an Edgewater ball dressed in a form-fitting harlequin outfit with a black swagger stick. Eventually she was accepted in town, and while her husband worked as a traffic manager (and indulged in ponies and booze on the side) she stayed home and raised three children—two sons, Ronald and John, and a daughter, Mary Jane. Ronald, the oldest, served in the Air Force during World War II and was killed while in the Pacific. John was thirteen years younger than Mary Jane.

Mary Jane, a real Titian beauty, grew up to be photogenic. Her first career choice after graduating from Dwight Morrow High School in 1943 was fashion design since she was an excellent seamstress. But because of her striking long red hair she became a model, then switched to a job teaching sewing in a West New York Singer Sewing Machine shop.

On the paternal side of the family, Johanna Ebneter, or Honey, was Harry's true blood grandmother. But Ernie was not his blood grandfather, though Harry didn't know this in his early years. Later, when he was old enough, his mother told him his father was an illegitimate child and that Honey had raised Harry, Sr., until she married Ernie when Harry, Sr., was fourteen or fifteen.

Honey's maiden name was De La Roche, so Harry, Sr., took that surname. As for the rest of his lengthy name, Harry was for his real father; William was for his grandmother—Wilhelmina Strudel De La Roche; and Frederick was for his grandfather—Frederick De La Roche. Wilhelmina, better known as Gram, often took care of Harry, Sr., when Honey had to work, and both of the women in the fatherless home took pride in Harry, Sr., and would do anything for him.

They couldn't protect him, however, from the taunts he got because he had no father, and some made it a point to mock him and call him a bastard. Occasionally he'd carry a knife in order to protect himself.

In stark contrast to the taunting was his friendship with Steve Madreperla, an all-round student and athlete. After graduation from Rhode Island University Steve started what became a successful career in the fire protection industry. He was also a deacon in the church he and his family attended, and since Steve had had a father who had been extremely strict, some people believe that Harry, Sr., felt that strictness played a part in his friend's success. He wanted success for his sons, too, so he may

Young Harry, Jr.

Harry with his uncle John Greer on Easter, April 17, 1960 in Montvale.

Harry, Jr., with Grandmother Greer in Montvale, December 1960.

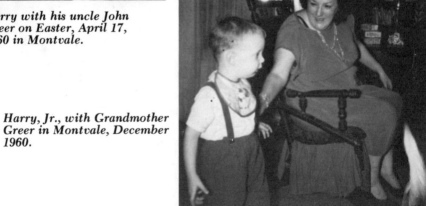

have patterned his role as a father on what he thought had started Steve on the right track in life.

Honey Ebneter had two brothers—Chris who lived in Wee-hawken and John who resided in Union City. Chris lived close to Honey and had children around Harry, Sr.'s, age. But Harry, Sr., never went to their house, either because he had been told he wouldn't be welcome, as an illegitimate child, or because he felt he'd receive that reception if he appeared at the door. Steve Madreperla played there, however, and was a good friend of the family, and Steve recalls that on one occasion when Harry, Sr., was twelve he cautiously approached that house for the first time in his life. From that day on he and Harry, Sr., began their lifetime friendship. But Steve was aware—and has sometimes said—that Harry, Sr., grew up with much hurt and, because he had no father, had a special need to be very strong and secure.

Following Harry, Sr.'s, graduation from Weehawken High School in 1950 he worked in a factory that manufactured Christ-mas tree balls. Then in 1952 he enlisted in the Navy and served on the destroyer—the *Douglas H. Fox*—during the Korean War. When he returned to civilian life after four years he took a job in West New York as a serviceman for the Singer Sewing Machine Company. On that job he met Mary Jane, who was then working for that company.

Before they were married in 1958 Harry, Sr., switched to his first job with Ford. The year they were married he was twenty-three and Mary Jane had just turned thirty. In the fifties that was "getting on" when a girl wasn't married.

History seemed to repeat itself, too, because the Greer fam-ily, as a whole, did not take to Harry, Sr. Mary Jane's father particularly opposed him and tried to prevent the marriage by telling his daughter again and again, "There's something about that man. . . .

"I won't attend your wedding," he warned, "if you marry Harry De La Roche."

Margaret Greer interceded, though, and when she saw the marriage was on regardless of the family's feelings she insisted that their daughter be escorted down the aisle and have the wedding she wanted. After a storybook wedding, on the surface at least, Harry, Sr., and Mary Jane honeymooned in Niagara Falls before settling down in the little house on Avenue F in Lodi. Soon Mary Jane discovered she was pregnant with Harry, Jr.

Six years later the De La Roches, now a family of five, made the move to Montvale, prompted by the fact that Margaret Greer—the owner of the Montvale house—was now a widow who needed someone to live with her. When she'd first moved to Montvale from Edgewater her son John—who works in field engineering for General Electric—lived with her and supported the household. Later he married Arden Mallè and they moved into their own apartment. But he still helped his mother financially, and together he and Arden did what they could for her.

Arden, a graduate of Green Mountain Junior College, was a slight, petite, attractive woman with wavy brown hair that came to her shoulders. She worked as a bookkeeper in the area and ran many errands for Margaret. John was tall with short-cut hair and a casual, fun-loving manner. But both Greers had a serious side and a real concern for people. In fact, when they'd been married awhile and were settled in a house they took teenagers from broken homes into their home in Maywood.

Although the Greers did all they could to take good care of Margaret she eventually needed someone to live in her house with her, not only because of money, but because she had several health problems that required many medications. Since she needed this kind of help—and her daughter Mary Jane and her family needed more space—the maternal side of the family got together and planned that Harry, Sr., and Mary Jane would sell their Lodi home and move to Montvale to help take care of Margaret and to assume full charge of the house. A financial arrangement was drawn up, making Margaret and the De La Roches joint tenants of the house and specifying that on Margaret's death the house would go to Harry, Sr., and Mary Jane.

The move to Montvale was a step up the ladder from living in industrial Lodi, and Harry, Sr.'s, initial expenditure was turning it into a two-family dwelling, so his family and Margaret would both have privacy.

To give his mother-in-law privacy, Harry, Sr., was more than anxious to turn the living room and den to the left of the front entrance into a two-room apartment for Margaret. He also put in a tiny bath. Usually Margaret cooked for herself on a hot plate in her room.

The kitchen was part of the De La Roche quarters, and Mary Jane made the dining room the family's living room.

Because she was so good at sewing Mary Jane decorated the house with chintz. She also furnished the De La Roche's quarters with braided rugs, books, plants and flowers, and lots of photographs. Since the dining room had no fireplace she went out and bought a fake one and placed her wedding painting above it. As soon as the boys grew older the family filled the basement with toys, a pool table and trains.

And while the boys played there for hours, no one anticipated the horrible discovery that basement would someday reveal.

3

As I look back from where I am now to the stories my mother told me I suppose my premature start in life may well have been the first imperfection in the perfect family image my father hoped to create. He always wanted the best for his sons from our earliest days and, certainly, my plucked-chicken look wasn't what he had in mind. But I guess all parents have great hope, especially for their firstborn, so my mother kept records of my progress for the weeks I was hospitalized. I later saw my baby book, and when I got to four pounds and five ounces she wrote (with an exclamation point), "He's out of the incubator today. We can *have* him when he weighs five pounds!"

By the time my parents brought me home my father was working for Ford, and since he was ambitious he'd already enrolled in Seton Hall University and was going to college at night.

As a father Dad had strong ideas on what a boy should be, so as long as I can remember he was strict and conservative. In a way I was like a proving ground since I was his oldest son.

I was short and thin as a child and, for my first few years, I was plagued with medical problems and my share of misadventures. My biggest problem was hearing and my ears were so sensitive that even the click of a light switch would start me screaming in pain. I also had a constant sore throat so by the time I was four, I was back in the hospital for an ear and throat operation. The following year I was hospitalized for bronchitus and breathing problems. Because of these experiences I was afraid of doctors, and whenever I had to have a shot two people had to hold me down. I can still remember those needles. And I'd get so sick on the way to the doctor's my father would have to stop the car so I could get out and throw up.

One misadventure that sticks in my mind is barely escaping an accident with a bulldozer in Lodi. A demolition company was tearing down brick buildings and since there were piles of bricks around that people were free to take, my mother and a friend were collecting some to build a patio. Unbeknown to them, I wandered away, and when a bulldozer was so close the driver couldn't see me I caught my foot in a layer of bricks and couldn't get it loose. Luckily, my mother's friend heard me scream and rescued me just in time. That same day I touched a bees' nest, and a bee stung me on my eye. Then, later, at my grandparents' house my grandfather swung me around playfully, and I accidently hit the other eye on the side of a table. That *wasn't* a very good day!

In Lodi I had my first beating up and, also, my first experience with female temper tantrums. It happened when a girl got mad and hit me with a baseball bat. At home I encountered a temper, too, because my father, along with his discipline, had a violent temper. I learned very early that he'd hit first and then ask questions later. If he wanted to teach me a lesson when I did something wrong he'd whip me with a Navy belt that had a metal buckle. Another punishment, since I was short, was picking me up by my hair. For minor offenses he'd put me in a chair and not let me move for two hours. My mother sat on the side-

lines and acquiesed to him. But when the two of us were alone
she taught me preschool skills and little prayers and blessings
like "God is great, God is good. We thank him for our food." She
was self-taught and an avid reader and when she was reading a
book she would get so involved in it the house could fall in on
her.

My father's strictness and punishments showed only one side
of him, because he was loving in his own way and he had my
well-being at heart. Whenever he could he'd spend time with
me—playing ball and that sort of thing—and some of my earliest memories are the walks in the woods that we took. For
years everybody who knew me would say, "Just take Harry out
in the woods and he'll be satisfied."

Some of my other happiest moments were spent with my dog
Flip, and I soon discovered, as the saying goes, that a dog can be

Harry, Jr., and Ronnie in 1964.

Harry and Eric in 1965.

a man's best friend. I've never forgotten the heartbreak I felt when my mother put Flip in a pound and said, to make it easier for me, that she'd taken him to a farm. That didn't help my heartbreak at losing my best friend, so after I was despondent for a week, she tried to get him back. Unfortunately, he'd been taken so my parents promised we'd get a new dog. Later we found Lucky, a lovable mutt who resembled Flip, with his long black hair and curled tail.

While we were still in Lodi Ronnie was born on March 24, 1961. He was outgoing from the first and my mother used to tell me he was known as "The Mayor of Avenue F." because of his talkative ways. When Eric was born on May 21, 1964, our family was complete, and according to my father's hopes, I was earmarked to be the example for the other two boys to follow.

I remember how excited I felt the day we moved to Montvale because I loved my Grandmother Greer—and I knew she loved me back. In fact, more of my happiest moments were the times I spent with her. I liked to go to her quarters, and since both of us loved to read I'd lie on her bed by the hour while she read out loud to me. She could tell many fascinating tales, and while she lived in the house the neighborhood kids would come and sit by her fireplace while she told eerie stories in her theatrical way. Before she told the stories—and when nobody saw her do it— she'd put what we called "magic" into the fireplace. Then when her stories got to a punchline the "magic" would explode. We loved to smell her incense, too, and we thought she was wonderful. But my father hated that incense and felt my grandmother was odd. She was a fairly good artist and sometimes she wrote poetry. I still have a valentine she made on which she printed the verse:

A valiant young man rides a coal black steed
My knight in shining armor, noble indeed.
It is Prince Hatchy and he is my love.
Brave as the eagle, tender as the dove
As roots the tree, close clings the vine,
So doth my heart to thine entwine
Charming Prince Hatchy, be my Valentine.

Grandma Greer and Grandma Ebneter liked each other a lot, so we'd all spend our holidays together with Uncle John and Aunt Arden. As far as the De La Roches went, we never had any contact with my grandmother's brother Chris, and we rarely saw her brother John who eventually moved to Paramus, New Jersey, from his Union City home. We called this uncle "Big John" simply because of his size. He had a son called "Little John" who was called by some people "Tough John." There was also a daughter Margie. She and "Tough John" both had children, so I have some second cousins.

On the surface our lives appeared to be good, and in our Christmas picture for 1964 we looked like the ideal American family people thought we were. But beneath this pleasant picture a war raged in our home. On our side, my father, as I've said, disliked my Grandma Greer's ways. From her side she objected to how he was bringing us up. His word was law and when we'd ask "Why?" he'd say "Because—and that's it." Sometimes he'd throw me down the steps for doing what he didn't like, and once when we visited Uncle John and Aunt Arden he swung at me and missed. But he swung with such strength his hand was bloody from the impact of hitting the wall. In fact, the ring he was wearing made a permanent hole in that wall. Sometimes his temper got so out of hand we'd be punished for something we didn't do just because we were there. Later, if he felt that he'd been wrong he'd try to make up for it, and just by the way he did something for you you'd know that he was sorry. He never said "I'm sorry," though. That wasn't in his nature. Because of their differing set ideas he and my grandmother fought, and soon there were constant conflicts—and open battles—between them. My mother, in a passive way, tried to keep peace in the house.

Two years after we moved, however, hostilities grew so bitter my grandmother conveyed her interest in the property to my Uncle John. This complicated financial matters, and there were even more fights. My father openly disliked Uncle John for standing up for my grandmother, so as relationships dwindled, Uncle John always visited us when my father wasn't home. My father also refused to keep on getting my grandmother's medica-

Harry, Jr., Eric, Mary Jane, and Ronnie in Lodi, New Jersey, Easter, April 1965.

Christmas, 1964. Harry, Sr., and Mary Jane; Harry, Jr., Ronnie, and Eric.

Ronnie, Harry, Jr., and Eric in April 1966, Montvale.

Mary Jane, Harry, Eric, Ronnie, and Harry, Jr., May 1967.

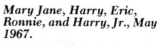

tions, so either Aunt Arden or Uncle John had to do that again. Eventually my mother yielded completely to my father's wishes and I'd hear my grandmother on the phone asking Aunt Arden to take her to the doctor's because my mother had indicated she couldn't continue to do that. Sometimes she'd call Aunt Arden for food and on those times she'd say, "Mary Jane 'forgot' my things when she shopped today."

I was too young to do anything, but I wasn't too young to see that, slowly but surely, Grandma Greer was being forced out of the house. I heard more fights than my parents knew, and later, when I was older, I learned that on one Saturday night my uncle and aunt were served with a summons instituted by my parents, stating my mother and father were taking my Grandma Greer to court to get her out of the house. There were many legal hassles I didn't understand. But I know, among some other things, my father itemized his expenses for taking care of the house from the time we moved to Montvale till he started the legal action.

Finally the matter was settled without going to court. But the day my black haired Grandma Greer, with her wise and loving ways, went out of the Montvale house for good, something went out of my life. Uncle John found an apartment for her close to where he lived, but my parents wouldn't take us to visit and I never saw her again. She used to phone my mother and beg her to bring us down, and after she died—with a broken heart— one closet in her apartment was filled with wrapped-up presents for Eric, Ronnie, and me. There were gifts for every occasion since she'd moved out of the house, in the hope my mother would change her mind and let her see us again.

That day never came, however, and when she died she said in her will: "I leave nothing to my daughter for reasons known to her and to me." Everyone but my father went to her funeral, however, and for a short time after that we occasionally saw Uncle John and Aunt Arden. All of us went to visit them when their daughter Kimberly was born since, in some ways, she was the daughter my mother never had. Later, at Christmastime one year, we all spent an evening together. But after that visit to their home, my parents never called them again.

For years I didn't see the Greers and they never heard from

me—until I phoned one Sunday and said in a broken voice, "Uncle John, this is Harry. I'm at the Montvale Police Station, and Mom and Dad and Eric are dead."

Harry, Jr., and Harry, Sr.

III

Growing Up
in Montvale

4

I enrolled in first grade in Montvale as the smallest, lightest boy in the class. But since I had gone to kindergarten in Lodi the school suggested that—possibly—I could skip first grade.

"Nothing doing," my mother declared. "He may have enough school problems because of his small size. We don't want him moving into a class where he'll be the youngest boy, too."

Unfortunately my parents were right about troubles over my size because, before I could fathom what was happening I was the butt of first-grade jokes and the kid who was always picked on and beaten up by others. When I had to wear glasses—by third grade—the kids mocked me even more. I didn't like talking about this and letting people know, so if my parents were aware of it they didn't do very much. Or maybe they thought I ought to fight back so I'd grow up to be strong. I wasn't one to fight, however. Instead I tried to please. But no matter what I did or said I got the reputation of being a whipping boy.

As the harassment continued from one year to the next, I'd often pretend I didn't care and hide behind different fronts. Some people said I was independent. Others called me shy. But no one ever got a look at what I was inside. Years later my pastor told me I had a strong will to survive and that, despite difficulties and defeats, this ongoing struggle to survive would see me through many hard times.

One of the best things in grammar school was meeting Steve Mahoney, now a student at Embry-Riddle Aeronautical University in Daytona Beach, Florida. Steve is freckled-faced and ruddy and looks like the Irishman he is. He's one of the persons who knows me better than anybody else. We became close friends in Boy Scouts and had good times together. Occasionally, with other fathers and sons, we'd go on good overnight trips. Sometimes, though, I was ribbed in Scouts, just like every place else.

I learned to love the woods early, but I took a taunting for this because I'd rather walk in the woods than participate in other things. One time some older campers tied me to a tree and left me in the woods for an hour before they thought they'd better come back and at least untie my legs. I decided to show them I could handle things and work out problems alone so when they started untying my hands I retorted, "I'll do this myself." Then I ran further into the woods and worked for about two hours trying to scrape the ropes off with a sharp rock I found. I got all sweaty and disheveled. But that was part of the stubborn streak some people saw in me. I stayed in Scouts for several years—till I was a senior in high school—and when I got out during that year I was ready for the rank of Junior Assistant Scout Master. During the years that I was in, I was in the Leadership Corps and, also, the Senior Patrol.

People sometimes called me a loner because of my avid reading and the way I liked to sit by myself and bury myself in a book. I was a speed reader from the word go and could read a thick book in no time. When our family would go to Uncle Steve's to swim and have a cookout I'd swim with the rest of the kids awhile. Then I'd go off and read. I also got interested in collecting coins because of Pop Pop's collection. In fact his collection was so valuable he kept part of it at our house because he felt it was safer there than in his home in Lodi. Little did he know what would happen to some of his coins in Montvale! As soon as I was able I got a paper route and also did some household chores for a widow on our street. That, plus coins from my family, helped me build a collection. My father was proud of what I collected and told me never to sell the coins—unless I was desperate.

At home there were often good times in spite of my father's

Baseball season in Montvale,
June 1970. Eric; Ron in his
American Legion team
uniform; Harry in his Huck
team uniform.

Harry, Jr., in his Boy Scout
uniform in Montvale, July
1973.

conservative ways and constant strict discipline. Mostly I think of my mother cooking or baking cakes—except when she was sewing or working for the town. She used the money from her part-time job distributing area papers to help pay for family vacations to Cape Cod or the Jersey shore. She wanted me, as the eldest, to understand my father, and she was the constant buffer as we sat at the dinner table. Whenever she sensed his mood would be bad she'd say before we ate, "Don't bother your father tonight."

When we did talk at the table one thing I learned very early was never to mention a girl's name in front of the rest of the family. Once I told my mother about a girl in school. But Ronnie and Eric heard the name and couldn't let it alone. I never mentioned a girl after that and I never brought one home.

We didn't bring many people home, except for one best friend. My friend was Steve Mahoney. Ronnie's was Andy Cannon, a personable guy with light blonde hair and a John Denver haircut. Eric played with Mitch Mulligan who lived a few blocks away. Those three were always welcome almost any time. But sometimes Steve feared my father, and when he heard him yelling he wouldn't come inside. In the summer we'd often camp in our yard or on our screened-in porch. And we'd go to block parties in Montvale as a family of five.

Church was big in our family, so we'd always sit together at the Woodcliff Lake Christ Lutheran Church where, among other volunteer jobs, my father was president of the congregation for one period of his life. Ronnie and I were confirmed there, and on confirmation day Grandma Ebneter sent me a card on which she and Pop Pop wrote, "We're proud of whatever you boys do. All of our love forever." I joined the youth group at the church and, also, the basketball team. I had great respect for the coach of that team, a builder named Roger Anderson who was head of the Luther League and who had a great way with kids. He called me the fastest runner he'd ever had on a team. I also liked Pastor Roy Nilsen, and I guess what I liked best was the way the church kids didn't put me down as much as others did. This wasn't allowed to happen. They more or less rooted for me.

Athletics weren't a big thing for me, but they were tops in our family. My father coached many Little League teams and played on a men's softball team. He was also manager and umpire for the Montvale Athletic League. I wasn't the natural athlete that my two brothers were, but I went out for Little League to comply with my father's wishes. I didn't really like it, though, because, as my father's son, I sometimes felt I got the brunt more than anyone else.

One of my other interests was the Park Ridge Pistol and Rifle Range—which my father always encouraged. Guns represented power to him, but my mother really despised them and tried her best to ignore the four my father kept in the house. As always, though, she deferred to him, so his rifle was usually under their bed. His 9-mm. automatic pistol was always under the mattress, and a loaded hi-standard .22 caliber pistol was in his bedside table. The other pistol—a .38 caliber revolver—was generally in his bedroom closet. My mother didn't know about that for a period of several months. As the eldest in the family, I was the first of my brothers to learn how to handle guns. I became an accredited marksman and, eventually, while in high school, I sometimes taught at the range. Usually I went there weekly, and after I finished shooting I'd pick up lead and shells. Later my brothers did this, too, so our house was full of shells.

My parents were all for our outside activities since they did so much in town. But nevertheless school marks came first, and if our marks were low my father made us stay in at night until the next report card. He always wanted to pull us up to our very best and highest, so whenever we had a low mark he'd give us work on his own and then he'd check on us every night and keep track of the progress we made.

The year I entered the seventh grade and Fieldstone Middle School I met a couple of other friends who have stuck with me. One was Bob Gantt, a real straight boy whose family is very religious, and who's now in college on a scholarship at Rutgers University. He had two sisters and a brother, and his family was very close. His mom was always nice to me, and she always had time to talk. Bob never came to my house, but I went to his a lot, and I liked the ways his family sat down and talked out their problems together. I'd often ride my bike there just to be with

Bob, and when he'd be on his mowing job at a farm across the street I'd give him a hand with that. When he had a couple of acres to mow he couldn't fool around so I'd take a sickle and cut down grass that had grown too high to mow. Once I got blisters all over my hands, and he never forgot about this. Bob knew how much I liked the woods, so whenever he'd go hunting he'd asked me to go along. Sometimes I'd go and take pictures. But I could never hunt animals. I couldn't shoot anything.

My other friend at Fieldstone was Jeff De Causemaker, who'd later have many ups and downs while he was growing up. He was the son of a school principal and we had some good times together, though I still had the problem of being mocked out that began in grammar school. Unfortunately, it almost increased when I got to the middle school because, instead of being short, I grew faster than anyone else.

The fact that my growth came all at once was a new cause for ridicule, and the more I'd try for acceptance the more I'd be the scapegoat I had always been. The athletes, especially, ganged up on me, and sometimes when I'd get to gym they'd all try to push me around. Once when they pushed me against a locker, Bob Gantt got really mad.

"Fight back," he begged, "at least just once. Let them know that you can!"

By the time I got to eighth grade two things happened to me. My height and the way I was growing up began to make me feel strong. At last I was getting too tall and too big to have my ass beaten all the time. I'd also decided once and for all to work problems out on my own and never let anybody know how I felt inside. I was starting to feel more capable—and better about myself. Then one things shot me down again at graduation time.

I picked up some kind of virus—I don't remember what— but I missed the second graduation practice and should have missed the third. My parents wanted me to go, however, so they'd see me graduate.

"Why don't you try?" my father said. "You'll probably be all right."

I forced myself to go that day and practice with my class. But the stage lights were so terribly hot they made me feel sick and faint. Then as the faintness continued I blacked out on stage. I couldn't help it that I was sick, but the kids wouldn't let me forget it.

So that was another mock out that followed me from middle school to my first year at Pascack Hills.

5

When I began my freshman year I tried once more for acceptance. But I soon found out that wasn't to be, because Pascack Hills, a regional high school with approximately thirteen hundred students, was full of cliques and castes.

I was still in a gangling stage—while getting my present height—so many of the kids who had mocked me for years still made me the butt of their jokes. Some just took it for granted that I was the one to harrass. Others said I was "different." Unfortunately this was emphasized because of the stringent dress code my parents insisted upon.

While most kids dressed in bell bottoms or jeans (and this made them part of the crowd) I had to wear straight-legged cotton pants when I left the house for school. My father would say "Dress correctly"—and that was the final word. In church we always wore jackets and ties and then we'd get laughed at for that, since all of the other kids we knew came in sports shirts and slacks. As time went on my brothers could dress the way they chose. But I couldn't wear my jeans to school until my junior year—and then only once a week. I saved money from my paper route, though, and as soon as I was able I bought eight pairs of bell bottoms at a neighbor's garage sale. After that I bought my own clothes, so my parents had to let me wear them. I liked to wear army jackets because they were comfortable, and I also started to wear combat boots since they were rugged and tough.

Some people called me a military buff because of those army clothes.

I was an average student during high school years, and one of the teachers I remember most was a man I had for American history in my junior and senior year named David Dierker. He was young and good looking in the "tall, dark, and handsome" way, and he was also an assistant football and baseball coach. I always got along with him, and I raised my hand a lot because he was a teacher who allowed no ridicule. I liked my English teacher, too, and I'd pull a few zingers there. Her name was Nancy Harmon, and she was attractive and young. Because I fooled around in her class she gave me the nickname O.B., though I never knew what O.B. meant—unless it was short for Obnoxious. But she was a very good teacher and always said this in fun.

The only sport I tried was track, as a freshman and sophomore. But I continued with baseball on a Montvale Athletic League team in order to please my father. I stuck with this three years in a row, but in my senior year I wanted to give up baseball and go out for the soccer team. My father said, "Join baseball." But, in one of the few times in my life I went against my father, I joined soccer instead.

Generally, instead of athletics, I preferred to stick with my reading, and as I got into music I especially liked the Beach Boys and some Led Zeppelin records. My favorite group was one called Cream that originally came from England. They did a song called "White Room" which I think about and play a lot. I had a great love for animals and they were attracted to me, so when I'd go to people's homes it always seemed that the animals sensed a friend had come to the house. Because of this love of animals I got the reputation of never hurting anyone or harming anything. One family I knew owned several raccoons, and I would go over to feed them. Another had a gigantic dog—and that dog would put his paws on my shoulders and, then, look down at me. Later when I got a job as a gas station attendant I was dubbed Dr. Doolittle because when a car pulled up with a dog I could not let the car drive away until I petted the dog.

I looked around for a gas station job as soon as I was able

because I wanted to buy a car and I needed to earn money for that. It was a high point in my life, and a really big day for me, when I landed a weekend-and-after-school job at a Garden State Parkway station. Elated, I rushed home with the news about my new employment. But my father was furious when he found out that all I knew was I had the job—and no further information. Jeff De Causemaker remembers the scene.

"Why didn't you ask questions?" Dad hollered. "Why didn't you get details? What about insurance and raises? Didn't you ask *anything?*"

"There's a right way to get a job," he announced, "if you want to get anywhere."

The year that I turned sixteen I joined the Civil Air Patrol with Steve and Vinnie Trojan, a guy I met at the rifle range. Vinnie, who went to Park Ridge High, was slightly younger than I. But he was another person I got along with well. We learned about the military in the C.A.P. and I really enjoyed seeing the films and going on an annual two-weeks' trip to McGuire Air Force Base.

We lived by rules at our house during my high school years and one of the things my father did was have what we called his "Spring Cleanings." Whenever the spirit moved him he would check our rooms, and he'd spend a long time in each of them searching through everything. He was very strict about magazines, so he'd always check them out, and if he found *Playboy* or *National Lampoon* he'd take them to the garage so they could be carted away. When he wasn't around, however, Ronnie would rescue the copies and cut out all of the pictures. Then he would put the magazines back and my father wouldn't know the difference until the next "Spring Cleaning."

One of the rules I hated most was having to get in early when my friends could stay out later. In my freshman year at Pascack Hills I had to be in at 8:00. Yet when Ronnie was a freshman he could stay out till 11:00. As always, I was a proving ground and subjected to the stiffest rules. When I was a junior in high school my curfew was 10:00 P.M., and even when I was a senior I had to be home by 11:00. This often caused more ridicule among certain people I knew.

"No Smoking" was the order of the day—in the house and my mother's car. My father knew that I smoked cigarettes after I started high school, but he was opposed to all smoking since my mother had had a cancer scare and been advised to stop smoking. She was told she'd had cancer at one time—though later her doctor insisted she'd never actually had it and he wouldn't be interviewed for this book. After she coughed up blood, though, she was hospitalized for a while and all of us were led to believe her illness had been cancer. That's why when we brought up smoking my father would always say, "Look what happened to your mother. We don't want it to happen to you."

Drinking in the house, or in any of the cars, was a "no-no" till we were eighteen. But since I looked older than my age, I had been able to buy booze from the time that I was fifteen. When I bought my car I kept my beer there. Then Steve and I, or other friends, would go down by the railroad tracks, since that was where the younger kids used to smoke and drink. Once when my parents were planning to stay out of town overnight, I thought I'd throw a beer party and ask some kids to my house. But the folks came home unexpectedly and arrived exactly five minutes before I brought in the beer. Luckily I could chuck it and stay out of trouble that way. Another time Dad found Ronnie with beer, but I took the blame for it. Then after he yelled at me for a while I put it in the refrigerator and said, "Okay, it's yours." He fussed a little while longer. But then he let me go—maybe because on second thought he decided finding a six-pack was better than finding pot, though if he'd known where to look he might have found pot, too.

As the drug scene increased in the suburbs, 90 percent of the kids in our school had tried drugs or were smoking pot. When you could show you had some it was a means of acceptance, and if you had hard-to-get stuff you went up in people's eyes. There was pot at most parties and you went out to smoke in cars. My father never asked me if I touched pot or drugs. But he always made it *extremely* clear that no son of his would *ever* smoke pot or take any kind of drugs. We knew if he ever caught us he would be tempted to turn us in. And once he said that he'd shoot us if he ever found us with drugs.

I'll never forget one evening when I had my mother's car, and while I was driving some kids around some of the guys were smoking pot, and another had cherry cigars. We also had beer and wine in the car, and the wine wasn't closed all the way. Somebody kicked it over while we were fooling around and, later, when my father checked the car he asked me what he smelled. At first he asked if he smelled pot. But I told him it was cherry cigars, and he accepted that.

I started pot as a junior, and in the beginning a friend of mine knew a guy who bought it for me. Then, after I got my job pumping gas I met some dealers myself. I smoked the most as a senior. But I wasn't deeply involved. It was only a temporary escape and couldn't cure everything. Once I had some stuff in my room when my father announced a "Spring Cleaning," but Ronnie was able to get there first and hide my papers and pipe. If he hadn't, Dad would have busted me in one way or another. Usually I kept my equipment in a fishing tackle box in my closet. I'd put the pot in the bottom and leave open fish hooks on the top. There was also a piece of loose molding above my closet door, and since it had space behind it you could shove stuff in there. It seemed that Dad checked everything. But he never thought of the molding or the bottom of the fishing box.

Ronnie began experimenting with drugs when he was a freshman at the Hills. My parents never knew this, nor did they know how he would change when on his eighth-grade graduation, they gave him a beautiful and expensive card with Rudyard Kipling's "If For Boys." They addressed it "To Our Ronnie" and dated it June 18, 1975. Inside, the lengthy message began, "If you can keep your head when all about you are losing theirs" and ended with "Yours is the Earth and everything that's in it. And—which is more—you'll be a Man, my son."

Both Ronnie and Eric had paper routes, and Ronnie always had money. My mother would sometimes question that because, when she'd check his newspaper records he hadn't collected for weeks. All of the people on his route liked him for his outgoing ways. He was also popular with other kids, and though certain persons around the town thought he was a wise guy the way he'd fly by on skateboards, most people summed up Ronnie as a

Ronald De La Roche.

regular everyday guy. He played the clarinet in the school band, but he didn't like that much. It was something he felt he should do to please my mother and father.

Ronnie and I became quite close during my senior year and we used to help each other out in any way we could. When I got my car he'd work on it, too, and if he knew there was beer in the trunk when my father went to check he'd always get it out of the car and into a hiding place. We'd also wear each other's clothes, and I would drive Ronnie places. If he was too late getting in, or if he'd partied too much, I'd try to get him upstairs to his room without letting my father see him.

Eric, at twelve, was a nice little kid who was always getting into mischief. He wasn't very big on school but he certainly liked to play football. He also played the saxophone and got quite good at it. The thing I'll always think about is the way he wanted to be like me—because I was the big brother. He could be a real scrapper, too, and he'd fight if he thought he had to. In fact, one friend of the family said that sometimes Eric could be so tough you damn near had to kill him in order to make him cry. But most of the time he was an imp who was always trying something.

I remember the way both Eric and Ronnie would rush to the back of the church so they could be first on Sundays to shake Pastor Nilsen's hand. Then, just before he got to the narthex, they'd rub their feet on the carpet so they could give him an electrical shock when he reached out his hand. Eric and his friend Mitch Mulligan were a Tom Sawyer and Huck Finn team, and once when they were eleven, they got into trouble with the cops when they broke into an old garage that they thought was abandoned. There were no signs of life around it, and when they found a collection of coins they pretended they'd found ancient treasures and buried the coins in the woods.

Eric wouldn't tell my mother. But Mitch told his mother about it and since Mrs. Mulligan happened to know that somebody lived in that house she explained to the boys that they had been stealing and had to return the coins. They took them back to the owner and explained why they had done it. But the owner was angry about it and immediately called the police. My parents didn't know about this till Mrs. Mulligan told them.

None of us told these things at home because we were all so closed, and a lot of the time it always seemed that all of us did our own thing. I couldn't really talk to my father and, even though I realized he had our well-being at heart, our conversations through the years would usually follow this pattern:

"Dad, is it all right if I do this?"

"No, I don't want you to do it."

"But why?"

"Because."

"But because why?"

"Because—and that will be it!"

As I grew older I understood how ambitious he was for us and so when he said I had to do something I usually complied. Sometimes my mother would tell him that he was being too tough, and once or twice I heard her say he'd drive us away someday. Occasionally, we'd have a thing where I'd assert myself and, after I did this a couple of times, he slacked off a bit. I particularly remember one evening when I asked for the car.

"Absolutely no!" Dad told me, not looking up from his paper. "The weather is bad, and it's raining. You're not going anywhere."

At that point I showed my stubborn streak and answered with "Everyone is going—and I'm going too."

"Oh, no you're not!" he retorted, as he put his paper down.

"Oh, yes I am," I answered, and I went out of the door.

I walked to where I wanted to go and when I returned in two hours he didn't say anything.

Ronnie and Eric stayed scared of Dad. But I wasn't as afraid after that, and eventually, as I grew taller, he couldn't pick me up by my hair. In fact, the last time he hit me, the most he could do was grab my shirt and pull till the buttons ripped off.

6

Even though I was not in a clique and the center of a crowd in high school I had some friends—and I owned a car—so I wasn't the withdrawn loner some people said I was. Neither would I do anything to make or buy a friend. It depended on where people's minds were when they said I would.

Whenever I had money to spend—and I did through working and drag racing—I'd like to be the one to treat when I was buying for myself. I'd also lend people money if they were my friends. But let some defiant kid come up and ask me for a quarter I'd tell him exactly where to go and say "Get out of here." Bob Gantt ate lunch with me every day during our senior year and whenever he heard somebody say I'd buy food to buy a friend he'd call that a great big farce.

Steve and I continued to be friends and through Steve I met Ed Mahoney—though they were not related. Ed was the oldest in a family of eight, and he's now studying engineering at the University of Hartford. He has a good personality and I liked hanging out with him. Sometimes he'd introduce me to girls and include me in some of the parties. Later we worked together at the Garden State Parkway station. Once Ed got really mad at me when I thought I'd try to be funny and jump on the roof of a Volkswagen he was driving to a party. I didn't mean to do it, but I made a dent in the roof. Luckily Steve was with me, and he fixed it right away. Then I gave Ed two cans of beer to make amends with him. But when he pulled out from where we were stopped he turned left where he shouldn't. A cop was nearby and pulled him in and when he saw the beer in the car Ed was in for it because he was only seventeen, below the legal drinking age in New Jersey.

Another guy I knew pretty well from school—and from pumping gas—was a quiet boy named Ed Zott who went to Wittenburg College after we finished high school. His family had a swimming pool, and they let kids come there a lot. I saw him most in my junior year, and we used to make films of our antics around the swimming pool. It was during my junior year that I started hanging out with Park Ridge kids instead of people from Montvale and the gang from Pascack Hills.

Park Ridge is more blue collar than the town of Montvale is, and the kids I met were more friendly. They didn't put you down. One that I got along with well was Jeff Fritts, originally from Montana. Sometimes in his coveralls he looked like a burly hillbilly, and when he referred to his parents as "My mama" and "My daddy" it always seemed out of character for his size and his sturdy build. He liked car racing and mechanics and our idea of fun was to drive around in a souped-up car looking for things to do. We used to go up to Alky Hill, a parking place in Orangeburg, New York, that was much like Inspiration Hill on television's *Happy Days*. Sometimes it was so crowded it was as hard to find parking spots as stools at a popular bar.

While working at my gas station job I met other Park Ridge people, and one family I felt close to was the Hennessys. I met their daughters—Patty and Vicki—through guys the girls were dating. Then I began going to their house, not only to see Patty and Vicki but to see Mrs. Hennessy, too. She was always kind to me, and we'd talk in a down-to-earth way. Sometimes I'd carry in her groceries for her, since her family was large. I'd also push her two-year-old up and down the block, and she could never get over the way I'd leave the other kids to take a small child for a walk. But, along with loving animals, I also liked small children.

Jeff Bickerton was another friend that I made down in Park Ridge, and we were drawn together because of our interest in cars. I went to his house often, and sometimes he'd come to mine. But he always thought my father was a crab, and he felt the look he gave him said, "What are you doing here?" It was just as easy to go to his house and I always felt comfortable there. His sister Allison was friendly and his father, a deeply religious man, would sit and talk to me. In fact, I'd often stay at their house, even if Jeff wasn't home. His mother shared our interest in cars—or at least she acted that way—and before I left for college, while I was at their house, she came outside to see my car after 11:00 P.M. so I could show her the engine and the work I'd done on it.

I usually got along better with adults than I did with kids, so I spent a good many hours at Roger Anderson's house. He was the basketball coach at the church as I mentioned previously, and he and his wife were active in working with the teens in town. They had a very beautiful home perched up on a hill and I'd either walk or bike up there many days after school. Mrs. Anderson was easy to talk to and sometimes I'd open up and tell her about the harassments and mocking out in school. When I'd sit on her steps and wait for her, if she wasn't home, she'd say I always reminded her of either a little lost puppy, or a huge St. Bernard, who just wanted to be around people. Coach Anderson used to tell me that when the kids said "Let's get Harry", I ought to go over and punch them so they wouldn't do that again. But I still wasn't really a fighter and I found it hard to fight back.

One of the cars the Andersons drove was a Pontiac Custom S—and I really wanted to buy that car from the time I was sixteen. I'd bug Mrs. Anderson about it, and we'd talk cars by the hour. Then finally both of the Andersons agreed to sell me the Pontiac since I had worked for the money and wanted it so much. My father wouldn't have agreed with the price, so I asked the Andersons to promise not to reveal it to him. Owning that car was a high point and I soon got it all souped up, so I'd have a loud car with squeaking tires that I could use for drag racing. I gained a reputation for driving very fast and some people called me a show-off for bragging about the car. I didn't know when I turned seventeen that I'd only have a year of driving. But the driving and racing I did that year was a happy time in my life. It also gave me status to be able to drive kids around.

The Pontiac's days were numbered, though, because soon after I bought it one of the doors was damaged in the parking lot at our church. I got the license of the car that hit it. But the cops never took any action, and I had to replace the door. Later when I had it parked in the driveway by my house an ex-cop, who was coming home drunk, turned the corner by the house and hit my

Harry, Jr., and Ronnie in 1976 with Harry's Cobra.

car with his van, knocking out the driver's side. The car was totaled and the incident was hushed because of the ex-cop's involvement. I finally collected insurance after a wait and some hassle. But my father wouldn't let me use the car after the way the van hit it. It sat in the garage a little while, then a junk dealer took it away.

As soon as I could I bought a new car—a 1969 Cobra Ford. But this one came to a bad ending, too, because in the middle of my senior year a gang of kids who were out to get me vandalized it one night. I'd parked it in an area right by our screened-in porch. But when I went out to get it the kids who'd sneaked in at night had punctured the tires, put metal in the engine, damaged the brake linings, thrown paint remover all over it, and cut the hoses and wires. We thought we knew who did it. But it was never proved, and I came out on the short end, since insurance didn't cover the damage. I was frustrated and angry, and my father said, "If I find those kids I'll blow their brains right out." Steve thought he was mad enough to do that, and Ed Mahoney said later on, "Right after that my friend and I came to the house to get Harry and saw Harry's father in the window. When he saw two guys coming toward the house he came out to see who we were and he looked as though he'd be ready to kill if we were the ones who'd damaged the car. I guess when you have guns around there are times when you're ready to use one."

My next car was a Ford Mustang, and this was such a powerful car it had a racing car safety belt. It was hard to control, however, and at first I was almost afraid of it because of the power it had. Mrs. Angela Blair, who lived up the street, let me use her garage for free, and I spent many hours there working on that car.

As I reached the end of my senior year I was starting to change a bit, and when there was too much "Let's get Harry" or taunting and mocking out I finally started to fight back for myself and stand up to the kids who harassed me. One day while I was on the job at the Garden State Parkway station a kid kept calling me an idiot and bad-mouthing me all day long. When he went too far I stepped on his foot. Then he punched me close to my glasses. After that we got into a physical fight, but usually I wouldn't slug someone unless it was for defense.

Another time I was walking to Steve Mahoney's house, and two guys with three knives between them made some comments to me. When I answered back one of the kids threw a knife that came so close to my eye it broke the lens of my glasses. That made me really livid since my eyes are so bad already I don't need anything more. I picked up the knife and turned the guy around. Then I saw a second knife—one for throwing and one for stabbing—so I put the first one in his back and said, "You drop that second knife right away or this one is going in you."

The other kid came up from behind and put the third knife in my back, but before anything really happened both of them ran away. We reported the incident to the cops but they never did a thing. My father was so mad, however, he threatened to shoot both of the guys if he ever caught up with them.

Despite my new defiance and attempts to stand up for myself, I was still anxious to win approval and please my family and friends. I let my hair grow longer and I bought myself gold-rimmed glasses to replace the heavy black-framed lens my parents always bought for me. I never smile in photographs because of my crooked teeth, so my yearbook picture was terrible and I hated everything about it. These days I know I'd have hated it even more than I did if I'd had a way to foresee that that awful yearbook picture would someday be shown everywhere in newspapers and on TV.

A few of the kids at Pascack Hills signed my yearbook for me. But some of the things that some kids wrote weren't for my mother to read, and, luckily, I worked things out so I never had to let her see it. My senior year had its good times, in spite of the various harassments, and so when I'm asked, "Have you ever been happy?" I say, "When I was a senior." I had mobility with my car.

And, sometimes as a senior, I felt like a top person, too.

Harry De La Roche, Sr., on graduation from Seton Hall University.
PHOTO COURTESY OF STEVEN AND DORIAN MADREPERLA.

Harry, Jr's., high school yearbook picture.

7

By the time I graduated from Pascack Hills in June 1976 I'd considered several different careers in my middle and high school years.

As a Scout I'd joined the Medical Explorers and served as vice-president, so for a while I'd occasionally think of following an interest in medicine. As a member of the Explorers I'd visit various hospitals for observations and films. But the operations turned me off, so I wasn't too sure of that field. I thought of switching to veterinary work, since I loved all animals. But I had to rule that field out, too, because I knew I could never put any animal to sleep. Two of my favorite subjects were history and government, so political science appealed to me, and I thought about that quite a bit.

I also liked the military from my Civil Air Patrol days, so in the end the decision was made that I should go to The Citadel, a South Carolina military college located in Charleston. Before we settled on that school I sent out applications to the Air Force Academy near Colorado Springs, the Military Academy at West Point, and the Naval Academy at Annapolis. I also applied to Ramapo College, a state school near my home, just so I'd have an ace in the hole if I couldn't go anywhere else. Later Ramapo accepted me and put me on a waiting list.

In the meantime my father was happy and proud that I talked of a military college, and he and the rest of the family began to pool all their contacts in the hope they could get me accepted. My parents joined a political club, and my father tried to pull some strings with his contacts in the community and at work. Grandma Ebneter cleaned for an influential doctor who knew Nelson Rockefeller so whenever she worked for this doctor she put in a word for me, too.

Everyone felt disappointed when the service academies rejected me because of my poor vision and the fact that I am legally blind except when I'm wearing glasses. When I applied to those schools, though, I signed a card that listed six other military schools—and The Citadel was among them. Later, when the academies turned me down, they sent all the information I'd given them to the six other schools. As a result, The Citadel wrote and accepted me. My family immediately felt this was it since a Citadel graduate receives a commission in the Army, Navy, Air Force, or Marines, depending on his choice.

As I considered The Citadel I wasn't sure that I wanted to go since it wouldn't be exactly the same as attending the academies I'd chosen. But it was the only acceptance I had, and I really couldn't take the chance of getting into Ramapo because of the waiting list. Besides, my father was terribly proud of The Citadel acceptance, and he wanted me to go so much I wanted to make him happy instead of letting him down. I reasoned I might like military law, and I'd be a second lieutenant. Little did I know where I'd go when I left The Citadel!

Not knowing, I decided to major in political science, and I looked ahead to more freedom than I had while living at home. I'd also be with new people, and I'd be in a different position than I'd been in all my life. Some people were shocked when I mentioned going to The Citadel, though my history teacher, Mr. Dierker, said he'd expected a choice like that because, with my army jacket and boots, he thought I seemed like a candidate for the military life. He also felt I was disciplined and willing to submit to that. But Bob Gantt had misgivings and didn't feel I was competitive enough to go to a military school.

"Military academies base everything on intensive competition," he warned. "They're always out running and drilling and doing all kinds of sports. I can't really understand you going to that kind of school."

Another person who couldn't understand was Paul Mulligan, Mitch's father. He had attended a military school and was now in the Marine Reserves. He said I wasn't like anyone he'd ever known in the service.

As I heard these viewpoints I had even more mixed feelings. But the real misgivings took over when I talked with Wilbur Boyce, a former Citadel cadet who lived in my area.

Wilbur, an intense and intelligent person, had gone to The Citadel for a year. It had been a good year, too, because he had played three different sports and was third highest in his company in grades. He wrote for the college paper, too, and he was outstanding in many different groups. But he left at the end of his first year because he decided the military wasn't for him after all.

My mother knew about Wilbur and thought I should talk to him, so she telephoned his mother and asked about the college. Mrs. Boyce sensed that my mother was concerned and wasn't sure I belonged. But she said my father felt I should go so that was where it was at. She asked Mrs. Boyce if Wilbur would talk to me about school. We didn't know each other well, but when I went over to his house he spent a long time with me.

"The Citadel is a very necessary institution for the right person," Wilbur explained. "But it's not for everybody, and I honestly believe that the system is as hard as—or harder than—any in the United States.

"It's so tough you'll see people in formation and parades pass out when it's hot," continued Wilbur. "And sometimes you'll get so tired you won't know what to do.

"But if you slack up things will get worse, so you have to keep on going."

"What happens when you get there?" I ventured.

"The freshmen go down to what is called a cadre period. This is a time when you train, drill, and run—and learn how the Fourth Class System works. As a freshman you'll be in the Fourth Class System, and it will be difficult. You'll find upperclassmen will play games with you because that's part of it.

"For example, you'll be walking along and an upperclassman may ask you who won the Civil War. The conversation may go something like this:

'Who won the Civil War?'
'The North did, sir.'
'You know where I'm from?'
'No, sir.'
'Well, I'm from North Carolina. What do you think of that?'
'No excuse, sir.'
'Who won the war?'
'I say the North did, sir.'

"When that happened to me," Wilbur pointed out, "the upperclassman racked me (the term for doing push-ups) because I wouldn't say the South won the war. I might have answered him that way but I'd seen someone the day before agree the South won the war and that was the end of it. That freshman got himself under their thumbs and they have no respect for that."

"What about the meals?" I inquired.

"There are about ten people at every table, and when the servers bring in the trays a freshman is delegated to go and get the food and serve the upperclassmen. My first meal was a quarter of a pancake because there were four freshmen at the mess and we had to divide the pancake. Sometimes before you can eat they make you learn certain things like the order of the buildings or the number of trees on the parade ground. But after a while you can eat, and you can get enough, too. If you heap anything on your plate, though, you're expected to eat it. And God help you if you let them know you don't like something—like grits.

"The school has a strict honor code," Wilbur went on to say, "and if you're caught lying you can be thrown out of school. You never, never tell a lie that can be easily checked on.

"You also have to be prepared to be inspected all the time. They look at your shoes and your belt buckle, and if you have the worst looking ones they make it a point to shame you and let people know about it."

"Don't worry, I know all those things," I said. "I'll shine my shoes and stuff."

"Well, in case you think you know everything," Wilbur said sarcastically, "don't go there with that attitude. It's the attitude you bring with you that determines how you'll make out. If you really show you're trying, you won't get as much hassle and embarrassment, even if you're not very good. And when you do something really well they can make you feel ten feet tall."

I mulled over Wilbur's warning as I spent the rest of the summer working at my gas station job and fixing up my car. I went out with Steve in my spare time, and Ronnie and I continued to be close, even though we were different and had different groups of friends. Ronnie was running with a new crowd, though he kept his old friends, too. But when he wasn't in summer school he was smoking on the railroad tracks or down at the bowling alley, a popular Montvale hangout for many of the kids in the drug scene.

Jeff De Causemaker, who had been my good friend, was becoming Ronnie's friend, and Jeff had a reputation for being involved with drugs. He was an excellent bowler, though, and he wanted to be a pro, and that was one of the reasons he was down at the lanes so much. I worried about my brother, however, and when he would ask me things about pot, I'd tell him he'd better watch out. A couple of times in August he asked me to buy some for him. But, again, I said, "You watch it. I'll help you with other things."

I kept my promise to Ronnie, too, and before I left for school I gave him all kinds of identifications that would show that he was old enough to buy beer and things like that. I kept my driver's license and Social Security card. But I gave my brother everything else, like my driving permit, rifle instructor's card, and all the insurance cards for cars I no longer had.

Two weeks before it was time for college I gave up the gas station job and got all my clothes in order. Then my last day home I cleaned out my dresser so Ronnie could move to my room. Since he'd roomed with Eric up till then he wanted a room of his own.

On my last night home I made a trip to the Bickertons to say goodbye. Jeff and Allison were both away and, because he gets up early, Mr. Bickerton was ready for bed. Before he retired, however, he wished me all the luck in the world and asked if I felt I could handle what he referred to as hazing. I answered, "Yes, I think so." But later he told Mrs. Bickerton he somehow got the feeling I was under some kind of a strain and didn't want to go.

I stayed at the Bickerton house for three hours and held their cat in my lap while I talked to Mrs. Bickerton and asked her to come out to the driveway so she could see my car. Before I left I promised that I'd come back in my uniform when I came home Thanksgiving. Then she asked me to make a mark for my height and write my name on a doorway.

I printed "HARRY 8/16/76"—and I hear the mark is still there.

8

In the De La Roches' twelve years in Montvale Harry, Jr.,—
understandably—saw both his family and himself from his personal introspection. But the views of others who knew the family
covered a very wide spectrum. What you heard depended on the
person with whom you talked.

To many of the members of Christ Lutheran Church, the
family was a model one as they sat worshiping together in the
church in the round. But others in the church and town saw
some other sides, too.

"They could all be great," said an engineer who knew them
through community work, "and they were engrossed in everything everywhere in town. But that doesn't tell you what went
on behind their own front door. I sometimes thought there was
something there you couldn't put your finger on. They gave a
very strong picture of family unity. But to me this unity was a
facade and something that wasn't there."

"The family didn't work together," said a grandmother in the
town, "and I always felt that the brothers teased Harry, Jr., a lot.
I was in that house just twice, and I never wanted to return.
Everyone was on young Harry's back. Nothing he did was
right."

On the other hand, the neighbor who let Harry use her garage
said all of the sons were three nice boys and very, very respect-
ful.

"They did many odd jobs to help me," she recalled, "and I felt
I knew all three of them as though they were my own."

Jeff De Causemaker, the slightly-built reddish blond, who
knew both Harry and Ronnie—and who got to know them
well—summed up the family by saying he sensed a great need
for recognition inherent in everyone.

"In Eric it wasn't really obvious because of his age," Jeff declared. "But the father *had* to be a leader. It made him feel
important and strong. The mother was respected for her community work. Harry was struggling for recognition through his
cars and the way he raced, and Ronnie was trying to find it by

57

getting involved with pot. It made him feel big to be able to say, 'Hey, look what I've got.' "

When the family was viewed individually most people agreed that Ronnie was well accepted and liked, though one peer who knew both Ronnie and Harry answered "What was he like?" with "Ronnie was a regular guy, and he never caused any trouble. But there was something about him. There was something hidden inside." Others spoke of his outgoing ways and his skill in sports. And some said that, as a sophomore, he started to go with a rowdier crowd and follow a different group.

"I don't know who Ronnie's friends were in grammar school so I can't compare them with his high school friends," stated one of his teachers. "But the kids he was with in tenth grade were not the malicious type. They were just a group that was going a little ahead of its time. I'd say he was exposed to drugs, but I saw no

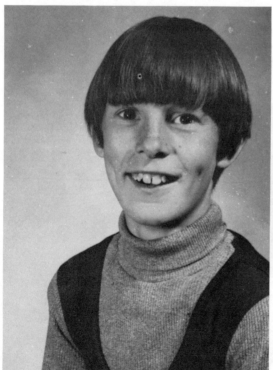

Eric's last school picture.

evidence of it, and guilt by association could be the very worst kind. He wasn't as neat as Harry, and sometimes his long, straight hair could look pretty terrible."

"He always had a smile," related another teacher, "And sometimes instead of disciplining him you'd just have to laugh with him."

Eric, with his Beatle-style haircut—and dimples and contagious grin—was summed up, as Harry put it, as "a nice little kid" and an "imp."

"Eric was full of the devil," said Patricia Mulligan, the mother of Eric's friend Mitch. "Once Eric and Mitch had a puppet show, and Eric was the Jolly Green Giant. I can see him working on it now. He was always grinning and playing jokes and then he'd look at you with that grin and say, 'Are you going to yell?'

"One time when we had a pajama party the kids all had those plastic sticks that light up and glow in the dark, and Eric ran out in his underwear in the middle of the night and flashed the stick in the windows to scare the rest of the kids.

"Mary Jane was always all for her children," Mrs. Mulligan continued. "She was a den mother for six years, and the kids can't ever remember hearing her raise her voice."

"Harry's mother was great," added Steve Mahoney. "Often I used to call her 'Mom' and she'd say 'Hi, son' to me."

"Sometimes after Luther League meetings or basketball games at the church she'd ask about Harry, Jr.," Roger Anderson said. "I know she was concerned about him while he was growing up, and she probably knew the pressures he endured in school and town. Maybe she didn't realize, though, the pressure they put on him at home.

"I'd try to encourage her as I could and say, 'Harry is doing great,' because I felt in his last year in high school he was coming into his own."

Roy Nilsen, the bearded pastor at Christ Lutheran Church and a very caring person who had five children himself, characterized Mary Jane De La Roche as a thoroughly delightful person.

"I can remember visiting her during her hospitalizations," he recalled, "and she impressed me at the time as a very real individual. So often people expect clergymen to come in with their collars on backwards and talk about lofty things. But she didn't cast me in a mold, and I appreciated her for that. She used to kid me about smoking a pipe, because she liked her cigarettes until they became a problem.

"I've often wondered about her role within the family circle, and my guess would be that most of the time it was 'Let's not make waves.' She probably tried as much as she could to maintain stability."

"The town was her life," reported the director of the Montvale Welfare Office, where Mary Jane was a volunteer who delivered gift baskets to the needy. "She helped many, many people. I was very close to her."

People saw many different sides of the master of the house whose hopes and dreams for his family were erased to nothing at all. In all fairness to him, however, and the image he envisioned, it has to be stressed again and again that he wanted the finest for his family, and as the friend who knew him best—Steve Madreperla—claimed, he thought the way to live the most was to discipline your children. If he got off target in calling the shots, one can't forget his boyhood and the father he never had. He *meant* to be the boys' mainstay—and he *meant* to be the guiding hand that would mold them into the image he had created for them.

A notebook of comments about him reads—on the positive side: "He had a very helpful side and was always right on hand for whatever needed to be done. If your house fell down and you needed help he'd be the first one with a hammer. Once when a dog was hit on his street he was the first one out of the house to move it from the road."

"He was the friendly usher in church who was there nearly every Sunday with the smile—and the big glad hand."

"He was always jovial and good natured at work, and he often went out to the stores to buy things for his children—as long as he approved of the games or the other things the boys wanted. He was proud of Harry, Jr., too, and just the Tuesday before he died he brought his picture in uniform to show to his co-workers. He was terribly disappointed, though, when he failed to make

Harry De La Roche, Sr.   **Mary Jane De La Roche.**
PHOTOS COURTESY OF *THE RECORD*, HACKENSACK, NEW JERSEY.

West Point. The kid was under pressure. There isn't any doubt about that."

"At town meetings he wasn't hard to take. He'd listen to other viewpoints, and when he'd make a suggestion he wouldn't defend it to the end, whether it was right or wrong."

Others had negative comments on Harry De La Roche, Sr.: "He *was* difficult at meetings. It always had to be Harry's way. That was the way that he wanted it. He was editor of the church paper once, and I was on a committee that needed an item included. I can still hear him saying in an overbearing way 'Either you give it to me right now or it doesn't go in at all.' "

"Yeah, he did a lot of things. But he was a son of a bitch. Not everyone in Little League—and his other activities—liked him."

"He was always telling Harry how to run his life, and he wasn't realistic in what he expected from the boys. He tried to make the decisions about everything Harry did. In fact, he was almost a Hitler-type and terribly harsh on his kids."

"I always had an uneasy feeling about Mr. De La Roche, and I certainly didn't like the idea of all those guns in the house. It's like an invitation to shoot if something every goes wrong."

A man who worked with Harry, Sr., in the Montvale Athletic League said he saw several negative qualities that he felt reluctant to discuss "because so many were exactly what I and other fathers do."

"But Harry had a Prussian-aura, and he was so full of his own importance he felt he was right about everything. He was a very hard taskmaster in pursuing his ambitions for his sons.

"This may have been a form of love. But I don't think the kids understood it, so it was hard for them."

In discussing the love in the family—and how little or how much was there—one person who grew up with Harry, Jr., says Harry was starved for affection and she can't remember any occasion when anyone really hugged him.

"I don't know that he was never hugged and that he was starved for affection," Pastor Roy Nilsen responded. "But I can conjecture that if Harry, Sr., was the ultraconservative person some people say he was he'd go along with the premise that men don't hug or kiss. That would be a lack of demonstration, though, rather than a lack of love."

Bob Gantt felt there was love in the family, but he saw it as the kind of love that expected a lot in return.

"Just the way Mr. De La Roche wanted Harry to go to The Citadel showed that he cared," contended Bob. "But you can be imprisoned by a love that expects too much of you."

Catherine Hennessy, with whom Harry felt close when he

visited her in Park Ridge, agreed that a well-meaning love in the family might have been a demanding one.

"I personally believe that Harry needed love badly," she confirmed. "But I think he got a love that said 'You are our son—and we love you by your doing what we want you to do.' "

9

While discussing Harry, Jr., and his childhood and adolescence many people who knew young Harry spoke of cruelty in the schools.

One teacher admitted regretfully, "It's something that has always existed—and something that always will—and some of the people who do it don't even know what's happening. It just becomes the thing to do every time they see a scapegoat."

"Harry never hurt anyone," said Joan Anderson, who was Harry's friend and a sociologist by profession. "But some of the kids are merciless here. They can be just as vicious in the things they do as any kid in the city slums. They take what they do so lightly, too, and they don't understand the ramifications of all the things they say. There's more of a sophisticated cutting here than on the city streets. But they're animals just the same.

"In the slums you can have your teeth knocked out and have a bridge put in. Then later the damage isn't there. But here they knock your insides out, and often, when this happens, the damage doesn't go away."

"Some kids at the Hills can be terrible," a senior's mother said, "and I know how they came down on Harry. My daughter didn't like those kids. She thought they were rotten-mean, so she went to school two days a week and stayed home the other three. I didn't argue with her because her grades were good, and I sort of understood."

A freshman who'd had friends in grammar school and not very many in high school said that the atmosphere of the school made a great many once-nice kids adopt a whole different attitude and think they had a new freedom to set the pace for everyone else.

"The kids who want to be popular feel if they keep pace with these kids they'll be accepted," he said. "They break down and conform to drugs—or whatever else is in—and this happens day after day."

Still another summing up came from Officer Michael O'Donovan of the Montvale Police Department. In an interview with Barry Wood, a New York sociologist, that was handed over to the defense attorney after Harry, Jr., was in Bergen County Jail, O'Donovan stated there were over forty different cliques in the senior class at Pascack Hills when Harry was in high school.

"The cruelty that exists with different cliques is phenomenal," he revealed. "The girls and guys go so far as to set up different members in cruel, humiliating situations to mock out people. It has become so severe that we have tried bringing in professional people, and some of our policemen want to get in there and start getting more citizenship and social interaction involved with the students.

"For Harry it was persecution," he declared. "There are something like eight entries in his entire yearbook. Six are mocking derogatory comments like—'You're the stupidest kid I met.'"

Then O'Donovan went on to say that Montvale is the kind of town in which people work very carefully to keep up images and façades. "Many families in the community shouldn't even be called families," he said. "They're related by blood, and they're parents of natural children. But the only thing they have in common is the fact that they live in the same house. The mother is doing her thing. The old man is doing his. The kids have theirs. There's no communication over the table at meals or anything, and the interaction and cohesiveness that is needed is absent."

While Harry grew up in this atmosphere he, like his father before him, was subjected to varying views. It was generally agreed by most of his peers—till his senior year, at least—that he tried very hard to please people and gain acceptance to a group.

"But everything goes on around him," one of his friends remarked. "Even when he's with a crowd he seems to be alone."

Ed Mahoney, one of his gas station friends, felt Harry's love of animals might very well stem from the unhappy fact that people didn't always accept him.

"If you're not accepted by people you have your animals," he said, "and when you talk to a friendly dog that dog can't really hurt you. I remember a party my best friend had, and all through the evening Harry sat alone dipping cheese doodles, drinking beer—and talking to the dog."

"Any way you look at it," a De La Roche neighbor said, "Harry was the 'different' one in the family, and he had lots of conflicts and frustrations. When he couldn't perform to his father's expectations, it was embarrassing."

"He was trying to live for his father and himself," Ed Mahoney added, "and I just got the feeling that Harry could never be what he wanted to be at home or anywhere else. He ended up by having no self, so it was the kind of situation that could tear anybody apart."

"Actually the military life would be the perfect way to please and appease his father," Wilbur Boyce, the ex-Citadel cadet, said while dissecting Harry. "Consciously or unconsciously, I believe that's how Harry saw it. And I can't think of a better way to make your father proud after years of feeling guilty if you think you disappointed him."

Around the Montvale area there was much speculation on whether or not a military school was the right place for Harry.

"In my opinion Harry was a guy who probably would have been far better off going to a city university and making it on his own with nobody setting day-to-day rules in a military atmosphere," Eric's friend's father Paul Mulligan believed. "But he wouldn't have been allowed to do that and be a free thinker and live in an apartment. That wouldn't have fit his parents' view of what their son should be."

"The family was really raring to go when they packed up the car for The Citadel," the De La Roche neighbor reported. "But when I saw Harry before they left and wished him a lot of luck he said 'I don't know how it will work. We'll have to see what happens.' "

Though Harry had many supporters he had his detractors, too.

"He'd be a misfit anywhere—in an apartment or whatever," one peer who disliked him said. "He'd show off and brag about his car and often he'd try to make you think he was smarter than anyone else. Sometimes he'd make up stories, too, and stretch or distort the truth. For instance, he'd talk about driving his car 115 miles an hour. It was a hard car to control, and I doubt he could drive it that fast."

"While some people called him withdrawn and meek I'd call him a nasty loud mouth," another classmate stated. "He was always trying to make an impression and sometimes he'd do something weird, like throwing a basketball at you—for no reason at all. Once he was down in the town park driving around in his car with somebody sitting on the hood. He was driving normally for a while. Then suddenly he took off fast before coming to a quick stop. Naturally the kid went flying and got a bit scraped up."

"Harry was quiet in the early years," added his friend Fred Zott. "But in high school he picked up different habits—like smoking, drinking beer, foul language, and pot. He knew how to be a wise guy then."

David Dierker, Harry's high school teacher, had his own views on Harry.

"I liked him," he declared, "and though I may be totally wrong it sometimes appeared to me that by the time Harry was a senior he wasn't always willing to do what it took to be accepted. He raised his hand a lot in my class and often I thought he might have been saying, 'Okay, I'll continue to be ridiculed and do what I want to do. If I want to raise my hand and answer—and you think raising your hand and appearing smart is dumb—I'm going to continue doing it even if I'm ridiculed.' I didn't allow ridicule in my class, but this is one measure of being noticed to a kid who is searching for something.

"In many ways Harry reminded me of the nervous, nail-biting

type. He'd shift around a lot in class, and he scratched his ear quite a bit."

"He was often shifty and sneaky," still another student put in. "He could be cunning and manipulative and not very easy to like. There were very few people who sought him out, and some of the kids who tolerated him weren't thrilled to be with him. Except for the few good friends he had none of us went out of our way to find Harry De La Roche."

Bob Gantt, one of the good friends, was quick to see Harry's better side.

"My mother was impressed by his politeness," he contended. "She used to say again and again, 'I can't get over that Harry and how well-mannered and well-spoken he is.' "

"I'd trust him in any situation," said Coach Anderson, another of the good friends. "I think he has capabilities, too, but emotionally he has a protective wall that he built around himself. He'll talk about anything in the world, but you can't get inside of him. I've had opportunities to do that, but it has never come out."

Bob Gantt is convinced the protective wall started as early as grammar school and that no one can get through it, no matter how hard he tries.

"I've seen him get really upset," Bob revealed. "But I've never seen him break down and cry. He keeps everything inside."

"Harry was very special," Irene Bickerton concluded. "There was a gentleness about him, and I can't think of once in our friendship that I didn't feel warmth for Harry. The night he invited me out at 11:00 to look at the engine of his car I felt a real sense of kinship. I felt we were really close then."

"Then a few minutes later when he left the house, after printing his name on our doorway, he said—at the same time he said goodbye—'My father has my whole life planned.' "

IV

The Citadel

10

The Citadel is a liberal arts military college that's rich in American history. Established in 1842 it was housed in a sturdy old fortress called The Citadel, from which it gets its name.

In the early days it was garrisoned, first by federal, then by state troops until the latter were replaced in 1843 by twenty students who made up the first Corps of Cadets. These cadets served as a guard for the state's arms at the same time they pursued an education designed for both war and peace.

During the Civil War—before the firing on Fort Sumter—cadets of the Corps manned the guns which drove back the *Star of the West*, a steamer sent by the federal government to relieve the fort. Later, from 1865, when a Union force marched into Charleston, until 1879, the buildings were occupied by federal troops and the operation of the college was suspended until 1882. In 1922 it was moved to a new location between Hampton Park and the Ashley River.

In outlining the requirements for admission the college catalogue says: "In general, The Citadel seeks to determine acceptability through a thorough evaluation of each applicant's character, maturity, motivation, readiness for college, amenability and obedience to authority, emotional stability, and potential as a contributor to cadet life. Where any of these factors are in question, the college will obtain additional information by means of any of the following: interviews with the applicant; interviews with parents and/or members of his community; a special report written by the applicant on such subjects as his goals in life, his reason for his choice of The Citadel, and/or reasons supporting his choice of major field of study; or a special test, to be taken by the applicant, designed to examine in detail any aspect of the applicant's character or potential."

Through the years the school has prided itself on its students and graduates—three governors of South Carolina, an All-American football star, and leaders in civilian and military life. Such prestigious military men as Generals Charles P. Summerall, Mark Clark, and Hugh Pate Harris have all been heads of The Citadel, and the list of distinguished visitors is a Who's Who in American history. The whole idea of the college is to develop leaders.

Harry was thinking of some of these things on August 17, 1976, when he and his family got into their car and headed toward South Carolina. He was the driver most of the way and, sometimes, while he was driving, he'd have a few uneasy thoughts about what lay ahead. But he kept those feelings to himself, and as the five De La Roches drove down Interstate 95, they looked like any family taking a son to college. The first stop was Virginia Beach for a short family vacation, and when they

En route to The Citadel; Ron, Eric, Mary Jane, and Harry in the Holiday Inn Motel, Charleston, South Carolina, August 21, 1976.

registered for their motel rooms none of them knew this vacation would be their last family trip.

It was a pleasant enough few days, and the family took lots of pictures. But before they knew it they were back in the car on their way to The Citadel for the due date—August 23. Once they arrived in Charleston they looked for Moultrie Street. Then when they got to the foot of that street they saw the imposing wrought-iron gates that led to the hundred-acre campus of the two thousand man state-supported school.

Since they'd never seen the campus before they were duly impressed by the many Spanish-style buildings and row after row of palm trees that served as protection from the hot southern sun. Mark Clark Hall, the museum, and many light-colored buildings bordered the large square parade grounds on which there were cannons and flags.

11

When we stopped beside the parade grounds to ask directions to the barracks parents and boys were scattered in small groups everywhere.

I fleetingly thought, "Okay, this is it. You can get a new reputation. Nobody really has to know what life was like before." I even thought of changing my name and instead of using Harry picking up on my middle name and saying I was called Bill. As my father snapped more pictures, I kept thinking of this. Then when he finished his roll of film—and we found out where to go—we climbed back into our station wagon and drove to Stevens Barracks.

I was assigned to Room 4449—and to Company "N" in the 4th Battalion. My roommate was Louis D'Annibale, a football player from Allentown, Pennsylvania. I also picked up uniforms and my

M-14 rifle. My parents got Citadel car stickers and tee shirts for
Ronnie and Eric.

The first night we went to a banquet for parents and new
freshmen (or knobs), and my family and I happened to sit with
Lt. Col. William Harris, dean of Undergraduate Studies. When
I talked with him he told me if I ever had any problems to come
and discuss them with him. I probably should have done this.
But I never did. That same night we met Frederick Chronis, a
cadet who came from Germany since his father was in the Air
Force. He was president of the Lutheran Club and he talked to
us for quite a while while my parents and Ronnie asked questions about the Fourth Class System. The family kidded about
this tradition that gives upperclassmen authority over freshmen.
But I just stood and listened. Then Chronis told me to see him if
I ever had any problems.

The next day I unpacked my gear and we did some silly things
like running around the parade group with little bags filled with
all kinds of crap hanging around our necks. I remember thinking
"I can still leave—they haven't cut my hair."

Actually, my hair wasn't long since I'd had it trimmed recently. But I still had to have it shaved to a stubble just like all of
the freshmen. This is so all fourth classmen start out in the same
way. All your identity is taken away and the school breaks you
down as much as it can before it begins to rebuild you. You're
made into a nothing on purpose, and as a knob in the Fourth
Class System you have to walk silently in single file with your
chin in and chest out. Upperclassmen bark orders and criticism.
But for freshmen it's "Yes, Sir" or "No, Sir."

My parents hung around for a little while, but since they were
on vacation they soon took off for their next destination and other
motel reservations. I had snapshots of them in my wallet, along
with pictures of our house and my car, so I wasn't homesick
when they left as many of the freshmen were when their parents
drove away. I made up my mind that since I was here I was going
to make it.

I was knocked down the next day, however, when I got into
trouble with my first squad sergeant through a misunderstand-
ing. A freshman's squad sergeant and corporal have the greatest

Citadel cadets resplendent in their full dress "salt and pepper" uniforms march across the checkerboard decking of the quadrangle in a Citadel barracks. Upper righthand corner: Cadet Harry De La Roche, Jr.

effect on him, and my first squad sergeant was a junior who made life miserable for me.

One of the activities at The Citadel is a thing called Junior Sword Drill. It's a precision team of juniors, and freshmen aren't allowed to see it. Whenever it came to the battalion to practice we were supposed to go to our rooms and close our doors behind us. I moved a little slowly—too slowly to suit the squad sergeant—so he ordered me to stay in my room until I was called to leave. He forgot to call me for afternoon formation, so when it was time for that I didn't know whether to stay in my room or report on my own for formation.

When I heard the cannon call for formation I figured I'd be late, so I thought I'd better stay in my room and wait for someone to come. For some reason the sergeant didn't miss me, and he gave an "All Present" report. Later, when he learned I hadn't been there he was extremely upset because his report "All Present" could mean lots of trouble for him and cause him to lose his stripes. He was angry when he came for me, and it certainly didn't help that by then I'd decided to leave my room since I didn't know what to do. He started screaming and yelling, and then he got his friends on my back because of what I'd done.

It was soon a case of "Here's De La Roche"—and more "Let's get Harry" again. In fact, when I arrived for mess I heard, "Look out for a waste product by the name of De La Roche." At first people knew the reason for putting pressure on me. But then it became a habit, and they didn't know why they did it. For a while I didn't know what to do about my troubles with the sergeant. But then I decided to leave it alone because if I made a big thing of it they'd hand it to me even more.

As we went from August to September nothing seemed to get better. For Cadre Week, and the weeks after that, upper classmen, as Wilbur Boyce warned, liked to throw everything at you to test whether or not you could take it. The school frowns on brutality and tries not to let it happen, and it's striving to end a lot of the hazing that went on in the past. But, still, whenever you do things wrong three people yell at you, and you're told you're lower than whale shit when you have to walk off sidewalks while going to a class.

We couldn't talk on campus unless we were spoken to, and we called upperclassmen "Mister!" and saluted senior officers. When we went to and from the showers we wore military hat, bathrobe, and slippers, and when we weren't polishing shoes and brass it seemed we were constantly bracing. That means you stand at attention with your body as rigid as a board and your chin held in till it creased.

Physical endurance was important, so, along with drilling and running, you got racked for punishments. When you were ordered to do push-ups with a rifle you held the rifle between your feet and balanced your garrison cap on your back. When either the rifle or cap started falling, you had to start again. You'd feel as though your arms would give out, and sometimes you got so tired you fell flat on your face.

Meal times were the toughest, and though Wilbur Boyce had filled me in on what would happen then I didn't expect the bullshit. Before you were allowed to eat you had to go through a silly routine in which you balanced your plate on two fingers and said some crazy thing like, "Would any of you fine southern gentlemen and high outstanding Citadel students care for anything on my plate?" Before you were permitted to take a bite you had to wait for a "No."

You were expected to be super-quick when serving the upperclassmen, and while you were trying to eat yourself you also had to watch their plates and anticipate their wants. When you served iced tea, for instance, you had to have just enough ice in the glass, and when a glass was half-empty you were supposed to reach for it and fill it up again. If you were slow on the pick-up you'd get shit from the upperclassmen, and while I was a student they'd throw their glass up for a freshmen to catch. I understand they've stopped that now but it happened twice to me, and once I was hit by flying glass when an empty glass shattered on my plate.

There were other crazy table games, too—like eating just with your mouth. About once a month we'd have cream puffs, and then there would be a contest in which you were told to turn your plate over, put the cream puff on the plate, and, while sitting on your hands, eat the cream puff solely with your mouth.

I said I wouldn't do it, and when cadre members persuaded me with threats I clammed up and didn't acknowledge they were even talking to me.

At first—except for things like this—I really tried for a while. I went to all of my classes and also played intramural sports—volleyball, basketball, and football. I even enjoyed the running, since I've always liked to run. Sometimes when I was the guide—and felt like being smart-assed—I'd speed up on the running so the officer would tire quickly. Then when I was told to slow things down I'd slow up for just a few minutes and then start speeding again. A few activities such as this got me the reputation of trying to beat the system and being a rebellious spirit.

When more and more things got to me I became more defiant. I developed a habit of explaining things which pissed everybody off, and instead of answering "Yes, Sir" or "No, Sir" I'd add something else, too. My company tactical officer was Capt. Matthew Sawtelle and he was an all right guy. But I'd ask the same questions again and again, and that drove him up a wall. One day when I felt like rebelling one of the upperclassmen who was drilling my platoon saw me laughing in formation, so he said "Come by my room." When I came he gave me a talk on discipline and rank and then, after he had racked me, he asked me if I understood why I was being punished. I answered "No, Sir, I don't understand" and that really got to him.

As time went on several stories circulated about me. Sometimes my roommate would mention that on occasion I'd wake up at night and sit in the dark and chain-smoke. There were other stories about smoking pot which we did a couple of times, though you're taking your life in your hands if you have pot on campus. Some people accused me of not taking showers and said that my room smelled foul. A corporal said I looked like hell and must sleep in my uniform.

I came in for several abuses because of this reputation. On one night, for example, two upperclassmen decided to throw me around for kicks to see if I would bounce. Then another time two others set out to teach me to fly. When they do this they spread your arms and legs and twirl you until you're dizzy. Then when they finally let me go they sent me into a steel dresser. Later a psychiatrist suggested I might have had a concussion as a result of this.

There were other uncomfortable incidents, too. One was a thing in which you were asked "Are you strong as a rock?" If you answered "Yes"—as expected—the upperclassmen would hand you a rock with your company letter on it. You'd have to carry that enormous rock everywhere you went, and once when it was handed to me I was sure it bruised my ribs since I heard something crack in there.

Since my roommate, Lou, was a football player I'd often be in my room by myself when he was at "away" games and once I was in there a little crocked—after being out on the town—when suddenly some visitors burst into the room and put a blanket over my head. Then they proceeded to cut my leg and put nail polish remover in the cut. And I didn't imagine this happened because when I awakened in the morning the slash from a pen knife was there.

Perhaps the worst occasion was the time a corporal asked me, "Do you want to bow?" I was company runner at the time which means you run all over doing errands and delivering mail. I was wearing sweat pants and a sweat shirt that day and I was feeling hot—as well as pretty exhausted—from doing all that running.

The heat was making me nauseous, too, and I was starting to sweat, so when, on arriving in an upperclassmen's room a corporal said, "Do you want to bow?" I misunderstood his southern drawl and thought that he had asked me "Do you want a bath?"

I answered "Yes, Sir, it's hot in here," thinking I'd get a shower. But instead they kicked me in the groin until I passed out in pain. I hit my head on a steel dresser again—and when I came to they were laughing. Some news of this incident eventually got out. But how can you really prove it when it's frowned upon by the college and done behind closed doors?

In spite of all this bullshit I had some good times, too, and I tried to listen to the upperclassmen who bolstered me by saying that every freshman gets picked on to some extent at least.

"It's a matter of how you take it," my second squad sergeant said. "And when you look back from an upperclassman's view you'll realize we've all been through it."

"I know," I replied, as I hid my real feelings. "Don't worry. I'm going to make it."

My second sergeant was Mark Coker, who was liked by everybody. He really loved The Citadel. But he was compassionate, and he didn't think that military men had to be blood-and-guts George Pattons. I used to talk to him a lot, and once when he asked us to write him a note about our feelings at college he said, "To make it easy tell it as though you're writing a letter to my girl." I wrote, "You're lucky to have Mr. Coker. He's someone to trust and relate to."

I made some friends at The Citadel, despite my reputation, and sometimes we'd go to Dino's, a King Street drinking spot. On Mondays I went to the Lutheran Club and met Pastor Wilfred Hendrix, who was called Rocky by everyone. He was the pastor of St. Barnabas Lutheran Church, a few blocks away from the campus. At meetings I'd see Fred Chronis, the fellow I met my first night, and I also got to know Pete Salerno, a cadet from Washington Township—a town very near my home. Pete was a really good guy, and he said at our first meeting, "Be sure to come and see me if you ever have any problems or think you're going to quit." I'm sure Pete Salerno meant this, as other people did. But none of the people who said this knew I worked things out myself.

Once I went on a camping trip with the Lutheran Club, and I talked a lot with Rocky while over at Sullivan's Island. Both of us liked philosophy and I'd read a lot of it, so while others were out playing basketball Rocky and I would stay inside and talk about such philosophers as Friedrich Nietzche and Bertrand Russell.

But even with these good times I had many troubled moments, and as early as mid-September I thought of changing schools. I didn't hate The Citadel, but I hated a few people in it. A change posed a major problem, though. What would I tell my parents? It would hurt them badly if I mentioned dropping out, especially since they'd taken a loan to cover my first year's expenses.

In the end I decided to stick it out and stay for the rest of the year. Then after I finished my freshman year I'd plan to go somewhere else. I wrote my parents about how I felt and brought up the subject of a transfer.

On campus I started to stay in my room as much as I possibly could. The physical stuff wasn't killing me. I could manage that. But I felt my grades were getting screwed up, and that meant more problems at home. It wasn't so much that the work was too hard. But the constant stresses and upsets made studying difficult. And then in addition to everything else I was concerned about Ronnie.

I'd never said very much to him about either pot or hard drugs except to tell him to watch it—and even when he wrote to me and said he was buying "J's" I flippantly answered on two occasions, "Have some on hand when I get home to soothe the savage beast," and, "Get a hold of your head friends and send some shit down here." But now I was starting to worry that something was happening to Ronnie while I was away at school. I'd learned from other letters that he was involved in shopping around so he could become a dealer, and when my family phoned on my birthday Ronnie was completely burned out.

My father knew something was wrong with him, but I think Dad thought it was drinking so when he said, "Isn't he sickening?" I didn't say a word. My mother was on the upstairs phone, and my father was talking downstairs, so after I talked to the family I said, "When we're finished talking together put Ronnie on again."

I heard my mother hang up the phone as soon as Ronnie got on, so then I said, "Listen Ronnie boy, unless you start cutting out this shit, I'm really going to bust your ass as soon as I get home." I tried to talk to him in a code. But he didn't know what I was saying, so after we spoke a minute or so I said, "Get Dad on the phone." It was then that I asked my father, "What's with Ronnie tonight?"

"I don't think he's feeling very well," my father said in disgust.

I continued to worry about Ronnie, and this nagged at me all the time, while my own difficulties compounded with every passing day. My parents opposed a transfer for my sophomore year, so when they gave me a solid "No" I decided there was no further point in staying at The Citadel. But I couldn't write back and tell them that if I couldn't transfer I was leaving school— and I wasn't ready to mention that maybe I'd even move out of the house and work and pay for another college as soon as I got enough money. My father wouldn't like that. But I'd tell him, "This is my choice." And if I were paying for it myself he couldn't do very much.

The more I looked ahead to this the more anxious I was to leave, so I had to come up with some way to get out of The Citadel fast. I didn't want to tell the school "You guys are fouling up my grades and running too much crap" because if I said something like that I would get even more. I had to think of a cover up that would save my face. I also had to have an excuse that no one would dare to check.

In the end I remembered my mother's cancer and decided to spread the word that my mother had terminal cancer and I needed an early leave. If I used the word "terminal" my story would really be strong and it would seem very logical to need a leave right away. While I was setting things up in my mind I decided to add that the illness was causing such money problems I might not be able to come back to school after Thanksgiving vacation except to collect my belongings. This would set me up in a spot where I could drop out at that time—or maybe come back till Christmas since my room was paid until then.

When I put my story together I mentioned it to several people and, as the story got around, the senior sponsor assigned to me asked if another senior would be able to take me on, since he already had a freshman who had problems at home. In the senior sponsor system that existed till 1977 all freshman had a senior who could either be a helpful "big brother" or a master who made you his slave.

My new senior was Walter Singleton from Beaufort, South Carolina, who planned to study pharmacy when he graduated from The Citadel. The first night I met Walter he asked me about the problems I had, but I only brought up the illness at home and kept the rest to myself. Walt wanted to phone my parents. But I told him I wished he wouldn't.

For the rest of my time at The Citadel Walt was a real "big brother." Almost as soon as I met him he invited me out on the town and took me to an enormous buffet where freshmen could eat all they wanted. We went to a Woody Allen movie next and then we went to the Officer's Club at the Naval Base.

When I knew that I was going to leave my feeling was, "I don't care," so I stayed in my room more than ever and began cutting most of my classes. By November I wasn't feeling well so I went to the infirmary and stayed for three days for diarrhea, plus nausea and vomiting. For my last two weeks on campus I was assigned a new roommate—Richard DuBois from North Caldwell, New Jersey. He was a really nice guy and I told him about my mother's health and the money problem at home. He knew that I was copping out. But he chalked it up to this.

As I mentioned to more and more people that I might not return from Thanksgiving everyone started saying I ought to do everything I could to try to come back till Christmas so I could get credits for a semester. Walt Singleton kept encouraging this, and I also got it from Captain Sawtelle when I told him I'd be leaving.

"You've already paid for the semester," he explained, "so it's going to cost you the same whether you leave at Thanksgiving or whether you stay till Christmas. Why don't you try to finish and then transfer your credits."

I guess I started wavering because, while I told some people "I may not be back from Thanksgiving," I also told some others "I'll probably stay till Christmas." I decided to keep the door open and not take my property home. Besides, if I had my things with me my parents would think it was funny, and I'd have to tell them right away that I was planning to leave.

Walt Singleton was really great in helping me get home and a few days before Thanksgiving vacation he personally persuaded Captain Sawtelle to submit a request for an early leave. Captain Sawtelle sent the request to the commandant, Col. Walter B. Clark. Then Col. Ralph Crosby, an assistant commandant, said I could leave on November 20 rather than November 24, when the vacation began. Once the leave was granted I had to let my parents know—fast—that I was coming home early, and I had to have a reason for the change in plans.

I knew the school had a system in which certain guys with good ratings as freshmen were asked to come back as corporals to train freshmen the following year. For lack of anything better I ran that story on my parents and added the guys with this rating were getting early leave for Thanksgiving. Two days before I was scheduled to leave Walt went with me to Colonel Crosby's office.

"We'd like very much to have you come back," Colonel Crosby declared. "But if you've really made up your mind that you won't be back from Thanksgiving it would be to your advantage to take your gear home now. It's open to pilferage if you leave it, and if you can't get back we'll only have to inventory it and ship it up to you."

"I don't want to take it now, Sir," I said. "But whether or not I return to school I'll definitely come back for my things."

I got the impression as we talked that the colonel thought I wasn't sure what I was going to do. But he said I could leave my stuff there, so I told everybody I'd be back to pick up my belongings.

And at the time I said this I expected I would.

12

I wrote a lot of letters while at The Citadel because I wanted to keep in touch with my family and friends at home. It was also a way of making sure I got some mail myself. My parents wrote a few lines each day, and Grandma Ebneter sent letters and cards. She was always saying she was proud of me and sure that I'd make good.

When the time arrived that I, myself, wasn't so sure of that I also wrote other letters. One was a special letter to Steve, to tell him to talk to Ronnie and warn him about the pot. Another was to Roger Anderson because I wanted to talk to him about dropping out of school. I trusted his judgment and advice so I wrote before coming home that I had some things to discuss with him during Thanksgiving vacation. However, I said that before we talked I had to straighten a few things out with my mother and father. Another letter that I wrote was to Patty Hennessy in which I confided in the last part: "They say this place makes a man of you, and I'm sure of it. But they also say the system when analyzed by psychiatrists will freak out the mind. I can agree with that."

Ronnie didn't show my parents any of my letters since the two of us had an agreement in which I used just one side of the paper. Then to make sure this couldn't be read right through the envelope I'd fold it in another paper as a double precaution.

Most of the letters I wrote and received have disappeared by now. But I have some between my family and me to keep for memories. Since they are part of this story, these are the ones I've retained.

Sept. 1, 1976

Dear Harry,

Mom's not home so I have the records blasting. I try to tell you everything that's going on here, but hey listen, I want to hear what's going on down there. I've been checkin' on your car every day. It's fine. I go in there to smoke. I'm trying to get some of the chrome

84

polished. If you write home to me make sure it's "clean." Mom and Dad censor everything. I found 2 Michelobs in the garage. I took the cookies out of the trunk. We're going to Uncle Steve's this weekend. I'm going up to the school to see who I got. Football practice starts today and I'm not going to play. I challenged some guys down in the apartments to a wiffleball game. Them and their wives tomorrow. I'm trying to find some carpet for your car. So you all have a good time, now, ya hear. Stay cool.

Ronnie

Sept. 3, 1976

Dear Harry,

We were all very happy to get your letter. You and the rest of us all figured it would be tough. No matter how tough they make it, you know you can take it. It can't last forever. This education and training is your whole career. The rest of your life will be easy and you will have it made if you stick it out and not only do well but excel and be tops in your class.

When we were there, Gen. Seignious gave us a talk and said that it would be hard for the knobs at the beginning but all the boys would turn out to be fine men. Harry, I believe that and I want you to believe it, too. I told Mom that it wouldn't surprise me if at the end of every school year, all the cadets were given a lecture and told that they are supposed to make it as hard as possible for the new knobs. Maybe to weed out the weak ones right at the start. Next year you can yell at a knob. Remember you can take whatever they can dish out. You are an outstanding young man.

Now, getting to the school work. Make sure you have the correct schedule of classes and that the advanced math course is ok. Also, keep up on the R.O.T.C. Find out all you can about scholarships and everything. If you need help, contact the right people both for regular studies and R.O.T.C.

We are going to Bambergers today to get you some more white socks and we will send them to you right away. Things have slowed down as far as visitors go since you left but make sure you prove the guys wrong who said that you wouldn't make it at The Citadel. You will make it. Let us know what happened on that first Wednesday. After that, when classes start, I guess things get better as far as harassment goes.

Lucky is fine. He will be anxious to see you at Thanksgiving. Let us know if you are making any new friends. Remember we are behind you all the way and we will help you anyway that we can.

We are all waiting for your letters. Mom can't wait each day till the mailman comes. We know that your studies come first, but when you get some time let us know how things are. I'm sure they are getting better.

Ronnie is not going out for football this year. Eric is starting town football. Both boys plus Mom and I brag about you to everyone. We are all proud of you. Grandma and Pop Pop will be up this Sunday. I guess that's it for now. Take care of yourself.

All my love,
Dad

Sept. 13, 1976

Dear Harry,

I will still always call you Harry. I can't seem to call you Bill.

We are happy to hear that you are coping with college. I always knew you could. You asked what we think of you changing to Freshman math. If you can handle Sophomore math easily with no problems then we suggest you keep it. But if you think it might be a little tough then switch back. Remember you need *top* grades to get a scholarship. *Never* go to a class unprepared and, especially, never go to a test being unprepared. Keep studying. It's much too important.

Things at home are a lot different with you away, but we will be looking forward to having you home at Thanksgiving. Ronnie checks your car frequently, but I don't give him the key. He only checks the outside. Remember you aren't working now and you blew your bank account, so you won't be able to spend money on your car except for necessities. Remember what happened in high school. When you got the car your marks went down. We surely don't want that to happen in college. It's too important. It's your whole future.

We will really miss having you here for your birthday but we will send something and you know we will be thinking of you always. We tell all our friends about you and The Citadel. They are all impressed and it makes us very proud of you. What do you do with your weekend time off? Do you study or what? If you go out, be careful. Did you get the package we sent? It had white socks and some goodies.

Ronnie started back at the rifle club tonight. Eric is supposed to start the training soon. The boys proudly wear their Citadel shirts. They are proud of their brother. Lucky sends his love. Muffins, too. Ronnie wears the things you gave him and tries to copy you in many ways. I approve because you did set a good example. I'm playing softball in the fall league again.

I'm glad you are learning to handle the upperclassmen. Don't get too frisky, though. Keep cool. Are you learning to eat more things? Have they let up at meal times? Will you have any social activities such as dances? Will they teach you to dance plus the social qualities, like it said in the book?

You know we can't afford to come down for Parents Day, but we will be with you in our thoughts. Mom and I are going to save some money so we can come down next year. We really want to be there with you.

Well, Harry, take care of yourself. Be strong and honest and always be proud of what you do. Never do anything you would be ashamed of. Follow the honor code. If you need me for anything ever just let me know. I will be there.

All my love,
Dad

Sept. 14, 15, 16, 17, 1976

Dear Harry,

I guess you will have to leave it to others to call you Bill. You're Harry or Hatchy to me. Dad and Ron just left for school and work. Ron looked a little like you in your Chinese shirt and blue jeans. Rather than send you a check for your birthday we will deposit something in your checking account here.

Yesterday I went to a meeting for the Republican Club to stamp envelopes for campaign literature. Then I acted as chauffeur for the rest of the day. Two cards and a letter have arrived from you. Much joy.

Please don't think of bringing your car down there. What would you do if you broke down halfway? Think of the expense to get it going again. Your grades would take a nose dive just as they did here when you got a car. Dad will probably have more to say on that when he writes.

I'm glad you are learning how to dodge the cadre. Keep cool. The upperclassmen really have it nice and that's the way it should be.

School will be one of the happiest times for you, and the best friends of your life will be made there. Uncle Steve and Aunt Dorian seemed awed by your going to The Citadel. It has a wonderful rating. People are quite impressed when they hear you are there.

Now about changing schools. Forget it. On every count it would be the wrong move. It would not be any cheaper to go to a good school up here. You couldn't work and go to school at the same time. You would lose too much of what college is all about. You have money in uniforms that would be wasted. To go to a school two years here, two years there you belong to nothing. A Citadel man is one who went through four years, not an in-and-outer.

This is the hard year and while you have no respect for upperclassmen now you will when you are a sophomore. You will understand a lot of what was done to you this year and why. The boys who want to leave have problems other than yours. They may need more adulation than they are getting.

To interrupt a course of study laid out for four years by jumping back and forth you'd lose out on your education. You'd lose all hope for an R.O.T.C. scholarship later on. Don't worry about money. We will take care of that. You study and succeed. That's your job.

Honey, I want to mail this, so I'll end.

> All my love,
> Mom

Sept. 16, 1976

Hey, Billy,

This is Ronnie. Well, I'll try to write down everything I can remember, but you know me, a stupid ass. I forgot to tell you I got Dierker for homeroom. This year's seniors are assholes. I had marching band practice. I think it's going to be all right. This year's frosh are dumb shits. I'm going shooting tonight. They say there's some pieces down there. Classes so far have been a bust. I had homework for the first night. It was hot up here and we ran the mile in gym. I did all right. I'm in jocks classes in the morning and heads classes in the afternoon. We went to Uncle Steve's last weekend. Steve M. has a silver Goat '67. Your car could blow his doors off. Dad went up to check on the car yesterday, but I got up there before him and hid everything. Since you left the closest I've been to a hot car are my models downstairs and, of course, hitching. What would you like a picture of? I got my own camera.

> Ronnie

Sept. 19, 1976

Dear Harry,

It's good to hear you are making more friends. That will make life better. Everyone thinks you are doing great.

We would like to get some idea of how your marks are. Do you think that you are doing well? Don't let anything throw you. Keep your head and you can and will handle anything that comes your way. If you go out on the weekend be careful. Don't go into the wrong places. We want you to have a wonderful time during your Citadel career. It is a top school and when you graduate you will have something that is very worthwhile. Citadel grads are looked up to. Your career and entire life will be made. You can even retire before I do. Wouldn't that be wild?

Mom mentioned our feelings regarding some of your thoughts from your one letter. I also feel that you would be making a very big mistake by switching schools. You would end up being nothing. You wouldn't have the true Citadel education or background and you need that to have your great life. Please don't listen to the guys who always knock the school and probably everything else. They don't want The Citadel or the military, so forget them. That kind of guy will always talk about how much better it is somewhere else. That's not you, Harry. You know what you want so you can cope with whatever there is and come out on top. Don't worry about the money. We will take care of that. You just take care of you and your grades. Don't let the upperclassmen get to you. They are supposed to weed out the weak ones.

I don't think you should take your car yet. Your grades are too important, especially in the freshman year. Get by this tough year first. Don't blow the whole thing. A car would take too much of your time and effort and you can't afford that.

We miss you and things are different without you. But we think how good a school you are at and how great a life you are making for yourself and, then, things are better. But we still miss you very much. Make as many friends as you can but good friends. Weed out the guys who play everybody for suckers. They are not friends. Look out for yourself at all times. I will try to find out about a rifle permit as soon as I can. Grandma and Pop Pop were here today. They miss you and can't wait to see you. Let us know if you get our birthday card. I enclosed $5.00 and stamps and we are putting $20.00 in your checking account. Your brothers will have birthday gifts for you when you get home. It's supposed to be a surprise. Don't expect too much from them. They are a little cheap, especially Ronnie. He can't wait until he can work at the Garden State Parkway gas station. Can you put in a good word for him? We will send your airplane tickets down later, but make sure you find out how to get to the Charleston Airport. We will meet you at this end. Be in uniform, and don't forget to bring a warm coat. Mom will have everything you like when you get here. It really will be a Thanksgiving!

Have you found out if you can leave your things down there *safely* over the summer or do you bring them home? Is there a problem of stealing in the school? I hope not. That surely would violate the Honor Code.

Well, Harry, I guess that's all for now. Be careful. We all miss you and love you. Have a Happy Birthday.

All my love,
Dad

Sept. 20, 1976

Dear Billy,

This is Ronnie. I'm going to try to tell you what's going on around here. I'll start from now and move back. Dad just left for a softball game. Last night me and a friend went tokin' but before that I met another kid and we were using the H20 pipe, but there was no H20 in it, and we got burnt. After that me and my friend had a "J" and, then, went to the Burger King. It was slow acting pot because we were sitting in the corner and we just started laughing at each other for about 10 minutes. People watched while we laughed. Then we just stopped. Before that I bought 5 "J's" and I lost them. Then I spent the whole night looking for them. I found them two nights before this. Me and some other guys did a cigar joint in a H20 pipe and a huge bowl. Later on when I went home I staggered and slurred, and my eyes were red and half closed, so I took the dog for a walk. But I couldn't stand when Lucky stopped. I had no sense of balance. It was outrageous. I have never been so wrecked.

School is now a ball-buster. I have to write up a bio-lab. The last few parties I've been to were great. Let's see, by the time you get this it will probably be your birthday. So, Happy Birthday and take it slow.

Ronnie

P.S. I got a pipe.

Sept. 23, 1976

Ronnie,

Are you fuckin' burnt out or what. Better cut down the bull shit before you are caught. Dad would probably shoot you. If you're too bad I'm going to break your ass when I get home. What types are you doing? What besides reefs? If you touch acid I'll break your balls. So when are you and Steve going to start work on the Mustang. Put in the Japanese tape player and carpet.

Boy, does this place ever blow shit. It looks and feels like a prison. One thing, when I come back, I'm going to be strong as shit. I've noticed that already. Hey, man, you better have some on hand when I get home to soothe the savage beast. (Me.) Can you see Dad's face when I come home with a couple of sixes and sit down and drink. I might let him have one. So write, you turkey.

Harry

Sept. 27, 1976

Little Punk Brother,

Yeah, I know you're a stupid ass, like you said in a letter. You don't have to tell me that. The only work I'm going to let Steve do to the Mustang is interior work and oil change and charge battery. Get Steve to get the car started one day before I come home. Tell Dierker if he isn't nice to you I'll come back with my M-14 and waste him. That's the rifle we all have.

Who has the bad-assed car in the school parking lot now? Get a hold of your head friends and send down some shit. Can always use that. What do you mean you hid everything when Dad checked the car? Get a clean shot of the engine. See who else you can get to write to me. Last night I got totally wasted.

How are your new proofs working. Soon you'll be 18 according to my proofs. See ya all later.

Bill

Sept. 30, 1976

Dear Harry,

It's been a long time since Mom and I got a letter from you. Ron has gotten two letters but he only reads us parts.

We got your bank statement. It showed two checks for $25.00

each. What did you spend $50.00 on. Please let us know. Also, you have about $50.00 in cash, plus the few dollars Grandma and I sent down. What are you spending that much money on? Remember you are no longer working, and your bank account is way down.

How are your studies going? Do you think that you will be able to get involved in any school sports, or would it take too much time from your studies? Studies are first. This first year is the hardest so you can look forward to better times. If you have problems there are all kinds of people to talk to. If you need me there for any big problems just ask and I'll be there.

Remember all those guys who said you wouldn't last. Well, you are proving them wrong (Mom and I knew you would) so keep up the good work. You will show them all how good a man you are. We were talking to our mayor at an Eagle Scout Ceremony. He is very impressed that you are at The Citadel. Everyone we talk to wishes you luck, and they are all impressed.

Harry, some of the things we hear about other colleges are pretty bad and the kids going to them really don't seem to be getting much out of school. We feel that you picked a good school and will come out better than all those other kids put together. We are so proud of you and love you so much that we want you to be the best you possibly can, so you just do your best and keep your cool.

We always tell Lucky that his big brother Hatchy will be home soon and he always perks up his ears like he is listening for you. I guess that's it for now. Be good and be careful.

All my love,
Dad

Oct. 6, 1976

Dear Harry,

Everyday Mom and I look for a letter from you but nothing. We really would like answers to our many questions and how things are going. How are your grades?

Some of the people you know are asking for you. They are all pulling for you so make sure you live up to the praise and pride people have in you. I hope things are easing up and you are enjoying college life more. We want you to be happy. But we also want to know if you are having any problems. We will help whatever way we can. Remember there is no one in the whole world who loves you more than Mom and I. You are our number one son, so let us know.

We want you to confide in us. Don't hold anything back. If we don't know, then we can't help. Sometimes you may not agree with us. But you know we are trying to do whatever is right for you.

We sure wish you would write more to us. I know you write to other people which is fine. But don't forget Mom and Dad.

All my love,
Dad

Oct. 11, 1976

Dear Harry,

We sure were glad to get your letter. But, Harry, don't give up your sleep to write. Try to do it on the weekend or some other time. You describe the Freshman year pretty well and we here at home also know you are in a very tough school, but we also know you can take it. The next three years will be like a whole different school world. You sure will be ready for anything when you graduate from El Cid.

How are your grades doing? When will we be sent your report card? Any chance for a scholarship? Keep trying your best. Don't let anything keep you from being the top student that you can be. Any new friends? We always like to know about that.

Eric got a card to start instruction at the rifle club. He's all excited about it. I guess he will do all right. He really looks up to you, even more that he does Ronnie. You are his idol. I'd say he picked a pretty good idol. Ronnie is in the "too cool" stage and he seems to get more and more lazy. He doesn't play football or run cross country. He says he is going out for spring track again. I hope so. I think he could do well in wrestling. He is thinking about it. He also said he may leave the school band, but we are totally against that. I think it is just a stage. I think he has had it with Scouts. He still needs one merit badge for "Star" but he is not trying. He really is a great boy, but maybe a little encouragement from you may help. That is, if you think you want to try. Ron also looks up to you. Some day he too will find out that Mom and I are doing things for his own good and not to bug him, but it takes time to understand that. Right now he thinks we are picking on him. But everything will work out o.k.

It won't be much longer before we send you the airline tickets— right after the Christmas Club money comes. Try to find out if there is a special car or bus or something that you can take to the Charleston Airport. If not, then take a taxi. We can't wait to see you. We have so much to ask and talk about when you get home.

Always remember that you can do anything you want to as long as you try. You can even become the top cadet at The Citadel if you want to. Just do your best. Work hard. Don't be afraid to sacrifice to get ahead. We have all the confidence in you so make sure you have it in yourself.

Love,
Dad

Oct. 14, 1976

Hey, Ronnie,

You sound like a real head and all that other bull in some of the letters you write. I used those words once in a while—but not like that. Cool the b.s. Who you trying to fool?

I might have to leave the company (transfer). I was racked by a corporal and when I left his room I left as slow as I could and to open the door I punched it open. Broke it right off the hinges. He yelled for me to get back in his room, but I told him where to go. Then his roommate, a mean mother, called me back. He may try to get me out of the company. But the corporal hasn't bothered me since. He knows next time I throw him off the 3rd floor.

Hey, don't overdo. Don't bum your head out.

When I come back Christmas I'll probably sell the Mustang and buy an old car down here. Maybe a Nomad or old Ford. Something good anyway. The hot cars are cheap down here.

Well, see you later, burn-out.

Billy

Oct. 26, 1976

Dear Harry,

I was waiting to get the firearm application before writing to you, so here it is. Remember you have to be fingerprinted up here. Then it goes to the FBI for review. Either bring it home with you or send it up in your letter. The two references for the gun application should be from N.J. For the reason for the gun use: TARGET SHOOT-ING.

I hope all the things you are saving to tell us aren't too bad or things that might get you in trouble. Mom and I worry about you. We want everything to go right for you. A little reassurance that everything is ok would be appreciated. But don't bend the truth to make us feel better. Tell us exactly how things are. We will stick by you in every way. Mom and I, Ron and Eric, Grandma and Pop Pop and Lucky and Muffins are really looking for the day when you will be home. We understand that you will want to visit your friends, but don't forget us.

I'm really sorry to hear that there are so many freshmen who don't have enough guts to stick it out. After the first year it's all different. Again, how are your grades and when do we get the report? How is R.O.T.C. going? Try to get a rank in it if you can. It won't hurt. Any chance at a scholarship?

Ronnie is calming down some. You know I won't let him get out of hand. I don't try to be tough, only to help and teach the best I can. Do you have it set up to work at the gas station during Christmas Holiday? Maybe Steve can help with that. We will be sending the plane ticket down soon.

Well, Harry, I'll say so long for now. Be careful and do your best. Don't let anybody bait you into any bad situations. Just take it as it comes.

Love,
Dad

Oct. 26, 27, 28, 1976

Dear Harry,

I'm glad to know the care packages are arriving o.k. Do you need something other than food—toothpaste, razor blades, shoe laces?

You say you will be out most of Thanksgiving. You do plan to have dinner here I hope? We are all counting on that. We know you won't be home much, but just enough time to let us really know how things are. Write and tell me what you want for breakfast, lunch and dinner while you are home. You should be home about 9:00 P.M. Wednesday *Nov.* 24 and your plane leaves at 1:00 Sunday, *Nov.* 28. You may not have time to go to church. About Thanksgiving Dinner, I can arrange to serve it at a time that's convenient. Do you want to eat early or late? 1:00 or 6:00?

Do you see any easing up yet? There's less than a month to go for Thanksgiving, and then a month to Christmas. If you take one day at a time, this year will be over, and recognition day will be here.

Your early A.M. letter to Dad has arrived. I would rather not have Grandma and Pop Pop stay overnight on Thanksgiving because that would mean they would be here all day Friday too. We can sit up late and talk and all that but I would rather they go home.

It was in the mid-20's this A.M. Warming up to the 30's. You will be wearing that winter coat with the fur hood for sure when you come home.

You know the prayer chain they have in church. They prayed away my cancer. Well, they prayed for four boys starting college for one month. Maybe that has given you the strength you needed to go through the knob year. I'm glad you were on that prayer chain. We know you can do it, no matter how hard it gets. You have a goal and as long as you keep it in front of you you'll make it.

Today I was stuffing envelopes again for the Republican party. Tomorrow night is the Republican Dance. Sunday I'm helping man the phones to get out the voters.

I love you, darling, and I'll pray for you every day. I'm very proud of you.

All my love,
Mom

Oct. 28, 1976

Hey, Harry,

Yea, I'm sorry I haven't written. Yea, I've been goofing out. I made myself a party kit. School's a bust but I goof out before school most days.

I went shooting last night. The way I got there was I walked down the tracks and when I got to the Burger King some girl knew me, but I didn't know her. She drove me around. Then Steve got in too. Last night I talked to Patty Hennessy.

Oh, yea. I've been to two parties. First was a sweet sixteen party with the goody-goodies. But I fixed that. I brought pot and beer.

The second party was for a kid from California with a lot of kids like the heads we know. We got messed. Did you ever see my pipe? I also had a cigar joint ¾" diameter, 5" long. I got it for $2.50. A steal. I don't want to send any down so you don't get screwed.

We all miss you. Do good. I'm proud of you.

Ronnie

Nov. 2, 1976

Dear Harry,

It was good to hear from you. I'm sorry that you didn't feel well. Did you get some aspirin? Did you see the doctor? Are you feeling better now?

I'm sending you a copy of the report card. We were disappointed, but we understand. I hope you can bring up those grades for the next report. Check with your instructors and class advisor to see what can be done. Don't let your grades slip. If you get "F" then they could drop you out of school. Please do your best. We can't wait for you to get home. The airline tickets are enclosed. We will meet you at Kennedy Airport in New York. It's getting cold up here. You probably won't be able to wait until you get back to the warm south.

Harry, don't let anyone get you down. Keep doing your best. Stay strong and smart.

When you thanked me for the way we tried to teach you when you were growing up it meant more to me than anything. Mom and I both felt so good when we read it.

Take care of yourself. See the doctor if necessary. Get those grades up for your own sake and pride. We'll see you in about three weeks.

Love,
Dad

Nov. 2, 1976

Dear Harry,

I'm in school now. The class is asleep except for an occasional joke.

I finished my party kit and I really haven't had a good chance to use it. Oh, yea, I used your I.D. I put the carpet in your car. I have been putting $5.00 a week away. In about a month I will be getting my social security. I've been to a few parties lately. Mom and Dad and Eric are going to Port Jervis for Eric's football games. I'll be alone for a day. I can hardly wait. Mom and Dad want me to get a haircut, but I am eluding it. I don't hang around the bowling alley any more. When you come back you don't have to bring anything because Mom bought you a new pair of dungarees, and I have plenty of tee shirts.

Ronnie

Nov. 5, 1976

Folks,

How are you doing? I'm doing ok. A lot of excitement over the weekend. When the seniors got their rings the barracks were destroyed. Paint all over the place, garbage cans were flying. And all the freshmen had to clean up the mess.

About Grandma and Pop Pop staying over. I want them to stay even if I have to be stubborn about it. I can drive Grandma to work so that would take care of that. The reason I want them to stay over is that I would like Grandma to cook breakfast like she used to do. Also, we all know that Grandma is getting on in years, so she might not be around. Since I'm down here I can't see her that much, so that is why I want Grandma to stay. About what I said about being stubborn is that I can be really rotten and leave early from home to come back to school at Thanksgiving and not come home at Christmas. I could stay at school or go over to one of my classmates homes who live around here. You know I will do something when I say it. If you can't do this one thing I really want then I guess I might as well stay down here—especially after all the fun and games I'm having down here. I already know how to get down here by car taking Interstate Highway 95.

Well, I hate to be like this, but this is the way it is. That's all. I hope you don't think I'm joking because I learned to forget how to joke down here.

Harry

Nov. 9, 1976

Dear Harry,

We got your letter with the rifle permit form in it. You know that before I can turn it in you have to be fingerprinted in Montvale. I'm sure we can do it while you're home.

Harry, we know that this first year is very hard, but please try extra hard to erase those bad grades. It's a lot to ask but please try to get A's and B's (mostly A's). Ronnie's grades aren't too great either. Maybe you can tell him how important good grades are.

We are anxious to hear all about the things that have been happening to you, so save us some time so we can talk.

I'm really sorry to hear about all those guys who are cracking up and the boys who don't have enough guts to stick it out. As I said many years ago, the guy who quits the first time will quit again and again. It's a hard habit to break once it's started. I wish I could talk to all those kids who want to quit. By the way, when you graduate, will you get a commission in the regular army or in the reserves? I think it would be better in the regular army if you can. What do you think?

Only about 2 weeks before Thanksgiving. See you soon. Be careful and work hard.

Love,
Dad

Nov. 11, 1976

Dear Harry,

Dad's softball team played today, a team on which Roger Anderson played. Roger told Dad you had written.

An offer of a ride home at Christmas sounds good but (1) is it sure, (2) how about the return trip, (3) how many boys will ride, (4) how much will it cost? I must know by return mail how you plan to come home at Christmas. Tickets are very tight at that time. If you can get a safe ride both ways that would be great.

You know, Harry, you could have told us your reasons for wanting Grandma and Pop Pop to stay. You didn't need to carry on with all those threats. I'm sorry you "no longer know how to joke." If you lose that capacity you lose a great deal, but I do think you came on a little strong. Since that is "one thing you really want" of course you should have it.

Harry, your last couple of letters seem "up tight." Please calm down and try to take it easy when you can. Vacation is almost here. We'll see you at the airport on November 24.

Love,
Mom

Nov. 11, 1976

Ronnie,

How are ya doin', burnout? Better hide the party kit well. What happens if someone finds it? A good place to hide it is in the fishing bag hanging on the inside of my closet on the door. Who's been having good parties lately? Do Mom and Dad check you out when you come in? Don't get too carried away when Mom and Dad go away. Remember when they told me they were going to be gone two days and came back the same day.

I come home in 13 days. I'm gonna see how many points I can rack up on my license before I come back down here.

Harry

Nov. 14, 1976

Mom and Dad,

I got care package #10 and the tickets o.k. Thanksgiving night is when I tell you about the school. Nothing before that.

I wrote to Steve to tell him to get the car running before I get home. I hear Ronnie put carpet in the Mustang. I wonder how it looks. I'm going to have a long talk with Ronnie when I get home.

I'll be home in 10 days!

Harry

V

Thanksgiving Vacation

13

By the time I was ready to leave for home on Saturday, November 20, I had changed the plane tickets my parents had sent for November 24. But by then I had my choice of flying or driving with another cadet. Pete Salerno, the cadet from the Lutheran group who lived in my area, had heard of my mother's illness, so he offered me a chance to ride home with the guy he was driving with. Pete was going home early since he'd come to The Citadel early for freshmen training in the fall.

"If you can wait till Sunday," Pete promised, "I'll see you have a ride. I can also get you a ride back to school if you want to plan on that."

I told him, "No, I have to get home." But then I asked if he could bring my shako and full dress uniform if there was room in the car. I'd be wearing my dress uniform on the plane. But I wanted my parents to see me in my full dress garb. Pete agreed, so before I left for home I took the uniform to him. He wasn't in his room, however, so I told his roommate about it and put it on Pete's desk.

The next day, which happened to be Homecoming Day, Walt Singleton drove me to the Charleston Airport after he set up traffic signs at the school stadium, where he worked. All I took home was a sweat shirt and my Citadel army jacket, and as we bucked traffic to the airport we talked about seeing my family until Walt put me on the plane that would take me to New York.

When I arrived at Kennedy Airport my parents and brothers

102

were there, and everybody looked the same—except Ronnie had put on weight. He was as heavy as I was at 6 feet and 135 pounds.

"Hey, turkey," I told him. "Wait till I wrestle you."

My father drove the long way home so we would have time to talk, since my parents were leaving when we got back to Montvale. They had planned a trip to Port Jervis for Eric's Mustang League games. The three of them would be away until some time on Sunday. This was the night that Ronnie had been looking forward to.

I didn't say much about college while riding home in the car, and when my parents asked questions I answered, "I'll tell you later on." Later there wasn't much chance for this, since I wasn't home a great deal.

Finally after the long way home we got to Grand Avenue. Then as soon as we walked into the house and sat down at the kitchen table my father gave me the shock of my life when he said, "Would you like a beer?"

"You're eighteen now," he added. "You're the legal age."

My mother had made a "Welcome Home" cake—and we talked till they left for Port Jervis. Then I went up to Mrs. Blair's house to take my Mustang from her garage and get started driving around. I was *very* happy to be back home, and I wanted to see *everyone*.

Naturally I looked for Steve first, and we made our plans for the night. Then I headed for Park Ridge to look for some of the people I knew and show them my uniform. My first stop was the Hennessys' to see Patty, Vicki, and their mother. Next I went to Jeff Bickerton's, and when Jeff saw my uniform he first thought I was a cop! We talked about cars a little while, and then we went out together, after I stopped at my house to change to a pair of jeans. Later I tried to see Vinnie Trojan. But Vinnie wasn't home, so I picked up Steve and we drove around and stopped at the A & P. At the shopping center I saw Jeff Fritts, who had never met Steve. Jeff asked what I'd be doing that night, and I said I'd be out with Steve.

When I wasn't looking for someone on that first day home, I was in my room at the house listening to my stereo. Ronnie had moved back to his room, and he was there rolling dice. We rolled a couple together and he said he was having a party that night since our parents were away.

He also confided, "Look what I've got!" And then he reached under his bed and pulled out a small green foot locker like you get with a G.I. Joe doll.

"This is where I keep my pot," he said, sounding pleased with himself.

I took a look inside the box and saw the scales and rollers, as well as several baggies that Ronnie had already emptied.

"You'd better be careful," I warned him. But I didn't say anymore.

Then later when we took my car back to Mrs. Blair's garage for a good look at Ronnie's carpeting job and the other work he'd done, Ronnie brought out a plastic bag and offered me some pot. He acted proud to give it to me and I said, "Well, okay."

I'll always feel guilty for taking it and not speaking to Ronnie then, especially since I'd already seen, from a close look at the carpet, that Ronnie must have really been stoned while he was doing the work. I should have talked to him that day as soon as I saw what he had—and I should have said, "Cool it, Ronnie, before Dad catches you." But I was starting vacation, so I let it go for the moment.

I wasn't with Ronnie very much during the rest of the week, and now I will always feel at fault that I was too busy to stop him from his involvement with drugs. Just saying he'd better cool it wasn't doing enough.

When I went out that Saturday night I drove around with Steve until we dropped back at the house around 9:30 or so. I wanted to show Steve something, and I wanted to check on Ronnie, since I felt he had something up his sleeve, but I didn't know just what. As we pulled up to the side of the house I heard the records blasting, and as soon as we walked inside of the door the place reeked of pot and beer. When Ronnie had mentioned earlier that he was having kids over I thought it might be a party and that, maybe, he would have beer. But I didn't think he'd be stupid enough to allow pot in the house.

"If you get caught," I informed him, "it will be your ass, not mine."

"You know your father's temper," Steve pointed out right away, "and you know the threats that he has made if he ever caught you with drugs. You're asking for a blow-up if your father finds out."

"I don't mind the beer," I put in, "but you're not smoking pot in here. Anyone who's smoking pot has to get out right now."

With that the kids went out of the house and Ronnie went along, probably down to the railroad tracks where no one would bother them. Steve and I waited till everyone left. Then we went out again.

I'll never know if my parents smelled pot when they returned from Port Jervis. But they didn't get home on Sunday in time to go to church. I was anxious to see Pastor Nilsen, so I drove down alone. A lot of people didn't know me in my Citadel uniform and Ruth Mohring, an intern for the ministry, asked Pastor who I was. Later she'd say she'd never forget me. But we didn't know that then.

After church I headed for Park Ridge to look for Vinnie Trojan. But he still wasn't home when I stopped by so I went to visit the Hennessys again before I returned to my house. When I finally got back my parents were there, and the first thing my mother asked me was, "What do you want for dinner?" I immediately answered "Pizza" and we had it that Sunday night.

I finally caught up with Vinnie Trojan on the following day, when I picked him up at Park Ridge High. By then I'd decided to fix up my Mustang so I would have it ready, whether I drove to The Citadel just to pick up my things or whether I went back and stayed there—without attending classes—for the two-and-a-half-week period until the Christmas vacation. I could always cash in my plane ticket and just before Thanksgiving I'd talked to an upperclassman who'd said if I brought a car back he'd put it under his name.

I was thinking of this possibility most of the day on Monday. But I also had another thought as I'd talked to a guy on the weekend who had a station wagon he wanted to sell for $200. I'd thought of selling my Mustang occasionally in the past, but I couldn't get a good price for it in its present form. If I spent some money on it, though, I should get $1200. Since I'd be leaving The Citadel—at the latest by Christmas vacation—I figured if I could sell it for that I'd spend $200 for the wagon and then use the rest of the money to set up some place to live. After that I'd get a job and look for another school.

Whatever I did, however, I had to fix up the Mustang so I made up my mind I'd cash in my coins for the money I'd need for the car. When I picked up Vinnie I told him that I had run out of money at school so I needed to cash in my silver which would go for a very good price. The coins that I cashed at a coin exchange were the ones in my own collection, though later when Pop Pop missed some of his, he accused me of ripping off silver from the collection he kept at our house.

I cashed the check I got for the coins—$1625.12—and I didn't tell my father because he'd ask why I sold them. As yet I wasn't about to tell him that I was leaving school.

By Tuesday I started dropping small hints that I might drive to South Carolina. But my parents never picked up on this so I don't know whether they got it, and I let it go at that. On Tuesday morning my mother was mad when Jeff Fritts came to the house. Jeff who can look like a hillbilly almost without even trying had been to a party the previous night with one of his other buddies. The guy got really loaded, and he was feeling no pain when he and Jeff came to the door to see me the following day. My mother didn't think much of the pair because of that incident, so she did her best to discourage me from hanging around with Jeff. Jeff was really a good guy, though, so I thought to myself, "He's my friend, and I'll do what I want to do."

Later that same evening I went out with Steve and him, and the three of us went to Nanuet Shopping Mall, where we acted like three stooges. We were so crazy we cracked ourselves up, and when I'd try to act serious I'd say, "I don't know you people." Eventually in a grim moment—and crucial time in my life—Steve and I would exchange a glance that said "Nanuet Mall."

Before I went out in the evening I drove around most of the

day, and while I was waiting for Vinnie to finish his afternoon classes I ran into Jeff De Causemaker. I hadn't seen him since I'd been home. He was standing by a snack shop where the Park Ridge kids hung out, so the two of us spoke briefly till Vinnie finished school. Then Vinnie and I raced my Mustang along Spring Valley Road.

I had a habit of taking that car up to its highest speed. Then I'd put it into neutral and just coast along. Usually while I was coasting I'd check in the rear mirror and when I looked this Tuesday I saw a cop's flashing lights. I'd never had any trouble with cops, except for warnings on speedings. But this time I said to Vinnie, "Oh-oh, he's going to get me."

If I'd kept on going he wouldn't have caught me, and he couldn't have seen my license. But I pulled over to the side, sure I was in for a ticket. I was lucky, however. It was a cop who knew me, and all he said was, "All right, De La Roche. What's your excuse this time?" He was in a very good mood, and all I got was a warning. Seeing the cop on Tuesday reminded me of the form I had for my rifle permit, and I meant to go down to the station and get my fingerprints. I got involved, however, and never got down with the form.

On Wednesday I spent the morning listening to my stereo and cleaning the .22 pistol from my father's bedside table. I was thinking of going shooting down at the rifle range, so my father said I could clean the pistol and load the clip with ten shells. I put it back in the table drawer when I finished loading it and, as · it turned out, the week went by and I didn't get down to the range.

After school I picked up Vinnie again, and then we drove over to Pete Salerno's to find out about the dress uniform I'd left for him to bring home. I wanted it for Thanksgiving when my grandparents came to dinner. When we stopped at Pete's he wasn't home, so we drove around for a while till I dropped off Vinnie at his house and went back to mine to eat. I left again at 6:00 to return to Pete Salerno's. I found him home on this trip, but he told me as soon as I arrived that he'd forgotten the uniform when he left school in a hurry.

"My roommate forgot to tell me you dropped it off," he explained, "and I was in and out of the room and didn't see it myself. I'll try to call him later tonight and if, by chance, he brought it home I'll let you know tomorrow."

Then Pete asked what I'd be doing about returning to school, and I told him I'd be going back for the two-and-a-half weeks till Christmas. I stayed and talked about cars awhile and then I went to find Vinnie. The two of us went to look for Jeff Fritts, and then we went out for the night. When my friends asked about The Citadel I kept pretty quiet, and I usually tried to make it appear that I'd be going back. I often just said, "It's okay" when people asked me about it, though I told certain people—like Steve and some of the others—some of the things that happened and how hard it really was. Steve and a few of the others knew I planned to pack it in. But even they weren't exactly sure whether I'd quit after getting my things or whether I'd stay till Christmas. I guess you couldn't expect them to know when I sometimes wavered myself.

The big thing on Thanksgiving was the football games, and I stopped in, first, at Pascack Hills and, next, at the Park Ridge game. By the time I got home from the two games Grandma and Pop Pop were there and we all sat down to dinner around the dining room table. The Ebneters asked lots of questions, but I kept making it clear that I didn't want to talk about school and would tell them about it later. By dessert I was getting restless and anxious to get away, so I decided to drive around to see who I could find.

No one was out, however, because it was Thanksgiving, so before too long I returned to the house, hoping Pete Salerno would call. I was beginning to feel uptight about the return to school. But each day it was harder to work myself up to talking to my parents about my future plans.

I waited till 6:00 for Pete to call. Then I put in a call to him. He'd just come home from a family dinner and hadn't phoned before because he'd learned that his roommate didn't have my uniform. I got more uptight than ever when I heard about this and I think I said something silly—like, "My parents will be ready to kill me."

Pete was upset and I was upset so he tried to calm me down by saying he'd talk to my parents if I wanted him to.

"Forget it," I said, as I tried to hang up.

"But what's the big deal?" he asked me. "I really don't understand it, especially since you'll be returning to The Citadel on Sunday."

Then he was silent before he asked, "You *are* coming back to school, aren't you?"

I told him then that I wasn't sure. But he said he could still provide a ride if I let him know in time.

I said "Okay" and hung right up. I never saw Pete again.

When I returned from the phone call I told Mom and Dad that Pete had slipped up on bringing the uniform. Then, since the Ebneters were ready to leave, I arranged to visit them Friday and spend the night in Lodi. My parents still found excuses why they couldn't sleep over, so the next best thing was to sleep over there for an extra visit with them.

On Friday Vinnie had a holiday, so we drove over to a tire place and I bought new tires for the Mustang with money from the coins. I figured I would have them if I drove to South Carolina, and even though I'd be cutting it close I knew that I could make it if I left early Sunday and drove for fifteen hours.

I didn't want my father to see my brand new tires because he'd ask why I bought them and where I got the cash. I still wasn't ready to answer that and face a confrontation. On Friday I went to Lodi in time to have supper there, and the Ebneters and I sat and talked until eleven or so. In the morning I woke at six o'clock since I was accustomed to that. But I laid around till 10:00 or 11:00 thinking about the next day. When Grandma had breakfast ready I got out of bed. A little later my mother called to see when I'd be home. That was the only phone call I had at my grandmother's house and when I said goodbye to her—and promised to take care—neither of us knew at the moment what a long goodbye it would be.

By the time I got back to Montvale my parents were having lunch, so I sat at the kitchen table with them before I went back out. Ronnie wasn't home at the time, and I didn't see Eric either. I tried to get in and out quickly but my parents both mentioned returning to school and said I should get my things ready for the 1:00 P.M. flight on Sunday.

"I don't have much to get ready," I replied. "Just my sweat shirt and army jacket." Then before they could say any more I got out of the door.

The first thing I did when I left the house was to go to see Freddie Caine, one of the kids from the Park Ridge gang who had an apartment beneath his house that I knew nobody was using. I suggested the two of us set it up and, then, have me move in. I figured if I could arrange this I could move out of the Montvale house when I came home for Christmas.

We smoked a joint while we talked about this and I suggested—real hard—that he go and ask his father if this would be all right. But Freddie answered, "No, not now." I tried to urge him to change his mind. When he wouldn't I said, "Make it soon."

My parents were planning to rake the leaves that Saturday afternoon, so I thought I'd go back and help awhile, if they wouldn't bring up school. They seemed to be in a very good mood and didn't ask any questions. After I'd done enough of the leaves I decided to call it quits and drive around to say goodbye to some of the people I wouldn't see till I got home at Christmas. Just as I had the Saturday before I dropped in at the Bickertons' and, also, the Hennessys'. When I went to look for Jeff Bickerton only his sister was home, so I stayed and talked to Allison for an hour or so.

"How's the Army?" she asked me, as soon as I got inside.

"It's The Citadel, *not* the Army," I declared, as I slouched down in the living room chair where I always felt so at home.

"Well, how's it going?" she continued.

"It's hard," I said, with finality. Then I switched the subject to cars.

Later Allison had a date, so after we talked for a while she went up to take a shower, while I stayed and listened to records. When she came down Jeff still wasn't home, so I said "I can't stay any longer. But tell Jeff I was here."

Next I went to Hennessys' and I talked with Mrs. Hennessy

while she took care of her baby and gave her a bath in the kitchen. I felt I could mention school to her, so I opened up a little, and we discussed how everyone finds the first months pretty tough.

"They're always a rough adjustment," she said. "You have to give it time. But if by Christmas you still don't like it no law says you have to stay. You could work and save money and go to another school."

There was still some time before supper, so I made a trip to Nanuet Shopping Mall and bought myself an expensive watch with some of the money that I had from the sale of the coins. I'd seen that watch at The Citadel and fallen in love with it. In twenty-four hours it would be gone. But for the brief time I had it, my $300 wristwatch was one of the nicest possessions I had ever owned.

I stopped to buy cookies and brownies at a bakery on the way home and just as I got back to the house Dad and Eric were coming in with pizzas. Ronnie and Eric ate by the TV and I sat down in the kitchen to eat with my mother and father. We talked of my plans for the evening and I said I'd probably stay out late since this was my last free night. Little did I know how truthful that statement would turn out to be.

I knew the time was getting short for talking about my plans. But, still, I couldn't bring myself to say, "I'm leaving The Citadel." There was always Sunday morning. Maybe I could say it then. I also had in the back of my mind that if I was questioned at supper I'd say, "I'm still on vacation. I'll tell you about school at Christmas. I'll tell you everything then." I didn't have to say this, though, because I was able to get out of the house before any questions arose.

There was never a confrontation about my leaving school, though newspaper reporters would later say my father and I had an argument about The Citadel. This was conjecture on their part every bit of the way because in my week with my family there was never a time that we ever discussed the big things on our minds. None of us knew what the other was thinking, and we left it at that.

When I left the house after supper—between 6:30 and

7:00—Ronnie left in the Mustang with me to collect his paper money. I dropped him off in the center of town to collect at Nottingham Apartments. Then I made plans for the evening that, unbeknown to me, was going to be the last good evening I'd have for many a year.

Steve was going to a party, and I had a chance to go, too. But I really felt like driving around, so I headed to Jeff Fritts's house. It wasn't cold, but there was a fog, and before the evening was over the fog would be so heavy you couldn't see twenty-five feet ahead.

While I was driving to Jeff's house my stick shift started to lock, so I stopped the car at a parking lot a few doors from where Jeff lived. The lot was crowded with cars and kids since it was by a tavern, and while I was working on the shift Vinnie drove by with friends. While we talked I put my new watch in my pocket so I wouldn't damage it. Then when I got the car fixed—or thought I had it fixed—I drove up the road to find Jeff.

His sister Lisa, who was waiting for her date, came out to talk to me. Then Jeff and I got into my car and rode all over the place. We never drove very far, however, without the shift acting up, so we spent the first part of the evening trying to regulate that. I must have fixed it twenty times in only a matter of hours. I knew I was getting nowhere, though, so I finally said to Jeff, "Let's forget about it and go back for my mother's car. I'll meet you at 7-11 as soon as I change the car." Then I drove up to Mrs. Blair's, and after I parked in her garage I walked down to my house.

My parents were both in the living room when I went inside, my mother by the fireplace, my father on the couch. I sensed at once that they seemed upset. But they said I could have the car. I walked out through the kitchen, and I noticed on top of the dryer a clean tee shirt that said "El Cid" that my mother had washed and dried. I'd wanted to wear that earlier, rather than "The Citadel" shirt, so I took off "The Citadel" right away and changed to the clean "El Cid." Before I got any farther, though, I heard my father's voice and after he asked me a question he told me something that, in its own way, contributed to changing my life. This added another problem to those I already had.

Despite the problems, however, the evening was a good one, and Jeff and I went everywhere in my mother's car. We drove up to Rockland County and ate at a Burger King and, later, took off for a parking lot where racing was often done. Since I'd put my watch in my pocket while I was fixing my car I don't really know what time it was when we got home to Jeff's house. Jeff's sister's date had had problems with the car he was driving that night, so Jeff and I followed him to his house and talked awhile in his driveway.

I didn't feel ready to go home myself while we were in the driveway, so I asked the two guys to stay out awhile and drive back to Rockland County. They both said they wanted to call it a night so after I dropped Jeff off I wondered where I was going to go and who I could find around next.

While deciding I drove to the station where I'd worked and bought a soda and gas. There was nobody much at the station, though, so I headed for Rockland County and another burger spot. Then I drove to "Maximus," a storefront bar and cocktail lounge, located in New City, where I'd been just once before. The place was buzzing when I went in, and strobe lights were everywhere.

I found myself a place at the bar and had two Michelobs while I listened to the records and watched the couples dance. When I noticed all the guys had sport shirts instead of tee shirts like mine I kept my army jacket zipped so the "El Cid" wouldn't show. But the bartender saw my jacket and boots, so we started discussing the Army.

While we were talking a black guy saw my army jacket, too, and since he was going into the service we talked while we sat at the bar. Later the bartender would recall that I was sitting at the bar at approximately 1:30. He'd also state for the record that I wasn't intoxicated. After I moved to a table with the black dude, whose name was Steve, I didn't see the bartender again, but Steve and I must have sat and talked for the next half hour or so. Before the evening was over we exchanged full names and addresses. But I didn't notice Steve's last name when I stuck the paper in my wallet.

When I decided I'd better go home I went to the men's room

first, and while there I heard somebody say the time was a little after 2:00. I left Steve at the "Maximus" and when I got outside the fog had become more dense. It was so thick I drove home slowly—ten to fifteen miles an hour.

I drove on Route 304 for a while. Then, instead of continuing on the highway until I got to Montvale, I took the back way to Summit to Grand then down by Memorial School. I figured I'd go home by that route because if any guys were still out I'd find them by going that way. I thought, "I have nothing better to do, so let's see who is out."

Most of the time on my slow drive home I'd been thinking about the next day and what I'd tell my parents just a few hours from now. By then I'd planned to say Sunday, "Look, I'm driving back." But now I was in a new bind with the shift trouble on my car. Maybe if it got fixed early I could still try to drive. And maybe the cops wouldn't bust me for speed when I had my uniform on.

But even more disturbing was the new problem that I had after my talk with my father when I went home to change cars. This was very much on my mind as I parked my mother's car and made my way through the thickening fog to the steps leading to our side door. I noticed the light by the door was off.

And this was very strange.

VI

November 28, 1976

14

The fog was still heavy a short time later—yet almost a lifetime later—when I got back into my mother's car and headed for the Montvale police.

By now I've told a thousand times (or so it seems to me) how I met Patrolman Olsen down by the village green and jumped from the car to yell at him, "Quick, come up to my house. I've just found my parents and younger brother dead and my middle brother missing."

After Olsen followed me back to the house and sent for additional help I stayed there till Captain Hanna drove me to the Montvale headquarters at 6:30 A.M. When we arrived at the station I was told I could leave at 11:00 and maybe go to a relative's if I had somewhere to go. There weren't many relatives I could call, and my grandmother was too old. But I asked Captain Hanna to place a call to my Uncle John Greer in Maywood even though it had been years since I'd seen my uncle and aunt. That call wasn't placed immediately, though, since the first calls went out to Ronnie's friends to see if they knew where he was. I was also told I'd be fingerprinted for the purpose of elimination. At different points throughout the day I was fingerprinted twice. I was questioned intermittently starting at 7:30 by Sergeant Parisi of the New Jersey State Police and Investigator Del Prete of the Bergen County Prosecutor's Office. Detective O'Donovan was in and out.

Apparently, around 8:00 A.M. they saw the state I was in so

116

they left me alone in the lobby by Chief Hecker's office. There was a cop behind the desk but he didn't bother me when he saw that I was crying while I was by myself. That was the only time all day that they let me be alone.

When the questioning started up again I was shuffled back and forth between rooms till after 10:00 A.M. and when I noted it was 10:45 and I hadn't seen Uncle John I spoke to Captain Hanna about calling him again. Captain Hanna didn't want to make the call, so I got on the phone myself. When a man's voice answered I plunged right in and said, "Uncle John, this is Harry."

At first he didn't recognize me. It had been a long while, so I told him my name a second time. And then I said in a broken voice, "Dad, Mom, and Eric are shot, and I'm at the Montvale Police Station."

Uncle John was obviously stunned. But he answered, "We'll be right there." Later my Aunt Arden told me he looked so shaken and white he had to sit down and compose himself before they rushed to the station. She thought the call might be a hoax so she took an extra minute to place a call to the Montvale cops to see if—possibly—what they'd heard had been an anonymous crank call. When she learned that it was the truth they came to see me at once. But though they arrived by 11:00 they were told that I was busy—and, maybe, they could see me later. I asked the cops if they'd arrived. But they said the Greers weren't there.

About 11:00 I reminded the cops they'd mentioned I could leave at that time. But the cops explained they weren't through at the house so I'd have to wait awhile. I noticed they kept their eyes on me, and now, looking back at this day, I know I was technically under arrest long before anyone said so. While I was still at the station someone suggested a lie detector test at the Prosecutor's Office in Hackensack.

"Take it," one of the cops advised. "It will prove your innocence."

By then I was moving around like a zombie and starting to feel really dazed. I thought if I said "No" to the test they'd think I had something to hide, so I felt forced to say, "Yes, I'll take it, whenever you want me to."

By then I noted it was 11:18 and, suddenly, a new face appeared. I was told it was Edward Salbin, a court reporter who'd been called in to take a formal statement concerning the questions I'd answered in the morning's interrogations.

I hadn't talked to anyone but cops since four o'clock that morning and as I'd never been at a station and asked to give a statement I was unfamiliar with the United States Supreme Court's 1966 *Miranda* ruling. As a result, I agreed to repeat what I'd said for the record.

The Miranda Warnings, as I learned too late, protect your constitutional rights and limit police in obtaining confessions from a suspect. They include five points and a waiver. If they are given to you—and if you continue talking after saying you understand them—you surrender your right to remain silent under the Fifth Amendment. When I finally learned what they were I learned that the five points and waiver state:

1. You have the right to remain silent.
2. Anything you say can and will be used against you in a court of law.
3. You have the right to talk to a lawyer and have him present with you while you are being questioned.
4. If you cannot afford to hire a lawyer, one will be appointed to represent you before any questioning if you wish one.
5. You may stop answering questions at any time.

Waiver

After the waiver (and in order to secure a waiver) the following questions should be asked and an affirmative reply secured to each question.

1. Do you understand each of these rights I have explained to you?
2. Having these rights in mind, do you wish to talk to us now?

No officer read these rights to me, and nobody mentioned a lawyer—though if one had been there beside me, the cops would have taken it easier, and there wouldn't have been any way in the world that I would have talked like I did. Not knowing, I gave the following statement at the Montvale Police Headquarters. It ran a total of sixty-four pages. Parts of the statement follow:

    Q. Harry De La Roche, Jr.?
    A. Right.
    Q. I am Investigator Frank Del Prete of the Bergen County Prosecutor's Office. This is Detective Michael O'Donovan of the Montvale Police Department. We would like to take down a statement from you, a sworn statement, concerning the death of your parents, Mr. and Mrs. Harry De La Roche and your brother Eric. Are you willing to give us a sworn statement at this time?
    A. Yes, I am.

Following this I was sworn in by the court reporter. Then I answered questions about my activities from the time I went to Lodi on Friday. When we got to Saturday evening Del Prete asked about changing cars.

    Q. Did Jeff go to your home to pick up your mother's car?
    A. No he didn't. There was another guy, a friend of Jeff's and mine, who came to my house drunk the other day and my mother didn't really want me hanging around him, so I told Jeff to go down to the 7-11, which is down the road from me and I would meet him there. I went into the house, I told my mother I needed the car keys. My father asked me did I know Ronnie smokes marijuana and I said, "I don't know."
    He said he found some and he said he was going to turn Ronnie in to the police.
    I was disgusted at what he said, at turning in my brother, his own son, and then he mentioned something about Ronnie saying burying my father under his bed. Probably because that's where Ronnie kept the "pot" and money and the supplies.
    Q. How do you know Ronnie kept the pot, the money and the supplies under the bed?
    A. Well, he had a box full of scales, bags, rolling paper or rolling machine, and some of the bags had marijuana and he showed me a Pascack Hills gym bag which had money in it. There were

hundred-dollar bills in little bundles with rubber bands around them.

Q. When did Ronnie show you this bag and the scales?

A. He showed me the box and money around the second night I was there, the first or second night I was home.

Q. How did he come to show it to you, you were talking about pot and drugs?

A. Well, I knew that he was getting a little burnt out, he was selling it all and I told him he better cut it out and he said he wanted to show me what he had and I said, "Well, okay," so he did and I let it go at that.

Q. When your father told you about this he asked you do you know if Ronnie smokes pot?

A. He asked me, yes.

Q. What were his exact words to you, try to remember that?

A. I can't be sure of the exact words because I knew he was going to get caught sooner or later and it was just that my father knew and trouble was coming.

Q. Was your father mad, was he really mad when he told you this?

A. He seemed like he was upset that my brother would do that, because one of his colleagues who worked, his son had dropped grades really low hanging out with the wrong people and all after he smelled pot and his father found out. The same for my brother, his grades all went down and he got interims in all his subjects, but the thing that really bothered me was my own father would turn in my brother and I was thinking I just had to get out of there, I couldn't listen to that, I was going to come back today before I went to The Citadel and say "You turn him in, I'm not going to The Citadel. I can't let you turn him in."

After this discussion I accounted for the rest of the evening after leaving the "Maximus."

A. I got onto Route 17 to drive around in the area of Seven Lakes Parkway. That was the last place I drove before I first went to school. So then I started heading back and I came to the Dairy Queen in Montvale, there are two overpasses on which the Park-

way passes over. By Summit Avenue I went under the first overpass off the side road and finished some beer I had in my car.

I then drove home and I happened to take my watch out of my
pocket, it was 4:01.

Next I talked about going upstairs and passing my parents'
room.

A. I had to pass my parents' room to get to mine and I happened
to look inside my parents' room and I noticed only one person
was laying in bed. I knew my father wasn't in the upstairs bedroom, so I decided to take a look and see what was up. I turned
on the light and I found my mother in bed. I then went into my
brothers' room, found my father laying in my brother's bed and
my youngest brother Eric lying on the floor with no sign of my
other brother Ronnie.

Q. Why did you choose the light in your mother's bedroom,
why didn't you put on your light rather than, you know, maybe
wake her up with the bedroom light on if she was sleeping?

A. Well, like I can't see anything out of my bedroom if I put my
light on, and I knew something was up because my father wasn't
there and I didn't hear him moving around, so I thought he might
have gone out for something, or whatever, so then when I found
that and when I saw my brother I thought I was going to get sick.

15

While Harry was giving his statement a great deal was happening elsewhere.

Inside 23 E. Grand Avenue the teams of Montvale, county, and state officers were continuing their detailed search. At 6:30 A.M. Investigator Del Prete told the investigative personnel that the State Police Identification Unit would be handling the collection and marking of all evidence so the evidence could be taken to the New Jersey State Police Laboratory for analysis or turned over to the Montvale police.

Among the things removed were possible .22 projectiles; blood-stained linens; pieces of blood-stained carpet; possible .22 caliber spent cartridges; two white socks with stains on them on the floor next to the right-hand side of the double bed in the master bedroom; throw rugs and towels from the bathroom; the contents of the trap underneath the bathroom sink; rubber mats from the bathtub; and a six-inch section of the box spring of the double bed in the master bedroom with a possible projectile in it. Later, additional things were inventoried and removed.

By 7:15 an all-out crime scene search was underway. The bedrooms where the bodies were located were photographed, and assigned officers began taking other pictures. Plastic bags were placed on the victims' hands and heads. As far as the officers could speculate, Harry, Sr., had been shot while sleeping in the master bedroom. They based this theory on the blood they found on the bed and floor. By the disarranged clothing and blood marks on Harry, Sr.'s, front and back it appeared his body had been moved.

The officers also speculated that Eric had been shot while in an upright position since drops of blood on the back of his legs indicated he might have been standing. Along with the blood on his pillow, headboard, and dresser, there were spatterings of blood on the ceilings and wall. There was also a substantial amount of brain and bone matter from the skull.

As part of the investigation, Police Dispatcher Frank Mottram confirmed that Harry had driven to police headquarters at 4:00 A.M. to report the family's deaths. He recalled the extension telephone lights operating at that time, but said no material connection or conversation resulted. Harry remembered picking up the emergency phone and trying to make a connection the way one would dial a normal phone. But what he was actually doing as he said "Hello, hello, hello" was hitting several of the call boxes that the policemen use. This was why he could not get through.

By midmorning the bodies of Harry, Sr., Mary Jane, and Eric were taken from the house, and Detective Ewings of the Montvale police was dispatched to the medical examiner's office to participate in the post-examination of the bodies, the removal of evidence, and the photographing of this phase of the investigation. The three bodies arrived at the medical examiner's office approximately 10:15 A.M. The first autopsy was performed on Harry, Sr. One bullet was recovered from the brain, and bullet fragments were recovered from his skull. There were noticeable bruises or abrasions on his inner right and left underarms, top of his left hand, and both knees. Bullet holes were observed in the right eye and behind the left ear.

The second autopsy was on Mary Jane. There were no observable bruises or abrasions on her body. Two bullets were recovered from her brain. After a preliminary examination of Eric, Dr. Denson determined that he had been shot three times. Later, he had died from a strike on the left side of the head that appeared to have been done by a blunt instrument. Following this determination, Dr. Denson suspended Eric's autopsy until 11:00 Monday morning.

While the searches and autopsies were going on, spectators gathered on the De La Roches' corner, and telephones started ringing through the area. As the Bickerton family returned from mass they noticed the crowd by the De La Roche house.

"Harry's family is having a sale," Harry's friend Jeff remarked.

"But then I saw the 'Crime Scene' sign," Irene Bickerton stated. "I said 'Oh no! Something terrible has happened' and Jeff turned white as a sheet. I thought he was going to get ill on the spot as he yelled, 'Don't let it be Harry.'

"Later Jeff was interviewed on TV. But the anguish he felt was so overwhelming he couldn't even look up."

All kinds of stories were passed around before many hours elapsed. But the multiple murders seemed so unreal that many people who heard the news refused to believe it was true.

"When we received the first call our immediate reaction was 'Don't tell us stories like that!' " remembered Roger Anderson. And when Eric's friends, the Mulligans, heard the news from a member of the Montvale Athletic League, Patricia Mulligan discounted it so much she said to Mitch, "Run over to the De La Roches and see if Eric is home.

"But then as people kept calling I had the terrible feeling there must be something to it, so I told Mitch not to go. I still refused to believe it, though, till 4:00 in the afternoon. The message we kept getting was the De La Roches had been killed, and it looked like a gangland slaying. When we heard one family member was missing, we prayed that Eric had gotten away."

Captain Hanna phoned Ronnie's friend Andy Cannon and asked if he knew Ronnie's whereabouts.

"I told him 'No' and I didn't worry," Andy said later on, "because I figured he'd probably slept over at somebody's house.

"Then at 11:00 A.M. a friend called up and said some De La Roches had been shot, and they didn't know where Ronnie was. I hung up the phone and got my bike. Then I rode everywhere that morning trying to locate Ronnie.

"Later somebody asked me, 'Do you think Ronnie could have done it?' I simply stared at the guy who asked. There wasn't any way in the world that Ronnie could have pulled the trigger."

Harry's friend Steve was pumping gas when he learned an alert for Ronnie had gone out.

"When I first heard it was for a brown-haired youth I didn't think of Ronnie," he reported. "But when I learned it was for a triple murder in Montvale I had a terrible feeling it involved the De La Roche family.

"As far as Harry doing it, Harry wouldn't have had the guts to do a thing like that. Harry De La Roche is my best friend. I know him better then anyone else."

Jeff Fritts, who'd been with Harry only hours before, received a call from a girl he knew who'd met Harry once or twice.

"There's trouble at that kid Harry's place," his informant re- vealed. "Someone has disappeared from the house, but I've just heard fragments of the story."

Jeff drove to Grand Avenue as fast as he could and when he learned several people were dead and Harry was down at the station he went to the station immediately to see what he could do.

Captain Hanna also called Jeff DeCausemaker and asked him to come to the station to help in locating Ronnie.

"If I remember correctly, the officer didn't say what was wrong," Jeff said in describing that morning. "But he stated it was very important to locate Ronald De La Roche.

"I was completely shaken up, but I left right away for head- quarters. Then on my way to the station I passed the De La Roche house. When I saw ropes around the house I stopped to find out what happened.

"I'll never forget the answer because the person I asked re- plied, 'They're all blown away.' "

16

The morning was growing endless down at the Montvale sta- tion and the constant grilling and interrogation added to my state of shock. Once I was asked if I wanted a doctor. But I answered "No." Later I said, "I do want a doctor," but I didn't see one that day.

I was starting to get confused. But the sworn statement went on as Detective O'Donovan and Investigator Del Prete con- tinued:

Q. Let's go back to when you found your parents and your

brother in the house. When you found them in the house did you go to any of the rooms to see if anybody was alive or see their condition?

A. I went to see my father. When I touched him he was cold and I couldn't feel any pulse at all. I did not want to try getting a pulse around his neck because it was all bloody. I tried his arm, tried to get any sign of life and I saw Eric on the floor and I knew.

Q. How many guns were in your house?

A. There are three pistols and one rifle.

Q. Who did these guns belong to?

A. They're all under my father's name. I used to use the rifle when I went shooting, but I haven't used them in the past almost two years.

More questions about the guns followed, and I told Del Prete and O'Donovan how I had cleaned the .22 and loaded it the previous week. Next came the questions about the coin collection and spending the $1600. Once Del Prete asked to go off the record to discuss the money in my possession. After we finished we discussed returning for my mother's car.

Q. At that time your father made you aware of the problem with Ronald?

A. Yes, he did.

Q. Were you, your father and Ronald engaged in an argument?

A. Not at that time. I did not see my brother Ronald.

Q. Where was Eric at this time?

A. I don't know, I did not see him.

Q. Could you hear Ronnie at all?

A. I really wasn't listening for him.

Q. Ronald apparently had come back to the house from Nottingham Court at this time?

A. He may or may not have.

Q. Was this argument between your father and Ronald taking place before you took Ronald to the Nottingham Apartments, or do you believe it took place sometime after?

A. I think it took place after, but with any little arguments they were having at home when I was home they kind of kept quiet because they didn't want to bother me with that. They said it was my vacation. They didn't want to bother me with that.

Q. In these arguments and discussions did your mother take part at all?

A. Not that I know of.

Q. Did your father become violent with Ronald as far as cursing him?

A. Not that I know of.

Q. Did Ronald become violent with your father as far as cursing him?

A. Not that I know of.

Q. Did your father relate to you that Ronald had threatened him in the course of the discussion?

A. Yes.

Q. What exactly did he say?

A. He said he would bury my father under his, Ronnie's bed.

Q. What was your mother's reaction at this time during the discussion with your father?

A. My mother did not say a word.

Q. Did she overhear the conversation?

A. Yes she did.

Q. Had Ronald ever threatened your father before either with running away from home—

A. When my father did hit him on different occasions he said he would get even or he would run away or something, but this was awhile before. My father had not done any hitting for a while.

Q. Approximately how long ago did you and your father discuss this situation involving Ronald?

A. A very short time, around five or so minutes. I said I did not want to hear it, that my father would turn in my own brother. I was going to come back today and say, "If you turn Ronnie in I'm not going back to The Citadel and that's money wasted."

Q. What was your father's reaction to that?

A. I did not have a chance to tell him.

Next I was asked about the beer that I had in the back of the car and drank on Summit Avenue.

Q. How much beer did you drink?

A. I would say about four and a half cans, I didn't finish the last one.

Q. About how long did you stay there?

A. I cannot be sure. I did not have my watch on and I didn't have my radio on.

Q. What did you do with the empty cans after you drank the beer?

A. I had them in the car. I put them back in the wrapper and then as I was going along the road further on down I cut through New York. I chucked them out the window into the woods.

Q. You went home and parked the car in the garage where you usually park it?

A. No I did not. I drove the car behind the station wagon.

Q. About what time was that?

A. At that point I wasn't sure what time it was. I pulled the watch out of my pocket. The watch said 4:01.

BY INVESTIGATOR DEL PRETE:

Q. What lights were on when you came into the house?

A. There weren't any.

BY DETECTIVE O'DONOVAN:

Q. No lights on anywhere?

A. No lights on anywhere. I went upstairs, there was a street-light outside my mother's window. From the light inside I could see a dim shadow. I noticed my father was not in his bed and I turned on the light.

At this point Lieutenant Scarangella of the Montvale Police knocked on the door of the conference room and asked to talk to Del Prete and O'Donovan. Both of the officers left the room, and I was told we'd stop for a moment while we took a short recess.

17

At Christ Lutheran Church—at twelve o'clock—services were nearly over, and Pastor Roy Nilsen and his intern Ruth Mohring had just made their way to the back of the church. Just one week ago they had greeted Harry and now they were waiting to do the same for the Thanksgiving weekend congregation.

"As we waited, a member of the congregation who had not been in church approached me from another direction and handed me a note," said Roy Nilsen. "Little did I know what I'd find."

But the message that the pastor found read "Some members of the De La Roche family are dead." Then there was the word "murder" as Roy remembers today, though in the confusion and the shock it's hard for anyone to recall the specific words that were used.

As soon as Roy got the message he turned and went back to the pulpit to tell the congregation he'd just received word a church family was in trouble, and, instead of greeting at the door, he had to go to their home.

"Since I didn't know what happened I didn't mention names," Roy explained.

When he left, Ruth Mohring took over, and as the congregation filed out more people heard the word "murder." The question was, "Who was it?" But Ruth couldn't answer that since she hadn't learned the name of the family. She got people out as fast as she could. Then she hurried to the church office, hoping she could see Roy before he left for the house.

"He was on the phone when I got there," she related, "and he told me it was the De La Roches. I decided to stay at the church while Roy went to the house, still wearing his clerical collar. When he got there he learned that Harry was with the Montvale police, so Roy lost no time in driving to the station in order to be with Harry."

At the station both John and Arden Greer were waiting restlessly for a chance to talk to Harry and let him know they were there. But whenever they asked to see him it was "Maybe later" or "He's busy now." Roy Nilsen received the same answer, so when he couldn't see Harry he offered to accompany John Greer to Lodi to break the painful and tragic news to Honey and Ernie Ebneter.

It's doubtful John Greer will ever forget that harrowing visit to Lodi because when Ernie opened the door he smiled, "Hi, John! How ya' been?"

"Ernie, I have some terrible news," John had to say at once. "Three members of the De La Roche family have been killed in their beds."

As soon as the words were out of his mouth—and before Ernie could recover—Honey came in to see John. And as she hadn't heard what he'd said he had to repeat to her, "Honey, I have terrible news. Three members of the De La Roche family have been killed in their beds.

"Harry, Sr., is one."

Honey collapsed on the floor at once and started to scream and yell. Then Roy tried to do whatever he could to solace and comfort her. Soon it was obvious, however, that she needed medical help so John and, then Roy got on the phone and tried to get a doctor. After several calls they were unsuccessful. But they finally located a physician who gave a prescription by phone. They also called Honey's brother, John De La Roche in Paramus. In almost a matter of minutes, Big John and his son, Tough John, got to the Lodi house.

While other family members were notified John Greer and the pastor left Lodi to go back to the station to see Harry. They expected that surely—by this time—they could both talk to him.

Arden Greer remained at the station while Roy and John were in Lodi, and for the hours the men were gone she sat alone while time dragged. Once she caught a quick glimpse of Harry. But neither of them could speak.

All kinds of things went through her mind. Then finally she asked Captain Hanna, "Is there any chance of a drug involvement anywhere in the family?"

At first he didn't answer. Then he said hesitantly, "Mrs. Greer, I wish I were home in slacks and in a position to talk to you as a friend of the family. But I'm on duty and in uniform and I can't answer you."

"I have my answer," Arden replied—and then she went on thinking.

One of the thoughts that went through her mind was, "What will Harry do tonight?" But soon the obvious decision was, "We'll take him home with us."

"I mentioned that to Captain Hanna," she said. "And I still recall his answer.

"He hesitated before he responded, and then he said quietly, 'Maybe you won't have to make that decision.' "

While John and Roy drove to Lodi and Arden sat alone, life was busy at the crime scene as the officers' search progressed. Eventually, it reached a climax when, at 12:15, Detective Smith of the New Jersey State Police and Investigator Nass of the Bergen County Prosecutor's Office removed the two laundry baskets that sat in front of the attic door.

Behind the door, the steps were steep, so the officers climbed up slowly. Then when they got to the top of the stairs they saw a brown metal locker directly to their left. There were cardboard boxes with Christmas decorations sitting on the top, and Detective Smith removed them to take a look inside. The time was approximately 12:25—and when Investigator Nass looked into the box he observed the feet of a human body.

On further investigation the officers saw a young boy stuffed into a locker, face down with his legs bent. There wasn't a shadow of a doubt that the hidden body was Ronnie wearing a tee shirt, white undershorts, and socks. There was no gun beside him, and he wasn't a suicide since he couldn't have climbed into the locker, shut the lid on himself and, then, put boxes on top.

Instantly both officers knew it was another murder, and soon the attic was as full of officers as the other two floors. Detective Sergeant Likus was called to take pictures and Detective Smith dusted the locker for latent fingerprints. He obtained two prints from the left end of the locker and one partial palm print from the right end. At 1:45 Dr. Denson returned to pronounce Ronnie dead. Rigor had begun. But the body hadn't cooled, and preliminary examinations indicated Ronnie had been shot once. The autopsy was suspended till 11:00 on Monday.

Because of the attic's low ceiling and lack of working space the locker with Ronnie's body was taken to the second floor hallway. Detective Smith took a sample of blood from the locker and Likus removed several woodchips from the attic floor and stairway.

The news that the missing Ronnie had been found at 12:25 was quickly relayed to the Montvale station, and five minutes later Lieutenant Scarangella interrupted Harry's statement to reveal — outside of Harry's hearing—that Ronnie had been found.

18

After the 12:30 recess, when O'Donovan and Del Prete came back, my formal statement continued till it terminated at 12:45. The questions began immediately. But my intuition told me the officers had learned something they weren't telling me.

O'Donovan started the questions.

Q. Do you have any problems at all with any of your brothers or your parents, any personal arguments that you were involved in with them.
A. None at all.
INVESTIGATOR DEL PRETE: I have a couple of questions.
BY INVESTIGATOR DEL PRETE:
Q. Why didn't you call the police from the phone in your house?
A. I don't know. I just got in the car. I remember, like one time I

called about my Cobra which is a Ford product car, and it was vandalized and at first I didn't get any answer with Tri-Boro. Then I had to wait and all, I don't know what I thought. I just jumped in the car and got down.

Q. And you say when you got to the house the lights that usually were on were off?

A. Right.

Q. And you went around to the porch, the rear porch?

A. That's the side porch. That's what we use for the main door. Everybody comes in and out of there.

Q. All right. Are you finished?

MR. O'DONOVAN: That's it.

Q. Is there anything you wish to add to this statement?

THE WITNESS: Not that I can think of.

Q. Is there anything you feel we haven't asked you that we ought to know about?

A. Not that I can think of.

Q. Do you know where Ronnie might be?

A. No, I don't have any idea. Captain Hanna called one of my friends who is also his friend and he suggested two places in New York, but I'm not sure.

Q. Is there anything you wish to add to this statement?

A. Nothing at all.

As soon as the statement was over I was asked another time if I would submit to a lie detector test to show I had no guilty knowledge about what had happened in my house. I was also fingerprinted for elimination purposes.

While I was still at the station nobody mentioned Ronnie, and I didn't see the Greers or Roy Nilsen before I was taken to a waiting car and driven to Hackensack to the Bergen County Prosecutor's Office. O'Donovan and Del Prete went with me, and on the way we talked about cars and, also, military life. I was becoming numb and wiped out since I'd had no sleep since 6:00 A.M. the previous Saturday. But I do remember hearing, "The person who did this needs help." I also heard an officer add that whoever did the murders would probably be going for help rather than to jail.

Next we discussed the polygraph test and the officers said the operators had never found anybody who was able to lie under it. I knew enough about polygraphs to know that this was bull because certain drugs or psychopathic liars can beat it or screw it up. We arrived at the Prosecutor's Office a little after 2:00.

At the same time—as I later learned—other officers were looking for a gun.

19

Before 2:00 P.M. in Montvale Detective David and Detective Lange of the Prosecutor's Office had been on a search outside the house, looking for possible weapons. Then at 2:00, they went down to the basement and divided it into two parts. Detective David's official report describes the search this way:

After a short time in the cellar, I came upon a pink chest of drawers at approximately 2:15 P.M. The chest of drawers contained various books, pieces of cloth, and fabrics. This chest of drawers was located on the west wall of the basement. Directly in front of the chest of drawers was an exercise bench, the type that is used commonly by body builders. The bench had a red vinyl cushion and on the red vinyl cushion was a red pillow shaped like a back-rest. On the bench also was a barbell that had two 15 pound weights, one on each end. This bench and the barbell were positioned snugly against the chest of drawers. I had to pull the bench out to gain access to the chest of drawers. I first took the barbell off and placed it underneath the pool table. I made a drawer by drawer search of the chest of drawers.

In the bottom portion of the chest of drawers which contained many items, I searched each drawer beginning with the top drawer on my left. I then started with the drawers on my right.

In the second drawer from the top I found the following item:
A hi-standard .22 caliber pistol, Model No. 9248, Serial No.
2428450. This pistol was wrapped in a blood-soaked piece of
terrycloth. The blood was still wet.

I called to Detective Lange who was approximately five feet
away and asked him to doublecheck to reaffirm my find. The
drawer was carefully pulled out, exposing the pistol, at which
time Det. Lange reaffirmed my find. Sgt. Paul Likus and he took
photographs of the weapon where it was found.

I called Det. Leroy Smith of the New Jersey State Police
Forensic Laboratory and he immediately came down from the
first floor and dusted the gun for prints. Neither I nor Det.
Lange, nor Sgt. Likus touched the pistol. I turned the pistol over
to Det. Smith who retrieved it from the drawer and dusted it for
prints.

Det. Smith's tentative finding was that the weapon was too
blood-soaked to raise any prints at this time.

Other things were happening, too, while Harry was in
Hackensack.

One was a search of his bedroom by Investigator Kunz and
Investigator Nass. There, inside his closet, they discovered a

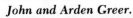

John and Arden Greer.

pair of long johns and a blue Citadel tee shirt under a pile of clothing. Both had possible bloodstains.

Back at the Montvale station Arden Greer was still hanging on, though Captain Hanna had told her Harry was in Hackensack. He mentioned that, maybe, when he was brought back she and John Greer could see him. Later he advised her the pistol had been found. While Harry was still in Hackensack the officers learned that, too. But nobody came to tell him about this new revelation.

When John Greer returned from Lodi, the Greers stayed till 5:00 P.M. Then Captain Hanna let them know they might as well go home. They left with the knowledge he'd call them when it was time to come back.

Before they left, John Greer asked, "Shall we call an attorney?" The answer he was given was that that wasn't necessary now.

20

At 2:05 I was taken into the polygraph room and, when I sat in the leather-like chair with its wide wooden arms, I was ready to bounce off the walls. The small blue room without windows was approximately eight feet by ten feet and the table with the built-in machine was directly behind the chair that seemed as formidable to me as an electric chair. I said to myself "I don't like this—I don't like this at all."

Before going into the polygraph room I'd passed through a waiting room, and between the two rooms was a two-way mirror with a curtain on the waiting room side. While I was still in this room, I met Lt. Herbert Allmers. He was a fairly stocky man with balding brown hair and brown sideburns.

I didn't know he was an officer and I didn't know, at the time, that as a polygraph operator who'd majored in psychology he'd given close to a thousand tests. But I felt he was using psychology on me even in the ante room where we discussed the polygraph test and where I was asked to sign a paper that was on the table.

It was a form to indicate I was taking the test voluntarily. But nobody read the paper to me, and I didn't read it myself. I would have signed anything that day, and I had no knowledge of the law.

Weeks later—when I read this form after my mind was clear—I saw what I had signed. I also learned what I should have known before I took the test. This is the form I signed:

BERGEN COUNTY PROSECUTOR'S OFFICE
CONSENT FOR POLYGRAPH EXAMINATION

PLACE: Prosecutor's Office

DATE: 11-28-76

I,_____ , voluntarily agree to take a polygraph (lie detection) examination to be given to me by Herbert H. Allmers of the Bergen County Prosecutor's Office.

I also authorize the Bergen County Prosecutor's Office to disclose, both orally and in writing, the results of this examination. I fully realize that I have the right to secure the advice of a lawyer or legal counsel before I sign this form or submit to this polygraph (lie detection) examination. I also realize that if I cannot afford an attorney at this time the State will immediately secure one for me, but I waive these rights. I realize that anything I say during this examination may be held against me at a later date in a criminal proceeding. I also realize that I may remain silent and say nothing. During this examination I know that I may leave at anytime and in no way can I be forced to stay. I have no objection to taking a lie detector test, and I do so voluntarily. No one has promised me anything, threatened me, or in any way forced me to take the test. I do it of my own free will because I have nothing to hide.

_____

(Signature of person examined)

This examination was concluded at 4:02 P.M. on the above date. Having submitted myself freely to this examination, I reaffirm my agreement as expressed above. During this examination I was well treated, and I knew that I could leave at any time if I so desired. I also certify that there were no threats or harm done to me or any promises made to me before or during the entire time I have been with any law enforcement agency or officer, either in connection with the examination or the signing of this form.

_____

(Signature of person examined)

My main recollection of the lie detector test is being strapped in the chair, with my back to the machine. The intricate machine, with its needle heads, registers changes in blood pressure, respiration, pulse, activities of the sweat glands, drug usage, and emotional disturbances. All reactions are recorded in waves or lines that go up and down on the chart that passes through the polygraph machine as questions are asked and answered. After the test the operator—who's behind you most of the time—interprets what the lines indicate.

When I was set up and ready to begin I was told it was very important to keep my arms very still as I placed them on the arms of the chair. My left arm got a blood pressure cuff—and I felt my pulse and blood pressure increase as soon as it was attached.

Finger electrodes were placed on my hand and pneumo tubes

that reminded me of the spring bands used on screen doors were put on my stomach and chest. While you are answering questions the needle heads on the polygraph machine bounce up and down when you talk—and when you say something that isn't true the needles really bounce. You can hear the scraping of the needles while you're taking the test.

Before the test Lieutenant Allmers went over the questions he asked me. He explained he'd ask the test questions first, then some stimulus questions the second time around, and, then, the test questions again. The stimulus questions were designed to show what the test is like and whether a person is capable of being tested. They'll calm a person who's truthful and excite a deceptive one. I was asked about dollar bills in this test.

As a starter, Lieutenant Allmers showed me three envelopes—one with a one-dollar bill, one with a two-dollar bill, and one with a five-dollar bill. After he gave me an envelope he told me to look at it and he'd tell me which bill it was. I took it but didn't look at the bill.'

"Is it a one-dollar bill?" he asked.

I answered "No." And the bouncing of the polygraph needle indicated the answer was false.

None of the questions and answers were taped, and none were shown in the evidence given to the defense. All were simple but tricky and required "Yes" or "No" answers.

It's hard to recall the specific ten questions, since I was so out of it. But, as I recollect it, Lieutenant Allmers asked such things as:

"Have you ever stolen anything?"

"Do you know where the murder weapon was found? Did you ever hurt anybody you loved? Did you kill your mother and father? Did you shoot your brothers?"

I answered "Yes" to the question "Did you ever hurt anybody you loved?" That wouldn't necessarily mean physical hurt—and everyone has hurt someone at some point in time. I said "No" to killing my mother and father. But when Allmers specified *brothers* in the plural I thought to myself, "Wait a minute." I knew then the cops had found Ronnie. But Allmers didn't tell me his body had been discovered.

For the rest of the time in the polygraph room the atmosphere seemed hostile and full of a lot of psychology when—as I recall it—the operator ran religious stuff like, "God is a forgiving father," and, "It's a better to confess."

After the test was finished I knew the markings on the chart would show what was true or untrue so I turned and looked at Allmers and said, "How did I do?"

He quickly snapped, "Don't you know?" Then he told me I was lying and that I had hurt them all. He also said—since the test was over—that Ronnie had been found.

The hands on the clock said 3:30, and my attitude was "Fuck it."

"I'm tired, hungry, and sick," I thought, "and now I've got no one left."

I sensed that the climate grew more oppressive with every second that passed, and I felt like such a defeatist I decided I'd cop to everything and check out myself. I hardly knew what was going on, but I wanted everything over and since the cops had been feeding me a lot of stuff all day, I said to myself, "I'll feed it back and give them what they're waiting to hear."

As soon as I opened my mouth, though, and told Lieutenant Allmers what turned out to be an alleged confession he asked if I would be willing to give a second sworn statement. Then he advised Del Prete and O'Donovan that I had confessed to the crime.

By 4:05 Richard Jennings, another court reporter, was set up and waiting for me. All I wanted was to get to jail.

Suicide was on my mind.

21

According to the record I was finally read my rights just prior to my second sworn statement.

But I was floating with the butterflies then and don't recall hearing them. I've been told Del Prete read them, but he left out the fifth constitutional right—"You may stop answering questions at any time."

I did stop twice in this formal statement, but I was encouraged to go on. Del Prete asked the first questions.

Q. We are here today because you want to give us a statement concerning the death of your family, consisting of your father, Harry De La Roche, Sr.; your mother, Mary Jane De La Roche; your younger brothers Ronnie and Eric.
Is that correct?
A. Correct.
Q. Harry, we took a statement from you prior to this, earlier today.
A. Yes.
Q. In which you gave us some information concerning the death of your parents.
That information you gave us this afternoon is false.
Is that correct?
A. Yes.

In answering "Yes" to the foregoing question I realized—later on—I didn't make it exactly clear that all I had said the first time around wasn't false information. Actually all of the facts were true until I got home from the "Maximus"—except for stopping at the overpass to finish the beer I had in my car and throw the cans away. In my illogical thinking I made up that information to account for one hour's time.

The next part of the statement led up to more details about getting home that morning.

Q. So, go ahead, that morning . . .

A. I went up to my room, about three o'clock. Then, sitting in my room, I had the pistol on the bed. I took my boots off downstairs, came upstairs with my socks, took my socks and my pants off. I was sitting in my room for a while thinking of what I was going to do, thinking I can't go back, and I really couldn't tell my parents because they wouldn't listen. I kept walking back and forth from the entrance to my room to the entrance of my parents' room. I walked in there and said, "No, I can't." Then I walked back in my room and sat down for a little while. Finally I walked into my parents' room and got real close to my father. I must have stood in his room about a half-hour just holding the pistol up. Then finally I said, "I can't go back," closed my eyes and pulled the trigger. That set it off. I shot my mother right then and there. I went into my brothers' room. When I turned on the light, Ronnie was laying on the side of his bed. His eyes were opened, like he was in shock, like he didn't know what was happening—I guess, he didn't. I shot him, and I went over to Eric. Eric started to get up. I shot him twice. He was still getting up, and then he started to go back down on his bed. Then I went back to my room and just sat there for a few minutes.

Then I heard some really heavy breathing and I thought, "Oh, my God!" I went back into my brothers' room and there was Eric. He was getting up and trying to get out. He was saying—he was saying something I couldn't hear him. I put my hand over his eyes and said "Eric, go to sleep, go to sleep. It's just a dream," trying to calm him down. Then he got up and he started screaming, and I hit him with the pistol butt in the head. Then he went down to the ground. I hit him again. He was still breathing. The second time I hit him he wasn't breathing anymore, so then I took my brother, put him upstairs.

Q. Which brother?

A. Ronnie. I tried wiping down the stairs to the attic. There were a few drops of blood there. There was blood on Ronnie's bed, so I took my father off his bed and put him on Ronnie's bed. Then I was just sitting there, like what am I going to do. The shirt had some blood stains on it from when I hit Eric, blood splattered up. I had some blood on the long johns from when I was carrying my father and Ronnie. I took them off and threw them in the back of my closet in my room. I went into the bathroom, showered off, and then I put these clothes on.

Q. All right, Harry.

A. Then I went down to the police station.

Q. Harry, why did you take Ronnie up to the attic?

A. To make it seem like I didn't do it.

Q. What did you do with Ronnie when you brought him up in the attic?

A. Well, we had these metal closets that we didn't use and that was the only place I could think of putting him. I was going to put him in the back of the car and bring him out to Seven Lakes with the pistol and hide him out there. I don't know.

Q. You put him in this closet, you said?

A. Yes.

Q. Then you went downstairs and you got your father?

A. I carried him into my brother's bed.

Q. Why did you do that?

A. There was blood on my brother's bed. How could I explain Ronnie did it if there was blood on his bed.

Q. You thought if you put your father on your brother's bed it would seem like it was your father's blood?

A. Yes.

Q. Is that why you made up the story about your father finding the marijuana—

A. No, my father did catch my brother and he was going to turn him in—

Q. About Ronnie putting the money under the bed?

A. No, that wasn't true. My father did catch him. He didn't know what to do—

Q. What did you have on?

A. Long johns and Citadel shirt.

Q. Long john bottoms and the Citadel tee shirt?

A. Blue tee shirt with white letters across it. It says Citadel.

Q. What did you do with the gun?

A. First I put it—there was a metal closet upstairs. I put it there, but I said, "That's going to be too easily found," so I put it downstairs in one of the drawers.

Q. When you first came home at three o'clock in the morning, where did you get the gun from?

A. My father's bureau, little nightstand drawer.

Q. On your father's side of the bed?

A. Yeah.

Q. What made you change your mind about taking Ronnie's body up to that Seven—

DETECTIVE O'DONOVAN: Seven Lakes Drive

A. I don't know, I really don't know. I think I was thinking I couldn't leave Ronnie out there, just out in nothing. I figured sooner or later he'd be found.

Q. Had you thought about this during the day at all?

A. Not really. I just was trying to think of some way to get out of going to The Citadel, and I came in three o'clock, and it was seven hours before I had to leave for the plane and there was nothing I could do to stop it.

Q. Do you remember how many times you fired the pistol?

A. I emptied the clip, it was a full clip.

Q. How many were in the clip?

A. Ten rounds.

Q. How do you know there were ten rounds in the clip?

A. I had cleaned the gun beforehand as I was going to go shooting.

Q. Do you remember how many times you fired at your father?

A. I think, I don't know, maybe two—well, one shot went through his pillow. It missed him completely. I was standing three or four inches away, and it hit the pillow instead.

Q. How about your mother, how many times was she shot?

A. I think once, maybe twice. Ronnie was shot once.

Q. Did your mother wake up at all?

A. My mother just started to stir. Ronnie was just like—I don't know. I don't know. He just saw me there or heard the shot or knew something was on. I don't know.

Q. Was Ronald sitting up in the bed?

A. He was laying on his side with his head out and eyes wide open like he was staring at nothing.

Q. How about Eric? Was Eric awake at this time?

A. He was getting up out of bed.

Q. Who got shot then?

A. I came and shot Ronnie. As soon as I turned on the light I shot him from across the room in the doorway. I had to go up to Eric. Eric—I couldn't believe Eric.

Q. Tell me about Eric again.

A. I shot him twice, and I figured it's all over. He's not feeling any pain at all. Then he started getting up and I figured—When I was in my room, I heard he was getting up and I figured "Oh, God what he was going through? What am I going through?" So I came back in. He was getting up and I hit him with the pistol butt.

Q. When you shot Ronnie, where did you shoot Ronald?

A. When I first came into the room, into his room.

Q. What part of the body did you aim for?

A. I shot him in the head.

Q. How about Eric? What part of him did you aim for?

A. I hit him in the head. He just kept on getting up.

BY INVESTIGATOR DEL PRETE:

Q. After Eric had been shot twice, you hit him in the head with the butt of the pistol?

A. After I got to my room, I heard heavy breathing. He was trying to get up. He was saying something. I couldn't quite hear what he was saying, I put my hands over his eyes—

Q. Was he facing you, Harry?

A. He was facing me.

Q. Did you get injured at all?

A. No.

Q. Did he scratch you or anything?

A. No, he didn't scratch me or grab me. I was told there was hair under his fingernails, but he didn't touch me. He tried kicking at me, but—

BY DETECTIVE O'DONOVAN:

Q. Did Ronald struggle at all after he had been shot?

A. No, he just laid there. He was just laying there. He didn't move. My father didn't—my father didn't move.

Q. Did you put Eric back on the floor?

A. No, he flung on the floor.

Q. Did you wrap the weapon in anything?
A. There was a rag around it. I had put that around where Ronnie had the bullet hole in him to keep him from bleeding all over the place.
Q. You wrapped a rag around Ronnie?
A. Put it on the side of his head. The rag slipped off. Ronnie slumped down.
Q. Is there anything else you would like to add to this, Harry?
A. No.
INVESTIGATOR DEL PRETE: Okay.

22

When I finished my statement at 4:34 I was driven back to Montvale—in handcuffs for the first time.

I can't remember the ride at all. I was completely dazed. But back at the station I do recall that somebody brought me French fries and a couple of Cokes. I certainly didn't need anything—except to calm me down. But Del Prete said I'd better eat since I wouldn't get food that night in jail.

At 5:35 O'Donovan announced that I was under arrest—and, though, this made it official, I still say that, technically, I'd been under arrest since early that Sunday morning. I was also advised that in a short while I'd be arraigned before Judge Fred C. Galda of the Bergen County Superior Court at the Montvale Municipal Court.

I was still not permitted to see anyone—like Roy Nilsen or the Greers—though prior to the arraignment the pastor had made one more request to speak to me a few moments. This wasn't granted, however, and when I was handcuffed and brought into court, I was directed to go to one side and stand there by myself.

My aunt and uncle, who had gone home at 5:00, had been called back to Montvale, and I saw them sitting in the court with the pastor and Ruth Mohring. Steve Mahoney was also there, looking as dazed as I felt. But even though I stared at him and tried to gesture a message, there was no way to get through. None of my father's relatives came to the arraignment, but I learned Vinnie Trojan and Jeff Fritts were standing in the lobby along with the TV people and newspaper photographers and reporters. Richard E. Salkin, an assistant prosecutor in the Bergen County Prosecutor's Office, was there to serve me with the warrants that authorized my arrest. He looked to be about thirty, and I was to learn at a later date that he was regarded as a lawyer who was destined for a good future.

As usual people commented that I showed no outward emotion when the warrants were handed to me. But in my spaced-out condition I would have taken anything without even batting an eye. It was almost as though I didn't hear when the prosecution called out the names of my parents and my brothers—and gave me a piece of green paper for the murder of each one. I was asked if I understood. I answered, "Yes, I do."

I saw Aunt Arden start to cry, and Steve who was sitting between two cops looked completely distraught. Then Judge Galda announced to the court he was entering four mandatory pleas of "Not Guilty" for me. I was ordered to jail in lieu of bail, and a bail hearing was scheduled for the following day.

"You are charged in four separate complaints with homicide," the judge told me. "I suggest you do not speak to anyone about this."

While we were still in the courtroom Pastor Nilsen and Uncle John asked to talk to the judge. Then they asked permission to have a few words with me. The judge announced he would grant their request and we went to a private room.

At first we all just stood there—and even though we'd waited all day for these moments together, there was an awful silence and no one knew what to say. Neither one pressed me for any details, but Uncle John had to ask me where to find certain papers, so funeral arrangements could be made. He thought he'd be called on to do this, not only because of my grandmother's age but because of the shock she'd been through. He also had to notify The Citadel that I wouldn't be coming back. After he left, Pastor Nilsen stayed on, and both of us stood there a moment. He put his arm around me, and I know he sensed how scared I felt because I stood ramrod stiff.

"I don't know what happened, Harry," he said. "But God hasn't abandoned you, and I won't abandon you either. I'll stick with you all the way."

I knew my lips were quivering, and I could hardly talk, as I answered, "I don't know what happened either. I just simply flipped out."

"We'll talk about it later," Pastor Nilsen said. "Right now we should get a lawyer. I'd like to call Mr. John Taylor, a member of our congregation who practices in Park Ridge."

I didn't know Mr. Taylor. But I had heard his name. So I asked Pastor Nilsen to call him to see if he'd represent me—at least for the bail hearing on Monday. Pastor explained that he'd tell Uncle John. Then my uncle, as a member of the family, would telephone Mr. Taylor and ask him to attend the bail hearing. I later learned when John Taylor said "Yes," Aunt Arden said "Hug him for me" when she knew he'd see me in jail.

When I left the arraignment and caught Steve's eye I rubbed my ear with my index finger as I so often do. This time, though I was trying to say, "I really screwed things up." But some of the papers construed it to mean that I was going "Bang, bang" and pointing to my head. Other accounts reported that I gave the finger to everyone who happened to be around.

While Harry was getting his warrants most of the spectators in the tension-filled court couldn't fathom the unbelievable tragedy. Ruth Mohring eventually became the person who described the climate best.

"It was only a week ago that I'd seen Harry, so tall and straight in his uniform," she remembered. "Then that Sunday evening, standing all alone in his combat boots and army jacket, the only thing that he had left were the four green papers in his hands charging him with four murders.

"Because of the circumstances many people weren't sensitive

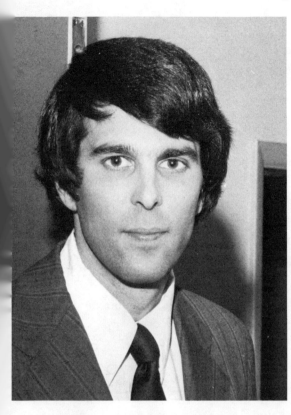

*Richard Salkin, assistant
prosecutor, Bergen
County Prosecutor's
Office, during the trial*
PHOTO BY *THE RECORD,*
HACKENSACK, NEW JERSEY.

to him. They were sensitive to what had happened and the emptiness that was left. But a reasonable number acted concerned and wanted to reach out to him to let him know we'd been trying to do what we could all day.

"As for me, the thing I wanted most was to go up to Harry and put my arms around him. I wanted to say 'You're not alone. Everything will be all right.' But society wouldn't permit that. Everything wouldn't be all right.

"All my emotions were turned around, and I wanted to cry out in the court room, 'Don't make judgments till you know everything. None of us knows the whole story.' "

Richard Salkin, the assistant prosecutor, looked almost as young as Harry as he stood on the opposite side of the court. A graduate of Fairleigh Dickinson University, he had obtained his law degree from Rutgers University. Later, after serving as law clerk for Judge Galda, he joined the Prosecutor's Office. He quickly progressed to chief of the grand jury section, and during Harry's hearings and trial he would be chief of the trial section. Salkin was good looking in a smooth, suave way and obviously very bright. And Ruth Mohring thought, as she watched the proceedings, that here were two dark-haired young men, both in the prime of life, brought together by a cruel twist of fate. One had everything ahead. The other—it appeared—had nothing.

After Harry left the court room to talk with his uncle and pastor, the room was cleared immediately and Ruth went out to the lobby.

"I noticed the freckled-faced, ruddy young man to whom Harry had gestured," she reported, "and since he looked so distressed and forlorn I asked somebody his name. When I learned it was Steve Mahoney I introduced myself."

"Is there anything I can do?" Ruth asked. "Would you like to sit down and talk."

Steve looked at her clerical collar. "Harry is my friend," he said.

Following the arraignment I was taken to O'Donovan's office while I waited for transportation to the Bergen County Jail. While I was there Detective David asked if I wanted anything, and I told him I'd like cigarettes.

When someone said we were ready to go I knew there were cameras waiting outside, and I didn't want my picture taken. I asked O'Donovan to cover my head, so he used his leather jacket and, then I was led outside. Because of all the television lights I could see the crowd through the leather. And as I moved my hands in the handcuffs the papers said—a second time—that I made an obscene gesture.

On the ride to Hackensack I sat in the back with John David. Frank Del Prete drove the car, and Richard Salkin sat beside him. We stopped on the way for cigarettes, and when John David brought back two packs that completed the eight packs I'd smoked that day.

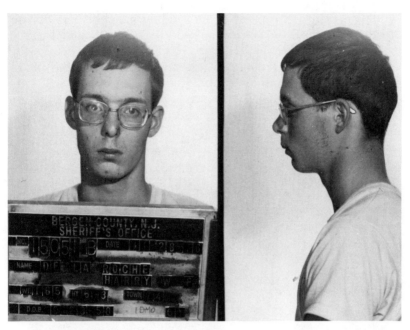

Harry De La Roche, Jr., mug shot on entering the Bergen County Jail, November 28, 1976. PHOTO BY BERGEN COUNTY JAIL.

It's hard to recall what we talked about as we drove to the jail but on the way John David asked what I had done with the shells. I told him I'd collected ten empty bullet casings and put them in my desk. Our house was full of shells, however, because I'd picked them up from the range and collected them in a bag. Once I talked about Lucky and asked what would happen to him. But Del Prete assured me that someone would take care of our dog. Within a few days, however, Lucky became very ill and had to be put to sleep.

At 7:31 we arrived at the jail and went to the booking desk. Then I was frisked and asked to strip, and after the officer in charge took any possessions I had left (including a disc from the "Maximus" that was good for a drink) my clothes were put in a plastic bag and the officers took a mug shot, along with finger and palm prints. Next I was given bedding and clothes and taken to the infirmary. Somebody locked me in a cell, and I saw a guard stay outside.

Nobody had to tell me—on November 28—that at the end of Thanksgiving vacation I was under a suicide watch.

VII

The First Days
in Jail

23

Bergen County Jail, which joins the courthouse, is commonly called "The Fortress." Outside, the five-story turreted building is a combination of modern ~~lines and medieval battlements.~~ Inside it reminds you of a wagon wheel with the corridors containing the cells going off from a circular, open-area spoke. In 1910 when it was built it was thought to be the finest jail in the State of New Jersey. But when Harry was admitted sixty-six years later, both the structure and electrical systems were badly deteriorated. The jail was located behind lower Main Street across from Hackensack's "Church on the Green," which dated back to the seventeen hundreds and was part of American history.

The courthouse, which was in front of the jail—and the scene of the subsequent trial—was built in 1912. It was distinguished by a massive dome, illuminated at night. The sculptured figures on the dome recorded the trial and triumphs of the families who built the church, and when the courthouse was first constructed it was called the "Temple of Justice."

But in the months Harry was in jail, he and others, too, would sometimes question the aptness of the words "Temple of Justice."

The fifth floor cell block of the Bergen County Jail.
PHOTO BY ED HILL, *THE RECORD*, HACKENSACK, NEW JERSEY.

24

When I awoke on Monday after an on-again, off-again sleep, induced by the trauma of Sunday I was in such a stupor that I felt out of it. A short time later when I met John Taylor he said I was practically in a comatose state. But life had fallen in on me. I was locked out of my skull.

The clock in the jail said 8:30 when I met my future lawyer—and the first thing I noticed about John Taylor was his six-foot four-inch height. He had dark hair and a mustache and—at that time—a beard. Five years before we met in jail he had had another murder case in which one boy stabbed another. But the case was worked out in juvenile court and never publicized.

When he introduced himself he said, "Harry, I knew your family, and last night I had a phone call from your pastor and Uncle John. They told me what had happened, and I'm down here to do what I can."

John (I called him that from the first) did most of the talking that day. But I liked him as soon as I saw him. Like me, he had once been involved with cars while working in an auto body shop. Then, in 1952, he went into the Army for two years. After that, he wanted more education so he enrolled in Fairleigh Dickinson University at night. I learned he had graduated cum laude from the School of Business and had worked in the insurance field while attending law school at night. After he became a lawyer he headed the legal department of a large insurance company, then joined a private law firm. Later, he began his own practice, then formed a partnership of civil and criminal trial work with Robert Kleinberg in Park Ridge.

"You don't have to accept me as your lawyer," John stressed. "But if you'd like me to escort you to your arraignment I'll be more than happy to appear with you in the courtroom this afternoon. After we go through the legal processes I'll talk with you if you wish. Then I'll see what aid I can give you or what other help I can get you.

We shook hands firmly after this and then John Taylor left for a meeting with my Uncle John and my father's relatives to talk about legal matters connected with the estate.

Next, Dr. Thomas Bellavia, the Bergen County Jail physician, came to examine me. He asked if I had physical problems or if I was feeling sick. Then he inquired about allergies and offered me medication if I wanted something to calm me. He also asked if I used drugs, and I answered, "Just pot." I didn't want medication then, and I told him I'd be all right, so he wrote on his initial report that I had no real medical problems. He also wrote that he saw no evidence of concussion or broken ribs, and no signs of bruises or physical abuses from hazing at The Citadel. I took issue with what he said since bruises and scars go away. I later saw him on other occasions for nervousness and insomnia—and other minor physical ailments.

After my time with the doctor I was shipped out of the infirmary to the Fifth Floor South Wing for two hours. Then I went to Detention Cell 4 where I stayed for the next few days. When they put me in Det. 4 they kept up their suicide watch, and I had to sleep in the front of the cell, where officers could check on me. When I first came in I didn't talk, and that made some inmates nervous. In fact, one got so paranoid he asked to be moved away from me, and whenever his tray of food came in he wanted to trade with somebody else for fear his would get poisoned.

Pastor Nilsen (whom I began to call Roy) came down for a visit on Monday to see what he could do, and I found out later that reporters asked him "What kind of boy is Harry?"

He answered, "He's a fine young man." Then when they posed the question "Suppose he is released today—where is he going to go?"

The pastor, in his compassionate way, said, "He can come to my house. I have discussed it with my family, and even though we'd all be scared we feel he needs a lot of love, and we have a lot to share.

"I don't condone the incident," he declared to the press. "But it's a matter of putting on the line what I've always believed. I need forgiveness. So does my family. So does everyone.

"With all of our reservations we would be willing to do this."

When this statement was aired on TV and reported in various papers it brought the pastor strong support. But it also brought threatening letters and, sometimes, it brought hate mail. The pastor never abandoned me, though, and on my first Christmas in jail he even left his family to sit with me in our visiting spot while I choked down Christmas dinner.

The Hackensack arraignment on Monday was scheduled for 2:00 P.M., so at that time I arrived in court wearing ripped black jail pants and a yellow shirt. Since all my clothes had been taken I didn't have underwear or socks, and the pants were so short they ended four inches above my ankles. I didn't say a word in court, and someone described me later as "looking like a teenage monk" with my pale gaunt cheeks and Citadel cropped haircut.

At first the County Prosecutor's Office asked that bail either be denied or fixed at one million dollars. Assistant Prosecutor Richard Salkin represented the State and during the twenty-minute arraignment he stated he was asking for high bail—$250,000 on each of the four counts of murder—because, as things stood at the time, I had no roots in the community.

"I'm being as candid as I can," Salkin contended. "The bail figures should reflect what the defendant faces—four life sentences. These are extremely serious offenses."

At the hearing, however, Judge Galda ruled that he was putting off any decision on bail until he received a full mental and physical report on me.

Following the arraignment Aunt Arden and Uncle John stayed to talk with me, and Aunt Arden said that I seemed confused when I tried to speak with them.

"If things were so terribly bad," she asked, "why didn't you run away? You're eighteen. You could take off. Lots of people do."

"But where would I go?" I responded. "What would I do if I split?"

When she asked if I'd like to send flowers to the funeral home and church I told her "Yes—and I'd like them placed right by my mother's head." I also confided on that first day that I'd thought of committing suicide as soon as I got to jail. Later Aunt

Arden would speak right up about certain things I'd say. But she sensed my mental state that day and just listened as I talked.

John Taylor returned in the afternoon, and when we talked about lawyers, I told him that I wanted him to handle my defense. He was the same age as my father had been and he also had sons of his own.

Later some guards put pressure on me to talk to more than one lawyer, and they mentioned a crackerjack criminal lawyer they thought I should have. One of the guards kept pushing him, so I said I'd talk with him. But after we talked I wanted John to continue to represent me.

"At this time we won't worry about fees," John assured me, "and whether you can pay or not I promise you I will do the same for you that I'd do for my own two sons. You'll get whatever I'm capable of doing. And if you ever wish to change lawyers I'll personally contact the lawyer for you."

I ran into a roadblock in keeping John as my lawyer when the Prosecutor's Office wanted him removed from the case because he was municipal prosecutor in Montvale, where the crime occurred. In this post he attended municipal court and handled minor complaints and violations. But the Prosecutor's Office contended this would give him access to the investigation. He would also be cross-examining the Montvale cops who aided in the murder investigation. Two days after the Hackensack arraignment there was a hearing on that, and in that December 1 session (which I attended in the black pants and yellow shirt) Judge Galda stated it would be a conflict of interest for John to continue as my attorney while acting as borough prosecutor. John agreed to resign from the post to handle my defense.

My family's funeral was scheduled for Friday, December 3.

"Would you like to go under heavy guard?" John asked the day before.

"No," I said. "I just can't go. There's no way I can go."

Later when I saw Pastor Nilsen I removed a cross I always wore and asked to have it buried by my family's graves. I had bought it when I was in high school, and it had meant so much to me that I never took it off. When I gave it to the pastor it wasn't my intention to have it buried with any one person. I wanted it with all of them. But later I learned that Pastor Nilsen had put it in my mother's casket at the funeral home.

I thought about this for quite a while and then I made up my mind that if this cross which I'd treasured had to be placed with one person I wanted it in Eric's coffin. Of all the deaths in the family his was imprinted most vividly. He was a victim of something that he had nothing to do with, so he shouldn't have suffered in any way. And he shouldn't have been beaten so badly.

"Put the cross in Eric's hands," I told Roy. "That's where I want it to be."

Starting with their first visit after the Hackensack arraignment, my mother's relatives, the Greers, came to see me each day. At first my Grandma Ebneter—as my closest living relative—indicated she was willing to come and see me, too. So did another person in the De La Roche family. But there are power people in the family structure and one member who pulls a great deal of weight said nobody was to see me. At that they all became hostile and wrote me off as dead. I wanted to see my grandmother, who meant a lot to me. But she was swayed by the others, and so she never came.

She was executrix of my parents' estate, and at first there was some legal talk of having her removed because of a general feeling that she wasn't in a position to do it. She agreed in the beginning. But then she changed her mind. Finally the situation was solved when John Taylor, the Ebneters, and the Greers had a meeting along with everyone's lawyer. John got the court to preserve the estate until a final determination of the criminal proceedings, and in the course of settling things—partially at least—everyone agreed that a small amount of money should be set aside to help me with the medical expenses and evaluations needed for my defense. When these funds were released, my grandmother was retained.

All of these things were happening in my first week and a half in jail, and though I came out of the comatose state I experienced on the first day, I was still, as my lawyer put it, floating along with the butterflies a great deal of the time.

I stayed in Det. 4 a few days. Then they moved me to Det. 3, where I was still watched over as a possible suicide. Sometimes this seemed like the answer, too, because I was lonely and scared inside, and, often, very depressed. But other times I'd say to myself, "Jail isn't the place to die." Occasionally I'd think of a dying declaration if my trial verdict was "Guilty" and contemplate having two razor blades so I could cut the jugular veins right there in the courtroom. After these thoughts of suicide, however, I began to calm down.

One day when I felt edgy, though, I asked to go to the green room. That was a very strange request so the officer I talked to gave me a rather shocked, "What?"

I answered, "Yes, you heard me."

The green room is a detention room, and if a prisoner acts up an officer sends him up there for protection or punishment. It's green tiled—which is where it gets its name—and while an inmate is there a ceiling fan is turned on. You freeze up there when the fan is on because, usually, you're wearing no clothes.

Nobody wants to go there, but on the day I requested it one of the cellmates near me had threatened suicide. The whole thing was getting to me, and I didn't want to be there when the suicide happened. I also wanted to blow off steam and be by myself for a while, so when I went there for the night I cried a little while. I wouldn't have wanted my cellmates to see me doing that. While I was there my arms were strapped to a bunk the officers brought in. Again they feared I'd kill myself and were taking no chances of that. I was up there for twelve hours, and when I came down the suicidal inmate had swallowed a TV antenna. He was rushed to Bergen Pines Hospital and operated on.

One of the things that kept me alive those first few days in jail was the mail that started coming in, not only from the people I knew but also from total strangers. The first to arrive was a card from my church signed by fifty people. Other letters I've saved said:

Dear Harry,

I don't quite know what to say to you. I guess most importantly I should tell you I'm behind you. I know, and I know you know, what you did is wrong. But who are we to judge? When I think about what you went through, I wonder how you did it. I guess I also feel very guilty because when you did stuff with us at church or when I saw you at school I treated you like everyone else. I could kick myself now because I feel like I only added to your problems. It's something I'll have to live with.

All I'm asking is that you accept me as your friend now. I know Pastor has said you could always stay at his house. Well, if anything goes wrong with that you always have a home with us. Don't think you have no friends because you have a lot, and you have a great friend in Steve.

Just remember you've got a friend, no matter what happens to you.

Love,
Debbie Weir

Dear Harry,

You may not remember me, but I lived across the street from you when we lived in Lodi. When you were a baby I played with you and cared for you. Then I walked you to school until you moved to Montvale. I'm twenty-five now with a family of my own.

Harry, I know you're going through a difficult time. But you mustn't feel alone because you are in my thoughts and prayers.

Sincerely,
A Friend

Dear Harry,

We all understand the terrific pressures you have been under. Don't lose your courage or hope. I am sure there are good, intelligent people like your lawyer and minister who will stand by you. Cooperate with them and trust them. I am a mother of two sons and I hope you will accept offers of friendship from people who understand your problems. *Just forgive yourself.*

A friendly neighbor,
Carol Roberts

I didn't answer those letters, since I didn't know what to say. But I finally sat down and wrote to Steve early in December.

Steve,

How are you doing, my brother. It isn't that bad. Only the food and being in my cell about 24 hours a day sucks. Steve, I will try to write as often as I can. Hope you will write me more than you did when I was down at The Citadel.

Don't believe everything you read and hear. What if I told you that I didn't fail my polygraph. The pigs can't understand what that means. They didn't ask the right questions. Someday I will tell you the whole story. I think you'll agree that what I did (the complete story) was right. I'll tell my pastor what it is but he won't be able to tell you for a while. You know me well enough to know I couldn't blow away my *whole* family. Read between the lines and you will start to see the truth. Yes, I gave two statements. There are bits and parts that are totally true. I wish I could tell you but I promised someone something, and I can't go back on my word. Anyway, you will know the whole story after the trial which should be a year from now. So, my little brother,

Till you write,
Harry

By the second week in December I started to come to my senses, so when the Greers came to visit on December 8 I asked them to contact Pastor Nilsen.

"I have something to tell him," I said. "It's urgent I see him right away."

VIII

"These Things Don't Happen to People You Know!"

25

Dr. Emanuel Tanay, a Detroit psychiatrist who has done extensive research on the causes of homicide, states in his book *The Murderers* that lives could be saved through a greater knowledge of what goes on in the minds and hearts of people burdened with years of personal frustration.

"In most homicides—between sixty and eighty percent of them—there is an intense emotional relationship between murderer and victim," he writes. "Homicide, so to speak, is most often an affair of the heart.

"Murder is indeed a family affair, because family members both love and hate one another, and the hate, if it becomes excessive, may explode in murder. People invariably kill the ones they love and hate, for no one else is important enough to provoke murderous rage. . . . Murder marks the end, the tragic end, of a very ambivalent relationship."

While Dr. Tanay and others provided psychiatric views of intrafamily murders, the shattered residents of Montvale were saying again and again, "They were a normal family—like any of the rest of us," or, "These things just don't happen to the people you know!"

In the beginning people talked about family breakdowns that could lead to crimes such as this—and those who saw it in this light viewed the murders as a strong indictment of the lack of communication that exists in some families today. They were the ones who were first to say, "We don't condone the shootings.

But we understand how it could have happened. If Harry got free tomorrow he'd be welcome at our home." In other circles there was hatred, and these were the groups who said from the first, "Make an example of De La Roche so it won't happen here again."

Along with this kind of hatred many people who'd moved from the cities to get away from crime were shaken by the awakening that the same crimes they had fled from were happening in the suburbs and in their neighbors' homes. Some who were highly sensitive to having this happen in Montvale wanted to suppress it and believe it had never occurred. Others with a social conscience called for a greater understanding of the need for counseling and therapy that can come to any family.

In an interview in *The Record*, the newspaper which serves Bergen County, the Rev. A. Wayne Schwab, a former Montvale pastor and, later, the Evangelism and Renewal Officer at the Episcopal Center in New York stated: "Our underlying assumption to this day is that seeking help is weakness, and strong people solve their emotional, behavioral problems in only one way—and that is alone. We make a stigma out of the problem, look the other way, and ostracize those who don't fit the assigned roles in our so-called serene suburban scene.

"I am speaking out of experience when I say people go on ignoring the troubled until, like Harry, they commit terrifying acts, or, stopping short of that, they live with limping psyches or simply deteriorate. It follows that we need to know what goes on within ourselves. Here in the suburbs the crisp neat lawns and the shuttered windows present a dramatic symbol, fine on the outside but what's within? Some families do thrive on the suburban style of living. But it can be difficult. In the accepted values, there is very little room for the Harrys who can't make the teams, who have mannerisms that are mocked. Nothing works for them.

"We have to penetrate the shuttered windows and the happy face that is a mask. We have to acquire a sense that our illnesses of the head and heart can be healed. We have to know that the best of us may become disturbed, deeply disturbed. We have to know what happens to oneself and to others. Harry's father didn't understand . . . because [Harry] wasn't cut out for a military school. But there's nothing in the climate to encourage a Harry or the father of a Harry to take a look inside themselves. And no one helped them to do it."

Interviews with the family's friends yielded a mixed bag of feelings during Harry's first days in jail.

"The newspapers keep calling me and asking me to talk about it," said Steve Mahoney. "But I won't say anything. Many of the kids who were interviewed for newspapers or TV stories were the very people who mocked out Harry or who didn't know him well. They agreed to talk to reporters just to get their names in the paper.

"I'm willing to say, however, that Harry couldn't have done it."

Some of Harry's other friends reacted in the same way.

"I didn't believe it when I heard it, and I'm still unable to believe it," Vinnie Trojan declared. "Harry didn't have it in him to do anything like that."

"The lid blew off for Harry," added Jeff De Causemaker. "If only he'd been able to let off steam and come to an understanding about his relationships with his parents."

"No matter what happens—even if it's proven that he did this—he'll never be guilty in my eyes," said Bob Gantt. "I saw the things that Harry went through, so if he reached a breaking point how many situations helped put him in this spot?

"The kids in school who called him names? His father who pressured him? The Citadel where he was told what to do—and couldn't fight back wisely?"

Other peers had different views ranging from compassion to an all-out dislike.

"The way I see it Harry's life is pretty well decided now," suggested a former classmate who said he couldn't stand Harry. "Basically he's taken care of, so I don't think the death of his family is any great loss to him. He has alleviated the problem, and the pressure is off."

"If Harry did it," speculated another peer, "he might have shot his father not only to get out from under him but also to keep him from being hurt because he was leaving school. Then he had to shoot his mother because he couldn't face her after shooting his father. The same thing would be true of his brothers. How could he look at either of them after shooting his parents? He may have thought when everyone was gone he'd really have his own life."

Lisa Fritts, Jeff's sister, who saw him Saturday night, had the feeling that Harry seemed sad when he came to pick up Jeff.

"I knew him for about a year, and I really liked him when I first met him," she reported. "He seemed to be very lonely and I soon got the impression he was hardly ever home. But there was a definite difference in Harry's attitude from the first time I met him to Saturday night. He just seemed very sad to me, and I felt sorry for him."

"Looking at things after the fact I believe that Harry may have always had an immaturity or instability few people were sensitive to," said a woman who knew the whole family. "He always needed friendship but not enough people sensed it. Instead they ribbed him and taunted him, simply because he was different. Maybe some kind of crisis was bound to erupt someday."

"When the newspapers came out after that Sunday I was astounded to read that Harry was mocked out and put down," said Irene Bickerton. "He was gentle and soft at our house."

"But from the things we read, and the little things we knew, we've kind of put it together and feel that he might have been justified," put in Ben Bickerton thoughtfully. "Certainly not to the extent he went. But we feel tremendous compassion for him, and the only thing that we can say is, 'He must have gone absolutely berserk like any one of us could if the pressure were that bad.' "

"You would have to be insane," a De La Roche neighbor reasoned. "How else could you kill your whole family and handle and move their bodies?

"I don't think Harry had a plan. I just think he went wild. If he'd taken the time to think things out why didn't he hide the bodies in an isolated spot? Why didn't he throw the pistol in a lake? Why didn't he take off for school?"

"Just a week before he came home from school I met his mother on the street," another neighbor revealed, "and I can hear her saying now, 'Harry will stick it out.' Later I met the father and when I asked how Harry was he said, 'He couldn't be better.' You could tell by the way he answered that he had definitely made up his mind that Harry was going to make it."

Paul Mulligan, a member of the Marine Corps Reserve and the father of Eric's best friend, recalled in the hours after the crime that the first week Harry, Jr., was at The Citadel Harry, Sr., wanted information on how Harry could plan to be a Marine Corps officer four years from that time.

Steve Madreperla, Harry, Sr.'s, good friend, spent much of his time in Montvale during those tragic days. And—as Steve Mahoney had said of young Harry, "Harry is my friend"—Steve Madreperla said the same of Harry, Sr.

"He wanted strength and security for his sons," Steve explained, "and while some people thought his approach to this was a too-stiff discipline, others might call it a dedication to what he thought was right. His family was everything to him. But there was something about his discipline and Harry, Jr.'s, chemistry that didn't mix."

While Montvale continued its post-mortems many of the residents added, "Let the family rest in peace."

"We can all offer our speculations and give opinions, but nothing will bring back the De La Roche family," said a husband and wife who had worked with them in many community activities. "Our hope is that Harry and Mary Jane never woke to see who killed them—for they loved all three of their sons."

"But I also think of Harry, Jr.," a neighbor said. "I have no animosities toward him, and I hope he comes out all right. Every day when I wake up I think, 'It could have been my son.' "

On Monday morning after the crime while Pascack Hills was in session the principal, Bart De Paola, spoke to the student body over the school's loudspeaker:

"We all need somebody to understand us," he said. "Let us hope that from this day forward we stop mocking each other out and start becoming more sensitive to each other as human beings."

26

At another school—The Citadel—the Sunday night phone call that came from John Greer also made everyone say, "But these things just don't happen to the people you know."

"I returned from Thanksgiving around 9:00 P.M.," said Harry's senior, Walt Singleton, "and all of a sudden a guard came to say Captain Sawtelle wanted to see me. I was trying to figure what I'd done wrong when I learned that Hank Gill, Harry's squad sergeant, had also been told to report. Captain Sawtelle seemed silent and stunned when we got to him."

"Have you talked to newspaper people?" he asked.

The two cadets both told him "No," and looked and felt perplexed.

"This concerns Mr. De La Roche," Captain Sawtelle finally said.

"What happened?" Walt Singleton asked him.

The captain hesitated before he said, "He killed some people today."

"On the highway?" Singleton inquired.

"No, he shot them," the captain answered.

That caught Walt Singleton completely off guard and, like many people in Montvale, he simply couldn't believe it.

"I had noticed a gentleness and sensitivity about Harry," he declared. "I'd also noted his feelings toward life so I didn't think he'd be capable of doing anything like that."

As the news started filtering to barracks and homes the state of shock continued.

"I heard it first on the radio," stated Capt. Harry Axson, Harry's military science teacher, "and I listened twice to be absolutely sure that what I'd heard was real."

Pete Salerno, who'd been unable to bring Harry's dress uniform home, was in formation on Sunday night when he heard the name "De La Roche."

"I turned and asked what had happened," he reported, "and then when I heard the story I said, 'You can't be serious!' I

171

absolutely couldn't believe it. I didn't know what to say.

"Now I wish I could have talked to him more when I spoke to him on Thanksgiving. But as soon as he found out about the uniform he hung up—and that was it. Now I realize his reaction was strange, but, of course, he was getting closer to the time when he'd have to come back. He was jittery and nervous and anxious to get off the phone. That was the last I heard of him. He wasn't like the Harry I knew.

"Harry didn't wait for the good times here. When he knew it was time to come back he must have been thinking about it and what was going to happen when he returned to school."

"Before Thanksgiving Mr. De La Roche seemed to be in serious need to go home," commented Col. D. D. Nicholson, Jr., vice-president for development. "But it's hard to conceive he had any ulterior motive. He could have picked up and left at any time, so why go through all this?

"Now that this has happened we're being taken apart by the media who say, 'In a military college wouldn't you verify the nature of an illness before granting an early leave?' We answer, 'Of course, we wouldn't. We work on an honor system and if somebody within the corps says he has a family illness we believe him.' It's not a normal procedure to grant an early leave as we did for Mr. De La Roche but both his tac officer and his senior were so zealous and concerned in their efforts to help him we felt we had a responsibility to let him go in this case."

On the surface the multiple murders were kept fairly quiet on campus, but speculation on the "Why's" was just as prevalent in Charleston as it was back home in Montvale. Some saw Harry as an introvert, a cadet who kept to himself. Others said he was quiet and shy but had only the normal difficulties freshmen would have adjusting.

"Maybe of all the freshmen he might have had it the toughest in 'N' company," admitted one of his former roommates. "But that was only because he brought it on himself."

"To some he was one of the worst guys in the company as far as getting along with other people," put in another cadet. "Something was boiling in him, and it just boiled over."

His tactical officer, Captain Sawtelle, thought he'd be back when he left.

"To me he was an average freshman," stated Captain Sawtelle. "He got into difficulty and he was uncoordinated. But you look at any freshman. He's confused. It's a brand new life. I didn't see him a great deal of the time, but I felt that in the time he was here he came along with the rest of the freshmen. He wasn't in the front of the class, but he was by no means at the rear either. The physical requirements didn't hurt him, and he was able to run as well if not better than many of the upperclassmen.

"I might say one thing that turned some people off was the way he'd come in and ask the same questions each day at almost the same time—like, 'What time is formation?' or, 'What time is the first bugle?' When you've asked that question once you've asked it. But he'd come to morning, noon, and evening formation and say, 'What time is bugle call?'

"In general, though, the way he walked in at the beginning of the year was just about the way he walked out before Thanksgiving. But something went wrong along the way."

"I was his squad sergeant for four weeks, and no squad sergeant is the most liked person on campus," admitted David Sullivan. "In fact, I know Harry hated me. But when I saw he was having a problem I'd get him in a room and say, 'Let's talk it out. What's your bitch?'

"As far as I can remember he never talked about problems. But sometimes I felt kind of sorry for him, and if I had to pull him for improper uniform or something like that I'd tell him to come by and work it out with push-up's instead of demerits.

"When I warned him at mess to be careful about what he put on his plate because he'd have to eat it whether he liked it or not, he'd slap everything on his plate. I don't remember his having to eat grits. But if he put them on his plate he had to eat them."

Mark Coker followed David Sullivan as one of Harry's sergeants—and while he was his sergeant he tried to be his friend.

"I often felt Harry tried," he declared, "though sometimes he made no effort. For example, in one instance, I specifically recall telling him that we were having a big inspection and I wanted to make sure he shined his brass and shaved because I didn't want everybody to jump on him. That day when he came to formation he was a mess. His shoes were dull and his brass wasn't shined. He just looked absolutely terrible. I blew up because here I was doing everything I could for him and I thought he should be doing something for me. You can only give a guy so many breaks.

"When he did things right I told him. Then he'd beam and grow eight feet tall. But when you told him he was doing something wrong, it made him feel he could do nothing right. That's the way Harry was. I found he deliberately hid his feelings, though sometimes he'd start to open up, and then realize he was doing it and stop.

"He was stuck between a rock and a hard place. He didn't know what way to go."

27

While people were assessing the tragedy—and trying to answer the "Why's"—the friends and survivors of the De La Roche family prepared to bury their dead.

On the Monday morning following the crime John Greer and his sister-in-law, Carol Mallè, drove to the Montvale headquarters to gain admittance to the Grand Avenue home where they hoped to find wills and cemetery deeds. Carol had taken time off from her job in the offices of a major department store because she wanted to spare John from doing more than he had to do in the upstairs of that house.

"The house was in disarray," she said, "and the scenes were very unpleasant. Violence was evident in the hallway and master bedroom, and on the attic stairs. We confined ourselves to the

Death Notices

DE LA ROCHE — Eric on November 28, 1976 of 23 East Grand Ave., Montvale, N.J. Beloved son of the late Mary Jane and Harry W., Sr. Brother of Harry W., Jr., and the late Ronald. Grandson of Mrs. Johanna Ebneter of Lodi. Funeral Service 10 A.M. Friday at Christ Lutheran Church, Woodcliff Lake, N.J. Interment George Washington Memorial Park, Paramus. Visiting at the Robert Spearing Funeral Home, 155 Kinderkamack Rd., Park Ridge, N.J. 7-9 P.M. Wednesday, 2-4 and 7-9 P.M. Thursday. In lieu of flowers kindly make donations to the Good Samaritan Fund, c/o Christ Lutheran Church, Woodcliff Lake, N.J.

DE LA ROCHE — Mary Jane (nee Greer) on November 28, 1976 of 23 East Grand Ave., Montvale, N.J. Beloved wife of the late Harry W., Sr. Mother of Harry W., Jr. and the late Ronald and Eric. Sister of John C. Greer of Maywood. Funeral Service 10 A.M. Friday at Christ Lutheran Church, Woodcliff Lake, N.J. Interment George Washington Memorial Park, Paramus. Visiting at the Robert Spearing Funeral Home, 155 Kinderkamack Rd., Park Ridge, N.J. 7-9 P.M. Wednesday, 2-4 and 7-9 P.M. Thursday. In lieu of flowers kindly make donations to the Good Samaritan Fund, c/o Christ Lutheran Church, Woodcliff Lake, N.J.

DE LA ROCHE — Ronald on November 28, 1976 of 23 East Grand Ave., Montvale, N.J. Beloved son the late Mary Jane and Harry W., Sr. Brother of Harry W., Jr. and the late Eric. Grandson of Mrs. Johanna Ebneter of Lodi. Funeral Service 10 A.M. Friday at Christ Lutheran Church, Woodcliff Lake, N.J. Interment George Washington Memorial Park, Paramus. Visiting at the Robert Spearing Funeral Home, 155 Kinderkamack Rd., Park Ridge, N.J. 7-9 P.M. Wednesday, 2-4 and 7-9 P.M. Thursday. In lieu of flowers kindly make donations to the Good Samaritan Fund, c/o Christ Lutheran Church, Woodcliff Lake, N.J.

DE LA ROCHE — Harry W., Sr. on November 28, 1976 of 23 East Grand Ave., Montvale, N.J. Beloved husband of the late Mary Jane. Father of Harry W., Jr. and the late Ronald and Eric. Son of Mrs. Johanna Ebneter of Lodi. Funeral Service 10 A.M. Friday at Christ Lutheran Church, Woodcliff Lake, N.J. Interment George Washington Memorial Park, Paramus. Visiting at the Robert Spearing Funeral Home, 155 Kinderkamack Rd., Park Ridge, N.J. 7-9 P.M. Wednesday, 2-4 and 7-9 P.M. Thursday. In lieu of flowers kindly make donations to the Good Samaritan Fund, c/o Christ Lutheran Church, Woodcliff Lake, N.J.

Death notices for the De La Roche family appearing in The Record, *Hackensack, New Jersey on December 1, 1976.*

master bedroom as we searched for strong boxes or other containers which might have the information we needed.

"The cops inventoried every item we removed. Then we sat in the car to go through papers. We also had to get underwear and things for Harry for jail."

When the morning search yielded no directions for burial arrangements, John and Carol drove to Park Ridge to the Robert Spearing Funeral Home.

"After conferring with Mr. Spearing I telephoned Harry, Sr.'s, family and discussed suggested arrangements in detail," recalled John Greer. "Harry's family concurred with them, so next we selected caskets, set tentative visiting hours, and made arrangements to purchase plots at George Washington Memorial

Park Cemetery in Paramus. Later in the evening we went back to the house, and Carol and Roy Nilsen went along to pick out clothes for the burial. Mike O'Donovan was there from the police to do what he could do.

"We selected a simple dress and pearls for Mary Jane, a business suit for Harry, Sr., and leisure suits for the boys," Carol Mallè remembered.

"I've tried to block this from my mind, and I seldom discuss it," she confided. "But when Roy and I went to the boys' back bedroom it was an absolute nightmare. The room was so bloody from the shooting and bludgeoning, I had to run out to the hall."

"Mike offered to get me some coffee, but I couldn't have swallowed a thing. The trunk that held Ronnie's body was blood stained and in the hall."

On Tuesday Arden ordered Harry's flower arrangement to be placed by his mother's head and asked that no card be included. Then she asked Robert Spearing not to discuss those flowers. Later, when the press asked if Harry sent flowers he honored her request.

On Wednesday night the viewings began, and the viewers filed through the funeral home till the funeral on Friday morning. Some came because they were mourners. Others were the curious.

Although John Greer originally started the funeral arrangements, Harry, Sr.'s, next of kin decided Honey Ebneter should do it for Harry, Sr., and the boys. The Greers and the Ebneters concurred with this so at the viewing and funeral John and Arden represented the maternal side, while the Ebneters and other De La Roches were there for the paternal side. There were also a number of cousins on the paternal side.

For the most part things went fairly well except for two disagreements. First, there was the matter of whether the caskets should be opened. Then there was the question of why anyone would feel anything but hatred toward young Harry. In fact, one relative felt so bitter that he said in front of three people—John Greer, Roy Nilsen, and Robert Spearing—that he'd like to kill Harry, Jr., for what he'd done to the family.

"When we took the clothes to Robert Spearing, I, as the pastor, saw the bodies," Roy Nilsen recollected. "The bullet holes were evident, and Ronnie looked so swollen I wouldn't have known it was Ronnie. What was left of Eric's face had been all covered by cotton.

"John Greer made it clear that Mary Jane's casket would be closed. But Honey Ebneter kept wondering about opening up the others. I knew the sight that she would see, so I put my arm around her and said, 'You know, Honey, there are going to be many people here, and people—being average—will look for the bullet holes. Maybe you don't want your son and his family to be remembered that way. We could keep the caskets closed and put photographs on top."

At first Honey seemed to concur. Then one of the relatives responded, "People have gotta see this. I also want to see Eric."

Roy with his usual compassion tried to protect him from this.

"I can describe everything," he hold him. "I can assure you he's there." But the relative had to see him, and when they opened the casket in private he naturally went to pieces. He agreed Eric's casket should be closed. Ronnie's and Harry, Sr.'s, were open at the funeral home.

Some of the De La Roches took a dim view of Pastor Nilsen for the way he'd befriended Harry from the moment he'd heard of the crime, and a few other people felt hostile, too, because of the pastor's offer to take Harry into his home.

"Although I got some very supportive calls and tender cards and letters from all over the country, I also received some crank calls," he said. "One of the callers—and my youngest boy took it—threatened to take a shot at me for offering to do this for Harry."

For the two days of the viewings, the caskets were lined in a semicircle with floral arrangements between them, and most of the time emotions were relatively well controlled. The Bickertons cried as they knelt by the coffins, and then they said to Roy, "If only we'd been home on Saturday when Harry came to the house. If only we'd had him for dinner and been there to talk with him." Later the girls from Eric's class filed by his casket and

The Reverend Roy Nilsen and Ruth Mohring following De La Roche family funeral services at Christ Lutheran Church.
PHOTO BY TED NEUHAUFF, *THE JOURNAL NEWS*, NYACK, NEW YORK.

when each put a nosegay on the floor beside it, Honey, who was sitting by Eric, was so overcome that she fainted.

On December 3, the day of the funeral, the weather was subfreezing. But news reporters and television cameras were gathered at Christ Lutheran Church as early as 8:30. Prior to the midmorning service the four caskets arrived from the funeral home, and the impact of the four coffins was something that was hard to describe. Arden Greer broke down and cried as the enormity of it struck her at that moment. The caskets were placed in a semicircle below a wooden cross, and members of community organizations carried the four coffins.

When it was time for the funeral nearly four hundred people were there, and the service began with the congregation singing

"A Mighty Fortress Is Our God." Then Roy Nilsen rose and said quietly, "Spirit of God, things are swirling through my heart and mind. You promised you would give your men the right things to say. God, how I need that help now.

"This tragedy has caused many parents and teenagers to reassess their relationships and, if parents and teenage kids can love and communicate, some strange good will come out of this. We are quick to assess blame. The solution is not in fixing blame—but in fixing hurts."

Then he paused before he continued.

"I can't stand here without praying for that boy in prison and hoping your love and wisdom might reach out and envelop him. May God do his work with Harry, too."

When Roy concluded his homily Cindy Christiansen, who sang

Johanna and Ernest Ebneter seated at burial services for the De La Roche family at George Washington Memorial Park in Paramus, New Jersey on December 3. Others are De La Roche relatives and friends of the family. PHOTO BY UNITED PRESS INTERNATIONAL.

like Julie Andrews, brought an unforgettable moment to the day
with her solo, "Love Them Now":

> Don't wait till they've gone away,
> Love them now while they're around.
> Touch them, hold them, laugh and cry with them.
> Show them, tell them, don't deny with them.
> Love them now
> Before they're just a guilty memory.
> Love them now, love them now.

At the graveside service at George Washington Memorial Park
relatives huddled in the freezing weather as Roy let a handful of
fresh brown earth form a cross on each of the caskets. The flag
from Harry, Sr.'s, was folded and given to Honey. Then the
funeral procession made its way back to Christ Lutheran Church
for a lunch that parishioners who had wanted to do something
had prepared for the family and friends. The emotional climate
was quiet and mixed with both grief and relief.

At last the unbelievable tragedy was over for one day at least.

IX

The Story Retold

28

When I told the Greers on December 8 that I had to see Pastor Nilsen they must have sensed it was pressing since he came the following day.

I was anxiously waiting to see him, too, because I had something I had to say to a person I knew I could really trust. Roy Nilsen was that person. I was released from my cell that day to go to the facilities provided for counsel on the second floor. John Taylor was in there with me at the time that Roy arrived.

"There's Pastor Nilsen," I told him. "Would you mind if I saw him alone."

"Of course not," John answered quickly, as he picked up his papers and briefcase and went to the reception desk to confer with his partner, Robert Kleinberg, who was at the jail that day.

Roy and I passed the time of day as we sat in the cell-like room at a table shoved against the wall. It had two chairs and a metal gate door like those that are used on our cells. But I was itchy to get started, so I opened the conversation with "I want you to hear this story.

"I know this will come as a shock," I warned, "but I didn't kill my family alone. Ronnie shot Eric and my parents, and I shot Ronnie in a rage. There are plenty of gaps in my memory, and it's like a twilight zone. But I'll tell you what I remember."

I can still see the look on the pastor's face. But he listened and said very little.

"As I said in my two statements both the light by the door and the light in our living room were off when I got home from the

'Maximus,' " I explained.

"I went upstairs without lighting the lights, and if you've been upstairs in my house you know we have a L-shape hallway with my parents' room at one end of the L and Ronnie and Eric's at the other. When I got to that part of the hallway I looked down toward the boys' room and saw Ronnie sitting on the side of his bed. His feet were dangling over the side, and he had a dazed look on his face.

"I started down the hall to speak to him. Then when I got to his door I saw Eric to the right of me. He was half lying on the floor and half propped up by his desk. The back of his head was bloody with something white around it, and blood was all over his bed. I can't describe what was in my mind, and I don't know what I said except, "Where are Mom and Dad?" He answered, 'In bed,' and when he spoke it was like he was in a trance. He didn't talk in his normal way, and his voice was a low monotone.

"I turned and ran to my parents' room. But even before I snapped on the light I knew what I would find. There was blood all over their bed. I touched my father and checked his pulse. When I didn't get any from him I figured Mom was gone too, because if something was wrong with my father she wouldn't have been just lying there unless she was dead herself."

"So what did you say to Ronnie?" Pastor Nilsen inquired. "You must have had some conversation, some kind of questions you asked."

"I'm not sure now," I answered. "I think I said some common thing like, 'What happened?' or, 'What is this?' "

I then went on to tell Roy how Ronnie kept on looking dazed and didn't answer at first. Finally he said in an abnormal voice, "Dad discovered me with drugs and is going to turn me in." I don't think Ronnie believed that, though. I think he feared Dad might beat him—or maybe shoot as he'd threatened—since nothing had ever made him as angry as discovering this.

"As I try to piece things together, maybe Dad had postponed taking any action because I was still on vacation or maybe my mother had said 'Let it slide till Harry leaves tomorrow.' "

"When did your father discover the drugs?" Pastor Nilsen put in.

"Ronnie didn't say," I responded. "But if my father had discovered it and known about it before supper I don't think that Dad would have let him out when he went to collect for his papers, and I don't think Ronnie was in the house when my father asked about Ronnie and pot when I went back to change cars.

"I guess sometime after 6:30 or 7:00 my father must have found the green G.I. Joe box that Ronnie used for his drugs, scales, and baggies. He would have seen some empty baggies since Ronnie liked to keep them so he could smell them sometimes.

"Dad might have been on a 'Spring Cleaning' spree or he might have been looking for something under Ronnie's bed, since Ronnie was sleeping in his own room while I was home from school.

"At any rate Ronnie was scared for his life as he said in a dazed monotone, 'I shot Dad and Mom, and then I shot Eric.' "

"When did he get the gun?" asked Roy.

"I think he must have taken it when he came home from wherever he was before my parents went to bed. I don't know where he was that night, and I don't know what time he came in."

I couldn't begin to tell Roy the feeling I had at that moment, and I can't describe the state I was in when Ronnie said in quick succession 'I shot Dad, I shot Mom, I shot Eric.' I'll never know why he killed Mom and Eric unless he cracked once he started.

"We talked for a little while longer—I really don't know how long. Then I heard Eric let out a groan. I also saw he'd been beaten and bludgeoned in the head."

"But if Eric had been shot," Roy wondered, "Why would he be beaten, too?"

"I don't know," I answered. "Ronnie might have hit him because he didn't die immediately. Or possibly he hit him before he went to my parents' room to make sure Eric didn't run. Maybe he hit him before the shootings. Or maybe it was afterwards.

"All I know is when I saw Eric it really set me off. I wasn't sure when I heard him groan whether he was dead or alive, so it's true that I went over to him and put my hand over his face. Then I said, 'Eric, go to sleep.' I wanted him to think it was a nightmare because there was no way he was going to live. When he slumped to the floor I just flipped. It's in my mind that he died in my arms since I had blood on my forearms and hands. After that I wasn't accountable. I screwed up an awful lot.

"There was nothing I could do for Eric, so I moved back toward Ronnie's bed. Then suddenly I had an impulse to kill him for what he'd done. When I began to approach him Ronnie lay over on his side. His eyes were wide open as he pleaded, 'Please help me—get me out of here.'

"I could have called the cops right then, and I don't know why I didn't. But I saw the pistol on the window sill at the end of Ronnie's bed, and when I saw some blood on the butt that freaked me out even more.

"I picked it up and held it. Ronnie's eyes were closed. Then I whispered 'Ronnie' and quickly pulled the trigger. There was only one bullet left and that shot killed my brother.

"After I shot Ronnie I freaked out totally, and the first clear thought that came to mind was 'Now I'm going to get the blame for all four of the deaths, so what I started to do at that time was completely illogical."

Roy interrupted me to ask, "Why didn't you turn and run for help when you saw Ronnie that night? Wouldn't that be a natural reaction when you walked in on that scene?"

"Who can know how they'd react?" I replied. "People can't put themselves in this spot until it actually happens.

"And look at the way I was brought up and, also, the way I lived. I had taken an awful lot, and you know how I control my emotions."

Roy looked at my face, and I looked at his, as he took out his pipe.

"I just went nuts," I told him, "and I know I did a lot of things that I should never have done. I moved some stuff around the house just to keep myself going. But now I don't remember getting from one spot to another. I wiped up certain spots of blood with long johns and a shirt on Ronnie's floor, and I even wiped off the light switch since there was blood on that. Later I chucked those clothes in my closet, and that was illogical, too."

My next concern, I related, was what to do with the bodies in order to protect myself from looking as though I was the one who had shot the entire family. I know that I was loose in the head, but my next move was to strip to the waist and leave only my long johns on. Then I put a towel around Ronnie's head and dragged him upstairs to our attic. I really can't remember putting him into the chest, but I guess my reason for doing this was personal survival and a half-assed way of setting myself up to say I didn't know where he was. When I told the story that Ronnie had said he'd bury my father underneath his bed that was erratic and stupid. But it provided a reason for why Dad was in Ronnie's bed.

"After I moved the two bodies I went in the upstairs bathroom and washed up in the sink. Ronnie had told me when we talked that he had used the shower.

"That Sunday the cops kept asking all day whether I'd used the shower, and when I had it up to here I finally said what they wanted and told them that I did. When I finished with the washing I put on the clothes I had taken off—the ones I'd been wearing that night. Then I went out to my mother's car. You know the rest of the story.

"We have a bit of discrepancy in Patrolman Olsen's statement that he saw me go through a stop sign and pulled me over for that. Instead I pulled him over when I came east on Grand Avenue and turned right at the intersection. There's no way you shoot through a stop sign when you make a right turn. I cut around his car right away and spun my tires to stop him. What are the chances of his looking in his mirror and seeing a car run a stop sign at that time in the morning?

"People have said I was planning to escape when I encountered Olsen. But if I'd been trying to run from the house I would have loaded my car with food, camping stuff, clothing, and guns, and any money left in the house in addition to what I had on me.

"If I'd been the criminal the cops said I was I could have headed for Route 304 and upstate New York. I could even have dropped the car I had, and stolen another one. Or I could have set my car on fire and then just kept on going.

"But I didn't do any of that. I went right to the cops. And I went there instead of calling because if I'd called at 4:00 A.M. and told them my family was dead they'd think I was drunk or something."

Roy didn't cut in while I talked. Then he spoke very softly.

"But what I can't fathom," he ventured, "is why you gave the police that first statement—and why you gave that confession—if this is the thing that happened. Why didn't you give this account from the start? People will wonder why you waited to tell anybody this version."

"There are several reasons," I replied. "I'd shot my brother. My family was dead. And I had no one and no place to go.

"They had me for Ronnie anyhow, so I figured I'd be a martyr and take all the blame myself. Ronnie and I were both guilty, it's true. But I feel more guilty myself because things might have been different if I had talked to him about drugs or if I had come home earlier instead of going for those beers.

"I blame myself for not doing more, since I knew about the drugs. I also found out he was getting money to buy some of his drugs by selling coins from the coin collection Pop Pop kept at our house. Now I hear I'm getting blamed for stealing from that collection for the coins I sold for my car.

"When I gave that confession," I explained to Roy, "it was based on what Ronnie told me, some of the things I had done and conversations I'd picked up from the cops.

"There was the matter of the pistol, too," I went on to say. "As I told you, there was one bullet in it when I picked it up from the sill. Now this gun was a semiautomatic one that's a ten-shot clip. You can hold an eleventh shot in the chamber, but this isn't always too wise. After I cleaned and reloaded the gun earlier in the week there were ten shells in the clip. I've learned from conversations that eleven bullets were fired that night, so, since I only loaded ten, the pistol had been reloaded with an eleventh bullet.

"It *had* to be reloaded," I explained to Roy, "because you could tell from the pistol butt that Eric had been hit on the head with that. When you hit someone with an automatic the gun is going to fire, especially when you hit hard enough to get some brain matter out. That brings up the question—who reloaded it and why?

"I've thought about that a lot this week, and if Ronnie opened the chamber and slid in that extra shot was he going to use it on himself or was he thinking of me? The bodies were warm when I found them so I feel the family must have been shot about fifteen minutes before I arrived. If I had been home earlier would something have happened to me?

"No one will ever know," I said. "But that extra bullet was strange, so now I've had a change of mind and instead of playing the martyr and taking all of the blame I want to tell the story to a few of the people I trust."

When I was finished Roy commented, "That certainly puts a different light on the entire story. Have you told this to John Taylor?"

"No, you're the only person I've discussed it with."

"I think you should tell John," he advised. "Shall I go out and tell him there's something he should hear from you?"

I nodded my head, and Roy shook my hand before he left the cell. Then John came in and listened before he asked a few questions—like, "Is this a jailhouse tactic?" and, "Have you been talking to inmates?" I told him, "No, this is the truth," and then he asked me to promise I wouldn't tell anyone else at this time. Later I got the okay from him to tell Steve Mahoney everything. I also told Uncle Steve Madreperla when he came for a visit with me. That same day Roy went to see the Greers to tell them another dimension had come into the picture.

On December 10 when Aunt Arden came I told her the story myself. Later I told the psychiatrists who came to the jail to see me. As the story leaked out, some believed me, while others discounted it. But this is the picture I have in my mind and the recollection I'll always have, no matter what anyone says.

For all the while that I was in jail I had one ongoing wish and that was to go to the gravesites the day I got out of jail. I knew I'd have a time of remorse when I actually said farewell. But I had to control my emotions in jail, or I wouldn't have been able to survive.

I'll never forget I killed Ronnie, though. That's a burden I'll carry with me for the rest of my life.

X

The Long Days and Nights
Till the Trial

29

December continued into January while I gradually accli-
mated myself to Bergen County Jail. It wasn't an easy adjustment, since paint was peeling everywhere, and walls in the
cellblocks were crumbling. Plus this, most corridors had foul-
smelling puddles from defective pipes and toilets. Fluorescent
lights were never off, and the din from doors and clanking
keys—plus people shouting back and forth—made a noise I'll
never forget. My cell, approximately seven feet by five feet, had
a bed, toilet, and sink. While I was trying to get used to it
several things happened in December.

One was going before the Bergen County grand jury and
being indicted on four counts of murder two and a half weeks
after the deaths. I knew, if convicted of these four counts, I
could be sentenced to four life terms in a New Jersey prison.

On December 18 a court-appointed psychiatrist from
Paterson—Dr. Joseph F. Zigarelli—came to the jail to examine
me. During our conversation I learned he'd been a neuro-
psychiatrist in the Army in World War II and now he was serving
as a resident psychiatrist at Greystone Park in Morris Plains, a
state hospital for the mentally ill. From his thick white hair I
decided that he was in his sixties. He spoke emphatically when
he talked and after we spent an hour together he submitted the
following information.

The Hon. Superior Court Judge Fred C. Galda
Bergen County Court House
Hackensack, New Jersey

Dear Judge Galda:

Here is the report of the synopsis of the neuropsychiatric examination performed on Harry De La Roche on December 18, 1976 at the Bergen County Jail.

The examination took place in the Chaplain's office. The patient entered the examining room alone. He was neat and clean in appearance and was wearing glasses. He was informed of the nature of the examination and that anything he said could be used against him. He willingly cooperated throughout the entire examination. Throughout the examination he answered questions relevantly and coherently. At times there was some circumstantiality. He preferred not to discuss anything about the episode for which he was placed in jail. He did, however, willingly discuss his entire background.

He tells how he was interested in going to a military college and how, after much effort, he had applied to all the military schools including Annapolis and the Air Corps Academy and West Point. He was not accepted primarily, he states, because of his eyesight. For this reason he did accept admission to The Citadel. He describes in detail how he attended this school and what had happened to him during his first year. He states that he was home on a visit in November from the school. He informs this examiner that he intended not to return to the school because he felt that he was not making a satisfactory adjustment there. He describes in detail how he became involved with some of his fellow students in certain altercations where he felt he was being picked on. He also describes certain episodes which occurred in which he injured his head and describes how since that time he has had some dizzy spells. He states that he has not been examined or treated for these dizzy spells since their onset at school.

Throughout the entire interview this patient's affect is appropriate. He expresses no psychotic ideas. The area as to whether he is depressed is probed deeply and he denies any suicidal ideation or attempt. He prefers not to discuss the episode and states that he has been able to accept what did happen by feeling that it did not happen. Occasionally he finds himself thinking about the episode and that he wanted to speak to members of his family and then realizes that they are no longer there. He describes how he spends most of his time while in Bergen County Jail. He has been reading but has limited activity. His intelligence is estimated as slightly above average.

A neurological examination was performed which was within normal limits except for his visual difficulty.

Impression: Impression gained from the initial interview with Harry De La Roche is that we are dealing with an underlying personality disorder and possible neurological involvement (post concussion syndrome with sequelae) which warrant further study and evaluation. At the present time there is no evidence of any overt psychosis in this patient and it is my considered neuropsychiatric opinion that he is not dangerous to himself or others. However, it is strongly recommended that he be maintained in a secure, controlled environment pending further study and evaluation. This should include a complete neurological workup, psychological battery, electroencephalogram and further neuropsychiatric interviews. It is also recommended that his previous physical examination performed in West Point, prior to his applying for entrance there, and any educational history during his High School and first year at the Citadel be obtained.

Note: The above examinations which have been recommended could be performed on an out-patient basis at the local hospitals and by specialists in their related fields. During his confinement at the Bergen County Jail it is recommended that he be given a program of some activity which should include occupational and recreational therapy and some counseling.

Very Truly Yours,

Joseph F. Zigarelli, M.D.

Except for the Greers, John Taylor and Pastor Nilsen—and one visit from Steve Madreperla—nobody came to see me, so the day after Dr. Zigarelli's examination I asked Aunt Arden to try to arrange to bring my grandmother down. I hoped that if the Greers talked to her she'd be willing to come regardless of what the relatives told her she should do.

That night Uncle John called Lodi and my grandmother answered the phone. But she said that she was too sick to talk, so Pop Pop took over for her. One of the relatives was at the house so while Pop Pop and Uncle John talked Uncle John heard a voice saying "Who the hell is that?"

When the relative heard it was Uncle John he got on the phone himself and when he heard about my request he announced that he'd speak for the family.

"We consider the boy dead and hope he rots in jail," he said. "He committed a bloody massacre.

"I also want to make it clear that we won't pay anything for his defense except what the court made us pay from the estate that's being preserved. We don't think much of you and Arden, so don't call any more."

The phone call was an upsetting one, so when the Greers told John Taylor he said to tell me about it. He also wrote my grandmother and asked her to visit me. Only a short time after—right before Christmas Day—Grandma and Pop Pop drove up to the Greers. Grandma told them she couldn't see me and had nothing to say anyhow. Then she went on to explain to them that the family wasn't speaking for her on the phone that Sunday night. Pop Pop listened but then he told them he couldn't understand why Uncle John would help me after what I'd done. He was also angry over his coins and convinced I'd stolen them.

As time went on my paternal relatives began taking things from the house even though the house was appraised and everything within it should have been sold for the estate. It seemed my grandmother didn't understand her role as executrix, so at first she took things out of the house and gave other things away. There was a lot of stink about this, and, eventually, the lawyers and two sides of the family had their day in court to decide whether or not my grandmother was acting as an appropriate executrix. After they came to an understanding, my grandmother was retained. Later she sold the impounded cars and still later—before the house was sold—there was a liquidation sale of what was left in the house. All of the money was preserved for a final determination of the criminal proceedings. My parents left everything to each other, according to their will. After that it stated it was left to the boys.

My Mustang was towed to a nearby garage, where a locksmith made keys for it. Then it was driven to Uncle John's and he kept it at his house till a kid who wanted a souped-up car bought it for far less money than I thought I'd get for it.

After Judge Galda received an oral report from Dr. Zigarelli on my mental and physical status he scheduled the put-off bail hearing for December 23. At first I appeared, as usual, wearing my tattered jail clothes. But John Taylor objected to them so Judge Galda ordered me to change. When I reappeared I was wearing clothes the Greers had brought to the jail—checkered slacks, a brown short-sleeved shirt, and a contrasting striped tie. In the discussion about my bail Assistant Prosecutor Richard Salkin continued to ask for $250,000 for each of the four murders. John Taylor said this was ridiculous and stated he might just as well request a $15 million bail.

A $1 million bail was discussed for a while. Then Judge Galda set $250,000. I thought to myself, "That's ransom, not bail," and it meant that I'd be staying in jail, since neither my relatives nor I could post it.

Two days after this hearing I spent my first Christmas in jail, and after Roy's visit for Christmas dinner, the Greers came at 4:00 P.M. As a gift they brought me another cross to replace the one I'd taken off to be put in Eric's hands. One of my special Christmas cards came from Jeff Fritts who wrote:

> Harry, I would like to say a couple of things that come from my heart and soul. If you ever need me I will be here and hopefully I would like to consider you as a close friend of mine. I would also like to say that your friends in Park Ridge miss you. Steve read me a couple parts of your letter. I wish you were here for some of the New Year's parties. Harry, Christmas is a time for loving. I hope

that the spirit of Christmas can touch you in that place. As I said, if you need me I will always be here.

Your friend,

Jeff Fritts

On December 29 I was pissed off when *Newsday*, a Long Island newspaper, published what it described as my purported confession. The story was based on the statement I'd given in Hackensack, and Kenneth Gross who wrote it had me describing in great detail how I had murdered my family. He even went so far as to say that I was more content in jail than I'd been at The Citadel and then he added that every night I had nightmares and dreams about Eric. I certainly don't know where he got these ideas since he didn't talk to me. And when it comes to reporting dreams how could anybody know what I was dreaming about?

As soon as the story appeared Joseph C. Woodcock, Jr., who was Bergen County prosecutor at the time, stated the publication of this story would make it difficult to provide a fair trial for me. John Taylor was incensed at it because many Bergen County residents—which meant prospective jurors—read the Long Island paper or had relatives living there. In addition, other papers paraphrased the story and radio and television covered it. John said that he might have to ask that the trial be moved from Bergen County because of the publicity about the alleged confession. He also intimated that this alleged confession would be denied in court. It was obvious someone had leaked the confession—and that someone had either discussed it with the reporter or let the reporter read it himself.

Because of this leak the prosecutor ordered an investigation of both his office and the Montvale police force to determine who had access to the case file. He stated the person who leaked it was guilty of misconduct and added that his office, or anyone working for his office, had a responsibility to insure a defendant's right to a fair trial. In early January Joseph Woodcock met in his office with Montvale Police Chief George Hecker and Det. Mike O'Donovan and told them to begin an investigation of the handling of my file. Later the county grand jury started its investigation. The first witnesses to be called were members of the prose-cutor's staff. After this start, however, all information on the leak was dropped, and nothing more was released or done till after the trial was over. We thought we knew the source of the leak and, later, we found we were right.

On January 2, I had my second examination by Dr. Zigarelli. He didn't mention November 28, and when he asked if I had any complaints I mentioned I still had occasional headaches and, sometimes, dizziness. On June 9 he examined me again in the presence of Dr. David J. Gallina, a psychiatrist who had exam-ined me on several different occasions at John Taylor's request. In this interview Dr. Zigarelli asked me what I recalled about November 28. I told him how I walked in and found Ronnie and what I did after that. He wrote at the end of the June interview:

> We are now seeing an individual who is in his own way at-tempting to control much inner emotional and mental conflict. The exact psychodynamics of this conflict still warrant some psy-chometric evaluation (complete battery of psychological testing) and some further probing into the actual experiences that Harry had at the time of the episode. At the present time there is no evidence of any overt psychotic reaction in this individual. At the present time he is mentally competent, is able to consult with his counsel in his adequate defense and is legally sane according to the McNaughton standards. From a purely clinical standpoint, however, it is still recommended that the previous examinations requested, including neurological examination, electroencepha-logram and other studies be accomplished in this patient. No previous attempt was made to probe into the area of the episode of November 28, 1976, not only because it was requested by his attorney but because of the possible emotional and mental trauma that could have occurred shortly after the episode.

January 7 was the date for a five-minute arraignment before Judge Galda in which John Taylor entered "Not Guilty" pleas to my four charges of murder. He said that after studying the men-tal examination Dr. Gallina would do, he might change the plea to not guilty by reason of insanity. Two months later, on March 7, he notified the state of an insanity defense.

I first saw Dr. Gallina on February 18. With dark brown hair, and rimmed glasses, he appeared to be in his thirties and looked extremely youthful. He'd been a psychiatrist in the Navy, and now he was associated with the Cedar Hill Medical Center in Wyckoff, a learning disability center where he specialized in treating young people with school or family problems.

I saw him on several occasions and was given a full battery of psychological tests. The reports we received on the tests follow:

Rorschach Examination: Harry gave an adequate number of responses to each of the cards with which he was presented and gave no indication of psychotic responses at any time. He gave a good affective response which included both color and form to all the responses and seemed able to spontaneously respond to many of the forms presented.

Thematic Apperception Test: To each of the picture cards that he was presented, Harry tended to respond in a guarded fashion. The chief defenses of denial and repression were indicated in the somewhat concrete descriptive answers which he gave to each of the rather emotionally stimulating pictures presented to him. There were no psychotic responses elicited and none of the situations elicited from Harry an extremely strong affective response.

WAIS: On the Wechsler Adult Intelligence Scale, Harry received a verbal score IQ of 119, a performance score of 113, and a full scale IQ score of 117, in the above average to superior range of intelligence. There were no signs of organicity or severe depression during the course of taking the ten subtests nor was there any pronounced scatter among the tests. His concentration and memory were good and he was able to direct his attention to the tasks required in adequate manner.

Sentence Completion: On sentence completion testing, the same process of guardedness and the defenses of denial and repression were indicated. For example, when completing the sentence— "When I was a child," Harry replied: "I was small." When completing the sentence—"My greatest worry is," he replied: "I am not worrying about anything." A clear example of denial. When completing the sentence—"Most women," Harry replied: "Are average citizens." Such sentence completions reveal little or nothing about his inner emotional life and tend to keep his correspondence with the outside world on a level which is designed and prone to cause as little interpersonal conflict as possible.

In his nine-page summary of evaluations Dr. Gallina stated:

It was felt through the evaluation that Harry was mentally competent to stand trial and that he could and would cooperate in his defense. On the basis of the mental status examination, he appeared to be legally sane by the common standards of McNaughton and was not considered to be a danger to himself or to others. There was nothing in his mental status examination or psychological profile to indicate that he was prone to crimes of violence or that he was a danger to society.

Then the report went on to say:

The following is a formulation of Harry De La Roche, Jr.'s, characterological traits based upon an examination and evaluation at the present time.

It is noted that he is extremely guarded about revealing himself in an open fashion, which might produce a conflict with his environment. He is rigid and holds to a perfectionistic view of himself, which is not flexible in adjusting to changing situations in his life or in his immediate environment. Acknowledging problems is seen by him as a weakness, which was the view held by his father, and is held to be unacceptable. He has a great need to be strong, capable, and completely invulnerable and has built his defense system to comply with these needs. He is, however, highly defensive and many of his actions and outward appearance are not, I feel, indicative of his inner emotional life.

The chief defenses which he employs are the primitive ones of denial and repression, although they are not utilized to a psychotic degree. It is extremely difficult to engage Harry in an intimate interpersonal relationship, although he has the social skills to be outgoing and sociable, although always quite guarded. He has a tendency to take on too much responsibility and is burdened by such responsibility but will not recognize the extent of the burden. His anxiety level tends to be quite high because of the lack of resolution for the many conflicts in his life and this can lead to him being impulsive. He ultimately does have a hard time in adhering to duties or ways of doing things which are imposed by others, and he will tend to resent such activity as he did adherence to the unreasonable demands of his father.

During the course of the evaluations, he at times showed undue sensitiveness and suspicion of those around him and does, at times, tend to misinterpret the motivation of people in his environment, leading to difficulties in allowing himself to experience close, open interpersonal relationships. The history of his family life does make such character traits understandable. He tends to be an extremely inner-oriented person who thinks carefully about his involvements before committing himself, as if expecting to be threatened or hurt at some point in the future.

He is also afraid of being in a passive and what he determines an effeminate state of non-competitiveness and will compensate for these fears with rigid patterns of behavior which will deny the existence of any soft, passive, or effeminate feelings in him at all. The application of these character traits to the incidents which led up to and culminated in the deaths of the members of his family can only be conjectured. The family situation certainly was an inflexible one in which conflict was not resolved among the various members through discussions or reasonable behavior. Rigidity was the hallmark characteristic, particularly of Harry's father, and such rigidity could not live with conflict. One side or the other had to comply. Harry seemed continually torn by the mixed loyalties that he felt to himself as an individual and to what at times were the unreasonable demands of his family. His actions on that evening appeared to be impulsive and not of the deliberate, premeditated type, but rather the explosion of emotions which resulted from internal conflicts that undoubtedly went back many years. The source of his conflict, therefore, appears clearly related to family members and to his father in particular and there is no indication that this conflict either was present or would reestablish itself with other members of society.

There is no apparent animosity or rage that Harry has felt or does feel for other people in his environment that would reach such proportions and it is therefore not felt that confinement would appreciably alter the basic personality or life style of this individual.

30

During my long days and nights in jail people continued to wonder about my lack of emotion—and they questioned why I could be so calm when talking of November 28.

But after you've told a story over and over again, it's easy to be matter-of-fact.

In a way I became even more closed while tolerating life in jail. But one thing that really sickened me was reading the autopsy reports and looking at the autopsy pictures. I didn't have to see them in jail, but I felt I'd control myself better if I had already seen them when I saw them in color at the trial. I only looked at each picture once, and John Taylor, who was with me, said, "Don't hold it in. You don't have to do that."

I answered, "John, that's the way I am." But when your last memories, of your family are pictures with their heads cut open—well, I can't talk about that.

I had to have things to think about, so I thought a lot about getting out of jail, and I planned to leave Bergen County and, also, change my name. Roy Nilsen and I spent many hours talking about my future, and one of the things we mentioned was a career as a mortician. He knew someone who could help me in another state, and sometimes when I thought of it it seemed like a good idea. I also thought of medicine, or international law, and at times I considered political science or studying philosophy.

Roy knew people in Europe so we'd talk about going there. I also mentioned Israel or, maybe, South America.

I slept a lot from boredom or else I'd read or think while I waited for my trial in Superior Court of New Jersey at the Bergen County Courthouse. County Judge James F. Madden was assigned to my case. I learned that he was fifty-seven years old and a graduate of the University of North Carolina and the John Marshall Law School.

While I was waiting I had so much time I'd often read three paperbacks a day, and once when I started a book after lunch I was up to page 738 by evening the following day. I kept a list of the books I read and some that stand out in my mind were *The Deep, The Court Martial of George Armstrong Custer, The Simarillion, All Things Wise and Wonderful, All Creatures Great and Small, All Things Bright and Beautiful, Wheels, The Gemini Contenders, The Rhinemann Exchange, The Eagle Has Landed, Jaws, The Exorcist, The Odessa File, The Dogs of War, The Hobbit, The Lord of the Rings Trilogy, The Day of the Jackal,* and John Jake's Bicentennial Series.

The Greers continued to visit me and each week they deposited money for me for cigarettes and commissary items. I had a few other visitors, too, since John Taylor made arrangements for Steve to come down with Jeff Fritts and Vinnie Trojan. It was hard to visit in a cubicle with a grill between visitors but it was great to talk to people who weren't deserting you. Bob Gantt came for several visits, and when Roy decided it would be good to have a girl visit me he suggested it to Tink Thompson, a girl I knew in Luther League who went to a nearby college and was often home weekends and vacations. She was a caring person, and even when she was very young, people came to her with their problems. Along with a lot of energy, Tink has great compassion so she agreed to come down with Roy, and we've kept in touch ever since. She visits, writes, and sends me cards, and fairly often I even feel that I open up to her.

By summer John Taylor was planning a plea of three counts of "Not Guilty" and one of "Not Guilty Because of Temporary Insanity." But the state still had investigative matter it hadn't turned over to him, and I often felt the state was unjust to delay things for so long. Sometimes I believe the prosecution was thinking I'd make a plea bargain if I had to wait long enough. But there's no way in hell I'd have made a deal. I'd never cop out to that.

If I wasn't acquitted I wanted to go to a hospital instead of a state prison. But if the hospital had been the Vroom Building at the Trenton Psychiatric Hospital, I'd have wanted prison instead. That building houses the incorrigibles and mentally ill state prisoners and I learned through the jailhouse grapevine that in a period of just a few months they had five suicides at Vroom. If I went down to prison I felt that at least I would be raped, and maybe, some other inmates might be after my life. In the county you can tell homosexuals, "That just ain't my thing." But down at state prison you have no choice. You have to bend over and they take it. The inmates also have a code by which they judge your crime, and they're ready to kill you for some crimes if they can get to you. Crimes with children and homicides are right on top of the list.

I occupied some of my time in jail and filled up some endless hours checking out relevant or irrelevant items that might help in the trial. For example, on November 28 a neighbor had reported she'd heard a car idling at 11:00 P.M. and then leave squeaking its tires. But this was never resolved.

There were also two notes found in my car—"Call Grandma" and "Call Police" and at first we thought Ronnie might have written them, but they both turned out to be nothing. The first was a memo to finalize the arrangements for going to Lodi overnight the Friday after Thanksgiving. The second was a note to me from my father to remind me to arrange for fingerprints to go with the papers for the rifle permit he'd mailed to me down at school. I didn't put either note in my car. Probably my father did. The coat with the fur hood was nothing either. That was my winter jacket.

Approximately eight months after the murders Father Norman Werling, a handwriting expert and lecturer, founder and president of GraphoDynamics, and a qualified expert witness for handwriting identification in various courts of New Jersey, analyzed my handwriting. Father Werling, a Catholic priest, has studied approximately twenty-two thousand handwritings, and is thoroughly convinced that a person's basic temperament, character traits, and career aptitudes can be determined by handwriting. I never met him personally and he didn't know who I was—or what my background was—when my handwriting was submitted to him. His report on a July 5, 1977, sample follows:

To understand this young man one must recognize his basic phlegmatic temperament. Thoughtful, methodical, and open-minded, he relishes the activity of the mind rather than physical effort. His slow manner of behavior could easily be misinterpreted as laziness, disinterest, even disobedience and rebellion. More aggressive and dynamic adults may put more pressures and demands on him than he can bear. Like a turtle that is being threatened and pulls into its shell, this young man, already withdrawn and isolated, can further recede into his own little world. Should he ever be driven beyond his limits of endurance he would escape in some way: physical flight, mental flight into schizophrenia, or by open hostility. In the latter case, his episodes of anger would come as quite a surprise to those who know only his usual calm and placid manner.

Caught between the demands of others and his own inclination to self-interest, a minimum of responsibility, activity and functional productivity, he is beginning to deceive himself and others. Secretive by nature, he is becoming evasive and dishonest, partly to conceal his unacceptable performance and partly to rationalize his own deficiencies.

Under the conflicts in such a situation it is to be expected that his social contacts will be kept to a minimum and yet he desires and needs more than the usual amount of sympathy, support, and companionship. But at the time of this writing he is frustrated, disturbed, and in serious emotional turmoil.

With all these problems, it is good to see that the writer's self-image and confidence remain at a high level. So, too, are his ambitions and plans for the future. In other ways he is asserting his independence as an adult, breaking away from the child's dependency and the traditions in which he was reared. He is showing his individualism but his new values and priorities are withdrawing from philosophical ideals to a more pragmatic, materialistic and sensuous level.

Although somewhat disturbed, his personality still has sufficient strength, balance and coordination to indicate that with proper professional help he could solve his difficulties and mature into a useful and productive citizen.

Life as a productive citizen seemed like a long ways off as I lived through some of the experiences in the county jail. One of my most unpleasant moves, as I was assigned different cells, was the time I spent in the same cell that Joseph Kallinger occupied while he was in Bergen County. He was the Philadelphia shoemaker who was convicted of robbery and murder, and as I lay in my cot in that cell I could still see the shit he wiped on the ceiling and the wood covering the pipes. He also liked to write on the walls and one of the things he left was "Forgive the guards for they know not what they are doing." Once I had a cellmate who had sniffed glue for ten years, and his brain was completely burned out. There weren't many people to talk to in depth, and one guy even asked me how to spell the word "hope."

Occasionally we'd have parties—either with jailhouse booze we made or with drugs someone managed to get. For booze we'd use juice from the fruits we got. Then we'd add sugar and yeast and let it brew in a sink with hot water. If we couldn't get yeast from the kitchen we'd use bread instead. We also made up applejack by straining applesauce through a handkerchief and adding a little water.

There were all sorts of drugs smuggled in, though people who were caught with street stuff got busted right away. Often guys would save up pills if they had to take medication. Then when they had a supply of pills everyone had a party. I only got involved in that once when I took two Mellarils. But they were mood-enhancing drugs, and they gave me a hangover in the morning that you wouldn't believe.

By summer I'd lost twelve pounds in jail since I didn't get very hungry in a place that was full of roaches and mice and other types of vermin. Two years before—in 1975—two grand juries and a commission had condemned the jail as a medieval dungeon unfit for prisoners —and while I was there it was announced that it would be shut down soon. But it was hot as hell that summer, and you smelled urine everywhere. The plumbing was backed up half the time, and when somebody flushed a toilet on the floor above your cell it usually started to leak. Once when I was on my john the water rained right down on me.

Rumor had it in late July that the jail would be closed in August and at that time all the inmates would be moved down the road to the annex, a minimum security jail, a quarter of a mile away. Even Sheriff Joseph Job declared "The Fortress" was unfit for human habitation.

When I heard of the move I couldn't wait to get out of that inhuman place.

31

The big day was August 2, and as the last inmate was brought to the annex Sheriff Job announced "The Fortress" would be closed permanently.

When the annex was opened in the 1960s the low, tan brick building intended for minor offenders, was regarded as a good example of a model penal institution. While I was there in 1977 it was being expanded to include more maximum-security cells, additional dormitories, and other up-to-date renovations.

The day that we were taken there we were brought down two at a time and it was a major event for me just to see the outdoors. I hadn't seen a tree and the sky—or the sun, moon, or stars— for the last eight months of my life.

The officers were taking no chances with us because, along with handcuffing us, the officer sitting in the front of the van had a gun which he pointed at us. Once we got to the annex I was put in a holding cell. Then I was taken to maximum security and placed in one of the thirty-eight cells used to house violent or dangerous inmates. One of the guys in with me was convicted of robbery, rape, and kidnaping. Another man shot his wife. Guards brought our food to the cellblocks on pie tins with a spoon. Then they passed around the knives which they always made sure to count.

Despite the improved facilities available at the annex, daily life wasn't very different than it was at the main jail. I wasn't able to get a job since I was one of the "bad guys," and in the yard I could only sit because I couldn't take the risk of breaking my glasses in a game. My only extras were sunglasses, and I couldn't see myself in court wearing sunglasses to the trial.

In August Roy Nilsen answered a call to a church in Maryland, and the interim minister at my church was Pastor Charles Immendorf. Until he answered a call himself he was dean of a Lutheran college where he taught several courses. I considered him quite a scholar and whenever he came to visit we had good conversations on philosophy and religion. Sometimes he'd bring me communion, too.

By the end of August it was obvious that the annex that had once seemed so promising was chaotic and overcrowded. It was ripe for racial tensions, and it was never intended for murderers—or rapists, and armed robbers. We had many problem prisoners who were sent from one county facility to another, as well as several convicted inmates who were waiting for space in state prisons. The latter caused problems for other inmates and understaffed jail officials, and sometimes it seemed that the inmates were really running the jail.

Some of the inmates called me a fink because I went for so many visits with my lawyer, minister, and the Greers. There were all kinds of rumors about me until I had to say, "Look, you guys, you want me to fink, I know enough to screw people in here. You really want me to fink?" After that a few guys shut up.

As soon as it was September I couldn't wait for the trial date—September 26. I needed some clothes for the trial so I gave Aunt Arden my measurements. Then the Greers went out and bought a blue suit with two pairs of pants and a reversible vest. Uncle John had my favorite boots repaired and polished for me.

The state had turned over the investigative matter John Taylor was waiting for, so after the months of waiting in jail it seemed we were ready for the trial. But ten days before the scheduled start, *The Record,* which served Bergen County, ran a provocative Op-Ed piece that took a dim view of cases built on the insanity defense. It didn't mention me by name, but the writer talked about people who had killed their families and pointed out that many of them—after winning an insanity defense—killed other family members when they were released.

John didn't like the timing right before my trial. Then a few days later he was more concerned when another newspaper story mentioned the liquidation sale that was held in our Montvale house. That in itself would have been okay, but the person who wrote that article said, "Harry De La Roche, Sr., his wife, and two sons were slain in their sleep by a third son." The word "alleged" wasn't anywhere, so John met with Judge Madden on September 23—the day I turned nineteen—to ask to have the trial delayed because of the newspaper publicity and the statement that I slew my family. I was upset about this. But Judge Madden postponed the trial, and a new date was set for October 24.

The annex continued to be overcrowded for the rest of the time I was there, and one inmate who really made trouble was a faggot named Harriet. "She" was black and built so heavily she made many guys' chests look small, and when she started to show me attention she really ticked me off. She was mostly interested in young white males, and after she arrived she and her clique beat a young guy who rejected her advances. The beating turned out to be so severe he had to be taken by ambulance for treatment at Bergen Pines Hospital.

When I spurned Harriet's advances, too, she came to my cell to attack me while three other blacks came along for support. That day the clique threatened me with knives, and I lost my commissary order.

The second episode was far worse, though, and it happened October 10 shortly after lunch. My cellmate and I got our commissary order and decided to leave our cell since inmates could go to the day room at any time they chose. We didn't usually lock our cells, so just as were about to leave, Harriet and her henchmen came storming down to our cell and proceeded to take our commissary order.

The gang had a stolen knife from the kitchen, along with a sawed-off broom handle which they used as a club. They started slapping and punching, and one guy threatened to kill me. Then they upended our bunk beds, and two of the inmates ransacked the cell while three or four others stood guard.

They totally destroyed my cell that day by breaking and ripping whatever they could, stuffing things in the toilet and stepping on what was left. My sunglasses and radio were totaled, and they tore up every one of my books, including my small address book. Then my cellmate and I were told to leave and not come back to the cell. All I had left was a pair of shoes and the glasses and clothes I had on.

I was so scared at the moment, I hardly thought of the loss, and the thing my cellmate and I wanted most was to get ourselves out of that cellblock before the gang really killed us. We asked to leave the wing for safety. But the officers were pretty helpless, so our only out was the day room where more of the clique threatened us. When I finally got off the cellblock I was almost stabbed when leaving.

It was about 1:30 when the authorities locked us in isolation. This meant that we were in a cell that had no running water and only a hole in the ground for a toilet. It stank of urine and feces and was cold without blankets or sheets. The only time you could have a drink was when the food arrived. I stayed there from 1:30 on Monday afternoon till I went to Bergen Pines Hospital early Wednesday morning for an electroencephalogram, brain scan, and chest and skull series. All the results were normal, but I felt like a slob when I went for the tests, since I hadn't been able to take a shower and my clothes were smelly and dirty. When I returned from the hospital I was moved to a material witness section. The authorities thought I'd be safer there since the persons in material witness were either work release people or inmates with petty offenses.

Nothing happened to my attackers in the way of punishment, so when the Greers heard about it they felt the matter shouldn't pass without an investigation. I was afraid to say much, though, except for telling John Taylor because I feared the retribution that goes on in jail.

Aunt Arden started things going by talking on the telephone with Under-Sheriff Peter Curcio, a stocky, gray-haired man who handled the annex's operations. She asked how the incident happened and why I was the one who was punished by going to isolation. The under-sheriff told her that isolation was the only place to put me at the time. Then he suggested that she come down and told her that, along with other officers, she could meet with me.

As we sat in Curcio's office on the following morning the officers tried to tell her—right in front of me—that they thought the fight was over my cellmate, who they earmarked as a homosexual. Then they went on to intimate I might be a homo, too, and that I'd wanted that cellmate so we could live together. He was my friend not my lover, and though he was labeled as a troublemaker he was good to me while I knew him.

The officers told Aunt Arden that the only way to investigate this was for me to reveal the names of the attackers and sign a formal complaint. But when I saw her for a moment alone I told her I couldn't press charges.

"There's no way I'll sign a complaint," I said. "They'd eat me alive if I did."

News of the incident traveled, however, and when Sheriff Job heard about it he decided to investigate it without my signing a complaint.

A young staff writer at *The Record*—John Banaszewski who covered crime—also got wind of the incident and showed up at the jail. He wanted to write about the attack for the next Sunday's edition, so he spoke at length with Sheriff Job and Under-Sheriff Curcio. Then he interviewed Aunt Arden. His story on October 16 got me back in the papers again.

After Banaszewski wrote his first account he decided to do a follow-up story exposing more details so he asked John Taylor to write Sheriff Job and ask for permission to visit me and ask questions about the attack. I told John I'd like to do this, so John wrote the following letter—which later turned out to be a controversial matter:

October 19, 1977

Sheriff Joseph F. Job
Bergen Co. Jail Annex
River Road,
Hackensack, N.J.

Dear Sheriff Job:

My client, Harry W. De La Roche, Jr., has expressed a desire to meet with a Mr. John Banaszewski, a reporter for *The Record* at Hackensack, New Jersey.

I have discussed the matter with Mr. De La Roche and it is his wish and desire that he be permitted to talk with the aforementioned person.

I have no objection to Mr. De La Roche meeting with Mr. Banaszewski. However, I will not be present at any of the meetings.

I would therefore appreciate it if you would be so kind as to permit Mr. Banaszewski to meet with Mr. De La Roche at the Annex so that they may discuss whatever affairs exist between them.

I have no further objection, as this meeting should occur immediately and I respectfully request that you honor my client's desire to talk with Mr. Banaszewski.

Very truly yours,

Kleinberg and Taylor

John R. Taylor, Jr.

JRT; lsb
CC: John Banaszewski

When the newspaper reporter arrived with his recorder we met in the small visitors' room where I usually saw my lawyer. We talked in general for a little while. Then he began asking lots of stuff that I was glad to answer because, since late in August, I'd wanted to see a newspaper reporter and let more people know what had happened on November 28. Except for a break for supper we talked for about four hours, and I told the reporter about coming home and finding my parents and Eric dead and Ronnie sitting on his bed. The reporter said he'd be writing that story, and that was okay by me. He didn't say when it would be printed, though, and I thought since the trial was scheduled to start he'd wait till the jury was selected.

All hell broke loose on Sunday, October 23, when the story appeared with the headline, "De La Roche Blames Brother For Murder." I was immediately criticized for telling the story outside of the courtroom, and John Taylor was accused of generating shocking pretrial publicity—and possibly a postponement or mistrial—by permitting an eleventh-hour interview. Later John would argue that the Banaszewski interview was solely to talk about the rape attempts while Banaszewski would contend there was no express agreement limiting the scope of his questions. *The Record* was put on the griddle for running the article on the front page on the eve of the trial, and in jail there was such a furor I wasn't allowed a razor so I could shave that day.

I also had to eat by myself instead of going to the cafeteria, where the guards thought I might have trouble.

32

The wire services picked up the story, and by 9:00 A.M. on Monday, TV and newspaper reporters were at Bergen County Courthouse for the start of the jury selection.

No one was sure that Monday whether my trial would get off the ground because of the newspaper stories. But I was put in handcuffs and driven to the main jail, so I'd be there and ready if the jury was to be picked. My blue suit was waiting at the main jail, so I dressed in that and a shirt and tie. Then I sat in a holding cell until 11:30.

Elsewhere in the building the Prosecutor's Office had served a subpoena at *The Record*, demanding the surrender of the tape recordings of my interview with John Banaszewski and ordering the reporter and the newspaper's custodian of records to appear at the courthouse at 10:00 A.M. Peter Banta, attorney for the paper, came to represent *The Record* and to meet in Judge Madden's chambers with John Taylor and Richard Salkin, who'd be trying the case for the state. Mr. Banta stated the interview tapes were in a locked file cabinet, and then he announced that the newspaper was not about to comply with the subpoena on the basis that recordings were privileged material and legally protected from forced disclosure by what was then a three-week-old amendment to the New Jersey Shield Law. The Shield Law prohibited the courts, legislature, and other office bodies from forcing newsmen to reveal anonymous sources. Supposedly the new amendment broadened the law's provision to protect the confidentiality of reporters' notes, tapes, and other material gathered while researching a news story. When Mr. Banta made that statement at the private hearing Judge Madden ordered an indefinite postponement in the jury selection so both the defense and state attorneys could file certain motions.

I didn't know about this until 11:30, when one of the officers in the jail put in a call to Judge Madden's court and learned about the postponement. Then I was told to take off the blue suit and get ready to go back to the Annex. I was upset about the delay and the fact that it meant more waiting, but Uncle John, who was angry that I'd given the interview, let me know that I was at fault for opening my mouth.

The next few days saw motions about turning over the tapes. As a starter, the attorney for *The Record*, who wanted Judge Madden to declare it was illegal for the prosecutor to demand tape records, filed a motion to suppress the subpoenas because of the amendment to the Shield Law. The prosecutor contended that *The Record* identified me as its source and, as a result, lost its right to protect tapes and other materials not included in the story. In turn John Taylor demanded that the paper surrender the tapes to him alone without allowing the Prosecutor's Office access to them.

The big surprise, however, came November 2, when I was informed in the afternoon that I was being returned to the condemned, deteriorating main jail for protective custody because of rumbles and rumors that my life had been threatened in the annex. At a private meeting earlier in the day Superior Court Judge Theodore Trautwein, who served as the assignment judge, told my attorney he was ordering the move and instructing I be kept under guard while waiting for my trial.

As usual I kept my feelings to myself and appeared to be quiet about it. But I certainly didn't like the idea of going back to that building. When I arrived I was placed in a cell on the second floor, and since I was the only inmate there it seemed like solitary confinement. The cell was white. But the window had been covered with black paint. I had nobody to talk to, and for the weeks I was there my visitors were limited to my lawyer, my minister, and the Greers. Both Steve Madreperla and Tink Thompson were turned away when they came.

I got a chance to get out of my cell on Friday, November 18, when I attended arguments on the tapes at a hearing in front of Judge Madden. By this time it had been revealed that the tapes were only two hours and forty minutes long because, in the four-hour interview, Banaszewski had shut off the recorder when I requested this. *The Record* was still unwilling to hand over the tapes, however, and its attorney had applied to Judge Madden for a quash of the subpoenas. Richard Salkin argued at length that the tapes should be surrendered. Later John withdrew his request for sole access to the tapes when we learned that if *The Record* gave the tapes to him it would waive any privilege to withhold them. "If there's a possibility of a waiver, then I do not want to hear them," he said. "The tapes should be sealed."

The previous day—November 17—Banaszewski stated in an affidavit that he had telephoned John Taylor on Friday, October 21, and told him the paper would be running a story based on the interviews on the following Sunday. In this affidavit he stated that he had asked John if John was trying to generate pretrial publicity by permitting the interview. He went on to state that

John denied this was his purpose and approved the forthcoming story. John, however, disavowed this and said that on Friday, October 21, he and his staff were moving their offices to new quarters in Park Ridge and, because they were moving from one office to another, he did not conduct business or accept phone calls that day—and did not speak with Banaszewski.

On November 23 in the first court ruling interpreting the new amendment to the state's Shield Law Judge Madden ordered *The Record* to surrender the tapes on November 28. *The Record* attorney responded by saying he would appeal the decision and seek a stay of the order to surrender the tapes.

Immediately after Judge Madden's ruling, Judge Trautwein ordered a change of venue to Camden, New Jersey, an industrial, marketing and transportation center across the Delaware River from Philadelphia. He set December 5 for the trial and said he wanted the change of venue because it would be impossible to get Bergen County jurors who had not read or discussed the newspaper articles.

John Taylor objected to the date and the move to Camden, 120 miles away because it would create a hardship on the defense and on witnesses who would have to travel. He also mentioned that if the trial were to begin on December 5 the jurors would not be in a good frame of mind if they had to be sequestered and away from their families before Christmas. He announced he'd appeal the change of venue and file a motion to delay the trial till after the Christmas season.

Things were quiet—too quiet—sitting in an empty jail, and not many things broke up the days except for occasional visits. Once Dr. Gallina came to see me because John Taylor had asked him to give me advance preparation for what was ahead in the trial. We went through everything that day and he tried to shake me up with Christmas pictures of my family that would call back memories. Both John and the doctor wanted to see if I would break when I saw them because they knew that the prosecution would barbecue my hide. I talked and I looked, however, and I didn't break a bit.

Finally on November 29, *The Record* agreed to turn over the portions of the two-hour-and-40-minute tape that had relevance to the murder. This was done to prevent the delay of a December 5 trial in Camden. Arrangements were made to submit both the edited version and the original tapes to Judge Madden. After he determined they were edited correctly he was to release copies of the edited version to the Prosecutor's Office and to John. On that same day Judge Trautwein turned down John Taylor's request to postpone the December 5 trial.

John's next move was to go before Judge Sylvia B. Pressler of the Appellate Court division to ask for a temporary stay of the ruling, pending a determination by a three-judge appellate panel. He also indicated that if all appeals failed and the trial had to be in Camden he was considering withdrawing from the case. That meant a public defender would be appointed, and this would delay things longer till the public defender got acquainted with the case. We didn't come to this, however, because Judge Pressler discussed the matter with Judge Trautwein, and Judge Trautwein reversed his decision. As soon as that happened it was arranged that the jury would be picked in Camden County on January 3 and, then, brought back to Bergen County to be sequestered during the trial.

I was relieved to have it postponed till after the holidays. But I was getting restless and more than a little disturbed. I've heard some people said at that point that I was going stir crazy and really starting to flip. But whenever I wanted to make some waves Aunt Arden kept telling me to cool it. I didn't want to cool it, though, because I'd decided by then that I hadn't been returned to the main jail for protective custody reasons. I believed that I had been sent there to get me away from everyone and from talking to the media again.

It was weird in that condemned jail, and it really pissed me off when three guards came in at midnight for a shakedown of my cell. They tore the entire cell apart and examined everything, and the question I wanted answered was, "Why did they do this at midnight?" I had the feeling they were getting scared I might try suicide. While they were checking everything they took a look at the walls, and when they saw paint was chipping one of the guards drew a circle around the chipped-off part.

I said, "Why are you doing that?"

He answered, "I like to draw."

They weren't fooling me, however, and I knew that they were keeping track of what was already chipped so they could see if I chipped off more and swallowed it for lead poisoning.

As time went on I had definite proof I hadn't gone to the main jail for protective custody alone. By December other inmates were there after incidents at the annex. Two of them were a couple of dudes I was being protected from. But since there were only two showers on the floor they came to my cell to shower. That wasn't what I call protective custody. It was a little strange.

I didn't look forward to Thanksgiving and the memories of a year ago. But as it happened I slept through the day, because I woke up feeling sick. I wasn't very hungry and couldn't eat a thing. At Christmas the Salvation Army gave us toothpaste and shampoo. I also received a great many cards from people from the outside. Some were from people I didn't know who had somehow heard of me. The largest was a card from Christ Lutheran Church with three pages of signatures. I asked Pastor Immendorf to say, "Thank You," so at the Christmas Eve service he expressed a "Thank You" from me.

Since Christmas Day fell on a weekend no visitors were permitted, so the only thing extra for Christmas was a piece of pie. At the annex there was a jail break which provided some excitement. Then I had my own brand of excitement—or whatever you'd want to call it—when the guy in the cell across from me decided to spend his Christmas constantly spitting out of his cell and throwing water and food at my cell. He'd started to do this the Friday before, and it certainly wasn't pleasant. But I thought since it was Christmas I would try and ignore it. I gave him some candy and a cigarette. But he threw them back at me. Then when he wasn't throwing things he'd bang his head against the wall and either moan or cry. Other than that activity it was just another day.

New Year's, too, was another day. But by then I was occupied with thoughts of Camden on January 3. I knew Under-Sheriff John Stasse and two officers would drive me down and, as I sat in my cell and thought, I hoped that, maybe on the way we could stop at a Burger King. I'd heard they sometimes did this, and I would have liked that a lot. What I wanted most, however, was to get out of jail and go home. But, then, when I'd think of the red frame house and mention, "I want to go home," I'd suddenly realize what I'd said and remember there was no home.

I understand that somebody wrote I had a nonchalant attitude the last days before the trial. But nothing could have been less true, since I definitely felt apprehensive. Now that the time for the trial had come I knew my entire future hung on whether or not Judge Madden would allow my alleged confession to be admitted as evidence. John Taylor would fight to have it excluded, and argue that I had made it after more than thirty hours of questioning without legal counsel.

But he'd warned me that if the confession went in I had to be realistic—and very aware of the obvious fact that the outcome didn't look good.

XI

The Jury Selection
in Camden

33

At 6:30 A.M. on January 3 I left for Camden County with Under-Sheriff Stasse and two plain-clothes officers. Once more I was wearing my blue vested suit. But this time I wore a belt with a chain and handcuffs attached to that. We made the trip in a county car—with no stops at a Burger King. But I couldn't have eaten anyhow since I felt nervous and tense.

Camden is a city full of factories, though many are abandoned, so the inner city is suffering as people move out to such suburbs as Cherry Hill, Haddonfield, and Mount Laurel. It was once a transportation center for all of southern New Jersey and because of its nearness to Philadelphia, the Campbell Soup Company and Radio Corporation of America established large plants there. I also learned that Walt Whitman, the poet, lived there for the last 20 years of his life.

As we pulled into the city the courthouse was easy to find since it towered above other buildings when we turned onto Federal Street. It was a light gray granite building with a modified Grecian design, and it had a tall tower with a huge clock rising from its six stories. The jail where I stayed overnight was on the sixth floor of this building. Photographers snapped my picture as I approached the courthouse, and since it was cold and breezy the haircut I'd had for the trial looked weird and disheveled in the papers.

The courtroom for jury selection was on the fourth floor of the building and when it was time for proceedings to start two guards from the Camden County Sheriff's Office brought me into the courtroom. All the while I was in court one guard sat behind me and the other sat off to the side. The courtroom had brown wooden pews, like you'd expect in a church, and from the windows you could see much of the city of Camden. The room could accommodate 150 people, and a 100-member jury panel was brought in to sit in the back.

Members of the press sat in the front on one side of the room. The Greers were on the other side, along with Pastor Nilsen who had come up from Maryland. Judge Madden sat on the dais, and, as he'd do each day of the trial, he loosened his robe when he sat down and let it slip from his shoulders. He was a relatively small man with short brown wavy hair, and often, going to and from court, he'd be seen in Sherlock Holmes' hats. He had all kinds of facial expressions—like wrinkling up his forehead, puffing out his jowls, and constantly letting his horn-rimmed glasses slip halfway down his nose. He saw everything that happened though, and everybody knew it.

His court clerk who did research sat at the bench beside him, and the court attendant who'd draw jurors' numbers stood by her wooden lottery box right next to the court clerk. The court reporter sat in front of the bench.

Richard Salkin and John and I sat at a table in front of the bench, and when the judge looked down at us Mr. Salkin was to his right (and nearest to the jury box). John and I were to his left. John wore a conservative tan suit and white shirt. Mr. Salkin wore a navy suit with a contrasting blue shirt. Later I heard that during the weeks of the trial one of the courtroom pastimes was to speculate on how many suits he owned, since he wore something different each day.

After Judge Madden made his introductory remarks and read names of possible witnesses he presented Mr. Salkin to the jury panel. Then he asked John and me to stand. I tried to smile slightly, but I guess according to the Greers, that I looked tense and white. From the prospective jurors sixteen persons were selected to fill the jury box. Judge Madden questioned each individually. If one was excused for one reason or another he or she was replaced.

Bergen County Judge James F. Madden reading trial materials at home before hearing testimony on the second day of the De La Roche case. PHOTO BY WIDE WORLD PHOTOS.

Sixteen jurors, including four alternates, were chosen at Camden, and Judge Madden explained that after the trial testimony was over only twelve—again chosen by lottery—would participate in the verdict. But the extra four would sit through the trial, so the trial could continue in case one or more members became ill or indisposed.

During the first day of jury selection Judge Madden questioned forty-one prospective jurors about their knowledge of the case, their attitudes toward crime, their occupations and marital status, and the ages of their children and grandchildren. He asked such questions as, "Would serving on this jury cause a hardship?" "Could you serve on a case of this nature and not have a prejudice toward it?" "Since police officers will be testifying would you give any more or any less credibility to a police officer's testimony than you would anyone else's?" "Have you ever been a victim of a crime?" and "Do you know or are you related to anyone in any level of government or in any law enforcement agency?"

On the first day it seemed the prospective jurors were reluctant to look at me, and I got the definite feeling they thought they would see a devilish monster if they glanced in my direction. John Taylor and I conferred on the jurors and as they sat in the box I told him which ones I liked. Later, both John and Mr. Salkin had peremptory challenges—gut reactions, so to speak —in which they could dismiss a juror without any explanation. The defense was allowed twenty challenges and the prosecutor, twelve. At times I thought some of the panel members seemed anxious for an all-expense winter trip away from their homes and jobs. Others gave a variety of reasons on why they couldn't serve, and during the first day Judge Madden dismissed twenty-five people. Some admitted they were prejudiced and could not be fair and impartial. Others asked to be excused because they could not be spared from their jobs for the three weeks the trial was expected to take. One man who was torn between his civic duty and the demands of his new business was excused when he said he'd have to declare bankruptcy if the trial ran more than two weeks. Another stepped down when he answered emphatically that he'd tend to take the word of police over any others.

In the peremptory challenges Richard Salkin dismissed a young auto mechanic with a mustache and long hair, a former military court attendant, and a young single female college student. John dismissed a state employee with a two-year-old child, and a mother of five who had previously served on a murder trial. After Mr. Salkin's third challenge the court was recessed for the day, and I was led up to the jail. I spent the night in a dormitory, and all the while I was there I wore a one-piece bright orange jump suit that you're required to wear in that jail.

When court commenced the next morning John had his third challenge. Then when it was Mr. Salkin's turn he surprised everyone by standing up and saying that the jury that was seated was satisfactory to the state. After John's sixth challenge he and I

Defense Attorney John R. Taylor walking to the Bergen County Courthouse on the first day of the trial.
PHOTO BY WIDE WORLD PHOTOS.

also stood up and John announced to Judge Madden, "Mr. De La Roche and I find the jury satisfactory."

The jury—composed of eight men and eight women—represented a wide range of ages from twenty to fifty-eight. Most of them came from the Camden suburbs, and ten of them had children. Five had children close to my age—between eighteen and twenty-two.

The jurors sworn in on January 4 were Marise Althouse, a housewife who had a son fairly close to my age and who, some other jurors later said, found her role as forelady very hard; Anthony Skokowski, a gray-haired office supervisor; Emmett Barkalow, whose son-in-law had been involved as a law enforcement officer in a police brutality incident; Paul McGuire, a disabled bus driver who, very much like my father, had been involved in Scouting and Little League and who, also, owned a number of guns; Sheryl Anyzek, the long-haired baby of the group who worked for an insurance company and was twenty at the time of the trial; Maureen Howard, an English woman and the mother of five children; Horacio Rodriguez, a bank teller who'd come from Cuba and who, as a new American citizen in the bicentennial year, was highly conscientious about his civic duty; Dorothy Krumm, a middle-aged housewife who'd lost a son very close to my age in a car accident; Michael Ronca, a twenty-four-year-old manager of corporate development for a life insurance company; Shirley Gear, a quiet, soft-spoken mild-looking clerk; Vincent Squazzo, a tall, dark-haired sales manager who found the trial a painful experience but who took the challenge of serving to fill a need in society; Joyce Saye, a recently married second-grade teacher; Mary Flexon, a bookkeeper and computer operator with a son who was born just two days before I was; Mae Neate, a black-haired, pale-faced clerk; Richard Kowlowski, a twenty-five-year-old tape librarian and computer operator; and Daniel McCarthy, a manager for RCA and the father of two grown children.

After the jury was sworn in Judge Madden announced a short recess while he telephoned Judge Trautwein back in Bergen County to see what the procedure and schedule would be. Later, when we returned to court, he announced the trial would begin the following day—January 5 at 1:30 P.M. After that, men from the sheriff's staff put the belt with the handcuffs around me and led me out of the courtroom.

I didn't know whether I'd be staying that night or returning to Bergen County. But officers from the sheriff's department came down to Camden to get me and we were back at the Hackensack jail by late in the afternoon—with no stops at a Burger King.

Unidentified officer with Harry in handcuffs on return to Bergen County Jail after Camden jury selection.
PHOTO BY BOB KRIST, *THE DISPATCH*, UNION CITY, NEW JERSEY.

XII

The Trial

34

The trial started with the state asking for a conviction on four charges of First Degree Murder and the defense seeking a verdict of "Not Guilty" on three counts and "Not Guilty Because of Temporary Insanity" on one count. It opened in Bergen County Courthouse in Judge James Toscano's courtroom, since that room was larger than Judge Madden's.

Just before the trial began John Taylor was called to Judge Madden's chambers, where he met with the judge and prosecutor and was told that the prosecution was willing to make a plea bargain offer in which I could bargain to accept a lesser charge and a lesser sentence than if I stood trial and was found guilty.

In this instance the prosecution was ready to offer me a non vult contendere on my father (which means no defense) and a guilty of second degree murder on Eric. Then the state would drop the other two charges and give me a joint sentencing of thirty years to life. Under that sentencing I would have been eligible for parole in ten years (really nine since I'd done a year in jail). After John talked with the judge and prosecutor he spoke to the Greers and Bob Kleinberg, and told them about the suggestion. He stressed it must be my decision, though, and then they all came to a holding cell and I was brought to them. When John explained to me what was up I immediately told him "No way!" I wanted to go to trial, and I wanted no part of a bargain.

"Why don't you think it over," he suggested. "Take a little time."

228

Opening day of the trial. Clockwise: Judge James F. Madden, Sergeant Carl Olsen (witness); Richard Salkin; John Taylor; Harry De La Roche, Jr. •

"No!" I answered emphatically. "If I walk away free from the trial, fine. But if I go to prison I expect to get killed in some way, so I wouldn't live the ten years."

With that decision the trial began at 1:55 P.M. when Judge Madden entered the courtroom and announced that this was the case of *The State of New Jersey* vs. *Harry W. De La Roche, Jr.*, Docket #2657-76. The jury, which, we later learned, was sequestered at the Hasbrouck House in Hasbrouck Heights was taken to and from court each day in a heavily guarded bus. The jurors were always accompanied by at least two sheriff's officers, and it cost the county $1,000 a day to sequester them for the trial.

The courtroom was a windowless wood-paneled chamber on the fourth floor of the building. Bright lights shone from the ceiling, and the American flag stood in the corner. The first two rows in the spectators' gallery were reserved for the press and courtroom artists.

The spectators sat behind the press, and during the days of the trial, those seats were usually occupied by Aunt Arden and Uncle John; Roy Nilsen, who came up from Maryland; Pastor Immendorf and Ruth Mohring; Uncle Steve Madreperla; family friends and acquaintances; parishioners from my church; high school and college students; and clerks, lawyers, and secretaries from the county courthouse. Jeff Fritts and his family came one day, and Bob Gantt and his family came another. Tink Thompson came whenever she could. And some days when I looked at the spectators I saw Jack Looney, a friend of my father, whom I hadn't seen in years.

Martha Terhune was court reporter for the opening day. But she took turns on other days with three other court reporters—Stephen Lithauer, Regina Dennehy, and Holly Schulz. John and I sat at the counsel table to the left of the spectators' gallery. Richard Salkin sat on the right with Anthony Cirello, his investigator. The witness stand was to the right between the judge and the jury. The court clerk sat at Judge Madden's right, along with two young law clerks who acted as secretaries. Henry VanderWerf from the sheriff's office was my security guard, and other court officers and security guards were at the door and along the walls.

The first day's proceedings got underway with the prosecutor's opening statement. After reading the grand jury indictment for four counts of felonious, malicious, wilful murder Richard Salkin portrayed me as a cunning and methodical killer who was trying to frame my brother. He compared an opening statement to the contents of a book and told the jury they'd see in Part One the ugliness and horror of the crime.

Detective Leroy Smith leaving Hackensack court with Detective Sergeant Paul Likus. PHOTO BY ASSOCIATED PRESS.

"But then there's Part Two," he stated as he walked back and forth in front of the jurors and sat on the counsel table. "That's when the games begin. That's when Harry told police that his family was dead, but he didn't know where Ronald was. That's where he was coming from then—trying to frame Ronald."

Mr. Salkin ended his opening by admonishing the jury members that neither he nor they would have a pleasant job, but he warned them that they had a duty to use common sense in judging the facts.

Montvale Police Captain John Hanna and Sergeant Carl Olsen leave courthouse in Hackensack after testifying at De La Roche murder trial. PHOTO BY ASSOCIATED PRESS.

"No one is looking for a lynch mob," he declared. "But we're not looking for sixteen Pollyannas either."

When John Taylor stood up he told the jurors that a grand jury indictment is one-sided—on the side of the state—and that no defense is offered them.

"But in this trial," he said, "there is a defense, and it will be presented at the proper time."

He went on to remind the jurors that the prosecution must

prove its case beyond a reasonable doubt and that the burden of proof is on the state.

"We welcome the state's scientific evidence," he declared. Later we would find it wasn't all that scientific.

In closing John asked the jury not to form hasty judgments as he moved to the back of my chair and put his hand on my shoulder.

"As Harry sits here at my side he's presumed to be innocent," he stressed. "He's not a criminal. He's like you and I. His future will be in your hands."

Sgt. Carl Olsen was sworn in as a witness that first afternoon. Both he and Mike O'Donovan had been promoted to sergeants some time before the trial, and when he was questioned by Mr. Salkin he told his version of flagging me down for going through a stop sign. But I *still* insist that I stopped him by coming up behind him. At one point in his testimony Olsen recalled that when he told me to empty my pockets I had a plastic bag. John objected to the mention of this, so the judge sent the jury out of the room. Then John presented an argument that the prosecution was trying to link me to the possession of marijuana when I was never charged with that. Judge Madden sustained John's objection and ruled that Olsen's possible remarks about possessing marijuana would be prejudicial to the defense. I started making notations during the first day of the trial and as I continued this during the trial I was often criticized for the way I took notes on my pad as though I were a "lawyer." But I wanted to help in my own defense, and there were many things to note, including inaccuracies in the prosecution's testimonies. At the end of that Thursday's session Judge Madden cautioned the jurors, as he did every day, that during the evening's recess they were not to read newspapers and magazines or listen to radio or television programs that commented on the trial. He also said they were not to discuss the case among themselves or with anyone else during their evenings.

Much of the testimony on Friday was without the jury's presence while Judge Madden listened to arguments on whether or not to allow my first statement to the Montvale police to be admitted into court and read in front of the jury. During the morning proceedings Captain Hanna testified that after he took me to police headquarters at 6:30 A.M. he personally dialed the Greer's telephone number at 6:45 A.M. and allowed me to talk with them.

As Mr. Salkin questioned him he talked about the phone call and said the Greers had come to the station and seen me right away. In John's cross-examination about making the telephone call, he gave this testimony:

Q. At what time was this, Officer, that he made this call?
A. To the best of my knowledge, within ten minutes after arriving.

Q. So, somewhere around quarter to 7.
A. Yeah, I would say so.

Q. Do you know who he spoke to on the phone?
A. It was either Mrs. or Mr. Greer. I don't know who it was.

Q. And how long did it take them to get to the police headquarters after Harry had contacted them?
A. I think it was about 20 to 30 minutes.

Q. So, about somewhere between 7:00 and quarter after you say they arrived?
A. Right.

Q. And when they arrived at the headquarters, where were you?
A. In my office.

Q. Was Harry still there with you?
A. Yes.

Q. And did you escort them into your office at police headquarters?
A. I don't recall whether it was an escort or whether I just invited them in. I don't recall.

Q. And you're telling me now that Mr. and Mrs. Greer came into headquarters, met you, and you brought them in to Harry, is that right?
A. Right.

Q. No doubt in your mind about that, Officer?
A. No.

Q. Did you excuse yourself from the room so they could talk privately?
A. No.

Q. How long did they talk with him?
A. Well, I think Mrs. Greer spoke the longest with him. As far as time goes, I don't recall.

Q. And you're telling me that this is all around quarter—7 o'clock to quarter after 7 in the morning?
A. If memory serves me right, yes.

Q. And what happened after they spoke with Harry at quarter after 7?
A. There was a period of time where they left my office. I don't recall now whether Harry had to go to the men's room, or whether they just wanted to talk outside, or whatever. There was no—no restricting his movements or their movements.

Later in the day the Greers took the stand and told a conflicting story outside of the presence of the jury. Both insisted I hadn't called till somewhere around 10:30 A.M., after which my aunt called right back to verify the call from the station. (At a later date she produced her phone bill showing a call to Montvale on November 28. The time was 10:53. John Taylor subpoenaed the Montvale police records to obtain their bill for that day, and the records showed no call to Maywood till the Greers received their first call from the station at 10:47 A.M. The second call at 5:42 P.M. was to tell them to come back for the arraignment.)

Both Greers went on to say on the stand that the cops refused their repeated requests to see or talk to me until after I was arraigned November 28. They also said Captain Hanna had told them I didn't need a lawyer. When I heard the captain testify that they had been free to talk to me from the moment they arrived I couldn't believe what I was hearing. I almost went out of my chair. Yet the prosecution shoved this lie under oath under the table and ignored it.

When Sgt. Michael O'Donovan took the stand he talked about his search of the house and conversations with me before he made the statement in examination by Mr. Salkin: "I then patted down and checked Harry out." O'Donovan said he had done this because he had seen a bulge in my pocket and wanted to establish it wasn't a weapon. John picked up on this "patting down" and emphasized his contention that the way I was patted down indicated that the suspicion had shifted toward me and that, because of this, the first statement I gave the police should not be admissible in court because the police improperly failed to read me my constitutional rights to keep silent and to have an attorney present. He pointed out that from 4:00 A.M. I was isolated from anyone but the police and that during that time they took my car keys, had me empty my pockets, patted me down, interrogated me and worked on me as though I were a suspect while I had my free movements restricted.

"I'm trying to point out to the Court that at this particular time Harry De La Roche was in fact a suspect, was in fact technically arrested," he stressed.

In his cross-examination he asked O'Donovan about when I got my rights.

> Q. Did you at any time advise him that he didn't have to talk to you?
> A. Yes, I did.
> Q. When did you do that?
> A. When he became a suspect in this case.
> Q. And what time of day was that?
> A. The latter part of the afternoon.
> Q. Not in the morning?
> A. No, sir.

The state—and the witnesses for the state—continued to emphasize that I wasn't a suspect in the morning and that I wasn't in custody then. Yet in a December 10, 1976, interview with writer-sociologist Barry Wood (which was turned over to the defense), O'Donovan discussed bringing me to the police station.

"Is Harry still a witness who is reporting a crime to you, or is Harry now a suspect," he speculated. "This is a matter of judicial interpretation. Our focus now did start coming in on Harry, since there was no forced entry, no robbery, no sexual struggle or evidence. The bodies were only dead a very short period of time, still warm and bleeding with normal finger movement, no discoloration upon the bodies. It therefore occurred within a half hour of our arrival.

"After Ronnie is found the investigation takes on an entirely new light," he added. "Every member of the family is accounted for dead, so now Harry becomes a suspect. Now the questioning of Harry is no longer inquisitive but starts to become accusatory."

Inv. Frank Del Prete also contradicted previous testimony when he testified that at 8:00 A.M. on November 28 he told a desk officer at the Montvale headquarters to notify the Greers about the murders. This conflicted with Captain Hanna's sworn testimony that I had called the Greers at quarter of seven and that after they arrived somewhere between seven and a quarter after they had been permitted to see me. Del Prete also testified that the police began considering me a suspect about 12:30 P.M. when Ronnie was found. Yet O'Donovan had said, a short while before, that I became a suspect the latter part of the afternoon. I know I handed out bull shit myself. But sometimes I had to shake my head at some of the things at the trial. In fact, someone said the tragedy of murder became a comedy of errors.

Despite the arguments about my Montvale statement Judge Madden ruled that I'd given it voluntarily and that it could be used against me. After saying the Miranda warnings do not have to be given while soliciting information he announced O'Donovan could read the first sixty pages of the statement to the jury. This was the portion the police took before Ronnie's body was discovered. The judge ruled against reading the last four pages, taken after police discovered Ronnie, because I had become the prime suspect and should have been advised of my rights.

The next day we had a Saturday session and, beginning on that day, Bob Kleinberg sat at the counsel table for the rest of the trial. One of the first things I heard that morning when I got to court was the news that Kleinberg and Taylor's office had been vandalized during the night. Cinder blocks were thrown at the windows and two of the large ones were broken. Then catsup was spilled on the building to resemble splattered blood. Catsup was also on the white front door. The damage ran to $500 and since it followed the Friday proceedings John believed it resulted from his being in the case. No witnesses or suspects were found in the area, but a large footprint was discovered.

On Saturday John made the first of several unsuccessful motions for a mistrial. The first one was on the basis I hadn't been advised of my rights after I became the suspect. But Judge Madden denied the motion, and the trial continued with O'Donovan on the stand. Many exhibits were brought out that day and as they were introduced into evidence I had to look at blood-soaked bed linen, blood-stained carpet samples, and recovered bullets taken from the house.

There was also testimony on the fingerprints that were taken, the paraffin test I didn't get, and the mileage between my Montvale house and the "Maximus." The cops only clocked the shortest distance. Yet I took a longer route home. The black guy I met at the bar came up for discussion for a while, and I'd like to know—since the state had my wallet with the guy's name and address—why no one tried to contact him and ask the exact time I left? Why wasn't the address turned over to my lawyer? Why weren't a lot of things done? Under cross-examination O'Donovan admitted he'd never tried to contact the guy to see how long he was with me.

Toward the end of the day, state police Det. Leroy Smith, a fingerprint specialist who stated he'd seen twenty-thousand fingerprints in his career, took the stand and described discovering Ronnie's body. He testified to dusting the locker for fingerprints. But the judge recessed the trial till Monday before Smith could tell the jury whose fingerprints he'd found.

Monday was my mother's birthday, and one of the exhibits that really hurt was the yellow nylon pajamas she was wearing when she was shot. A court table behind the counsel tables was filled with cardboard boxes and crumpled paper bags which the prosecution had brought as evidence in a large shopping cart. There were wood chips from the attic floor and steps, the gun and the towel that was wrapped around it, bullets from Eric's and Ronnie's skulls, white long johns and a Citadel tee shirt, and Ronnie's green G.I. Joe box. Some bags contained the undershorts my father and brothers had been wearing.

When Detective Smith got back on the stand, he testified he'd lifted three fingerprints off the metal locker door. Then he told the jury he matched one fingerprint made by my left index finger with copies of the fingerprints that were taken at police headquarters. So far this fingerprint indentification was the most incriminating physical evidence the jury had heard about. But why shouldn't my fingerprint be there? It's logical my father, Ronnie, and I would carry things to the attic. As far as the other fingerprints went, there were not enough characteristics present for Smith to make a match. While testifying about fingerprints, Smith also told the jury no fingerprints could be taken from the .22 pistol Det. John David found in the basement because it was too smeared with blood. Yet the very next day a senior forensic chemist with the State Police said there was only a small amount of blood on the gun. I think there were no fingerprints on the gun because of the towel that was wrapped around it.

Stephen Kunz, who had been an investigator in 1976 and who, at the time of the trial, was an assistant prosecutor, took the stand and testified he'd found the blood-stained long johns and Citadel shirt buried beneath sweatshirts and sneakers at the rear of my closet. Then the state brought out Ronnie's green box, and showed that it contained rolling papers for making marijuana cigarettes, a small scale and two empty plastic bags but no marijuana.

Mr. Salkin slammed it on the table and said, looking at the jury, "When you sell marijuana you need marijuana to sell, right?"

John implied that the evidence might have been tampered with. Then he looked in the box himself and pulled out a pair of scissors. The box also contained a few seeds. But they were too small to identify.

Because of a four-month delay by a state crime lab, the state really goofed on the blood tests and most of them were inconclusive on the evidence taken from the house. In fact, out of forty-five pieces of evidence delivered to the State Police by the

Montvale police in November and December only nine items could be identified for blood type when tests were performed on them in April.

The nine items that could be identified for blood type were:
1. Ronnie's left hand which showed Type O and Type A blood
2. My mother's pajama top which showed Type O
3. A mattress cover which showed Type O
4. One piece of carpeting which showed Type A
5. An undershirt which showed Type A
6. A second undershirt which showed Type A
7. A bedspread which showed Type A
8. A sheet which showed Type A
9. A second sheet which showed Type A

My father, Ronnie and I were A. Eric and my mother were O. Gary Onken, a forensic chemist for the State Police crime labs, said the fingernail scrapings taken from Ronnie revealed the presence of human blood but not in a large enough quantity to establish the blood group.

There were several reasons why the blood tests were botched. The State Police—the first to receive the bed linens, clothing, and other items—sent that evidence to the West Trenton State Police lab. At the time the prosecution requested no priorities but probably assumed the lab would automatically give something of this nature priority. This didn't happen, however, and the evidence was kept on a shelf at the lab, waiting its turn in a four-to-five month backlog of cases. In April the Prosecutor's Office put a rush order on the evidence. But between December and April, the blood was exposed to air, humidity, bacteria, and even detergent residue. All of this made the blood work pretty useless. This was unfortunate for the defense because if the blood tests had been conclusive they could have helped determine whether Ronnie had significant amounts of blood on him from other family members. John objected to the blood-type evidence and argued that the tests were too inconclusive.

"They had the information in November but did not do the tests until April," he declared. "Are you telling us you let your own evidence be destroyed?"

Lab tests on the .22 automatic were performed immediately

after the deaths because the pistol was needed for ballistic tests, so John Nichols, another State Police forensic chemist identified Type O on the pistol's magazine clip and muzzle. Blood tests on the towel wrapped around the pistol were inconclusive.

The testimony on the blood tests was tedious, and by 9:45 A.M. I noticed a juror yawning. I often thought the jury looked bored, and one member rocked back and forth in his chair during the afternoon.

On Wednesday, January 11, Capt. Matthew Sawtelle, my tactical officer at The Citadel, was subpoened to testify about my emergency leave. He testified in full uniform and I noticed that he looked at me when he took the stand. Dr. Lawrence Denson, the county medical examiner, was also a witness that day and much of what he had to say was damaging to me. The jurors looked grim, as they listened, and when really destructive testimony was given I noted some jury members seemed to study me. Dr. Denson began by saying there was no trace of cancer in my mother's vital organs.

"Terminal cancer is usually very diffuse," he testified, "and whitish material would be found in various organs."

I could see a few of the jurors wince when Dr. Denson went on to say that Eric survived two bullets fired at close range and died when his skull was cracked open by a blunt object. He said powder burns on Eric's face showed he was shot with a gun held less than two inches from his face. Then he added that there were superficial wounds on the back of Eric's hands which indicated he had been trying to fight off an assailant. When the prosecutor showed him the gun and asked if the gun could have caused skull injuries Dr. Denson answered, "Yes."

This was a difficult day to take. Then on top of this, Dr. Denson said that the only place in my whole house where blood splatters (caused by an object hitting a person with force) were found was near Eric's body and on the tee shirt in my closet. To show that Ronnie, who was 5'8" might have been the one who had worn the clothes in the closet John, who's one inch taller than I am, suggested the bloody long johns would be too short for me by holding the underwear up to his waist and walking in front of the jury as he asked Dr. Denson, "Are these the long

Dr. Lawrence Denson,
Bergen County
Medical Examiner,
leaving courthouse
after testifying.
PHOTO BY *HERALD-NEWS,*
PASSAIC-CLIFTON, NEW JERSEY.

johns worn by a tall man? A little short aren't they, doctor?"

As soon as he finished speaking Mr. Salkin's investigator produced a second pair of long johns—the ones I had on when I was arrested. Mr. Salkin took this second pair and held them next to the blood-stained ones.

"The ones taken from De La Roche are actually shorter than the other pair, aren't they, doctor?" he asked. Some spectators said I pursed my lips and let out a silent whistle when the prosecutor made this point.

When he was testifying Dr. Denson said he could not tell the *exact* time of death of any person but he estimated it was about 3:00 A.M. Under questioning, however, he went on to say that the deaths could have been within an hour earlier and could have occurred at 2:00 A.M. Ronnie's time of death was put at 3:00 A.M., too, but since his body was still warm when it was found Dr. Denson stated his death could have occurred 1 to 1½ hours after the others when he was asked that question.

The fact that my family could have been killed somewhere between 2:00 and 4:00 A.M. is something I think of a lot. A little after 4:00 A.M. the police were at my house, and at 2:00 A.M. I was still at the disco. Moreover if Ronnie could have died up to 1½ hours later than everybody else why wasn't that checked out closer, since I stated that I shot Ronnie at approximately 3:30 A.M.

The day after Dr. Denson testified, the jury had a day off while we had a Miranda hearing to determine whether the investigating police detectives violated my constitutional rights to remain silent and consult a lawyer before the confession I later recanted.

Throughout the day various detectives from the Montvale police and Prosecutor's Office took the witness stand and testified I had been given my rights and was aware of them before confessing to the slayings. From our side of the courtroom John maintained I was not properly advised of my rights until I had already given a confession to Lt. Herbert H. Allmers, the officer who gave me the polygraph test.

Lieutenant Allmers testified that before the polygraph test—and before I signed my consent to take the test—he read a consent form that contained an extensively worded Miranda warning. When I signed the consent form I waived my right to an attorney. Though Allmers said he went over this orally, I say that nobody read it to me, and I didn't read it myself because of the state I was in. The form was on the table and I simply signed it.

Allmers said it took me three to five minutes to read and sign

Detective Lieutenant Herbert Allmers demonstrating polygraph with which he tested Harry De La Roche, Jr. PHOTO BY ASSOCIATED PRESS.

it. But the judge interrupted him to wonder out loud whether I could have read the form and digested the information in a time frame of five minutes. He took a look at the form himself, and then he pointed out that, even as a lawyer, it took him thirty-eight to forty seconds to read the consent for the test.

Lieutenant Allmers also said that he told me Ronnie's body had been found before I took the test. I don't remember it this way, and according to what I recall, I wasn't told in so many words 'till after I had the test.

When Lieutenant Allmers described the test he said that when it ended it was quite evident by the charts that my answers were deceptive and that I'd killed my family.

"I told Harry the polygraph charts indicated he was lying, and as far as I was concerned, he had murdered his mother and father and two brothers," Allmers declared. "Then I asked him if he wanted to tell the truth. A second later he asked 'How much time can I get for the murders?' "

Allmers maintained that after I learned I failed the test I confessed to four shootings and described what I'd done in vivid detail. He said my eyes filled up with tears when I talked about Eric's death. Then he told the court that after this oral statement I agreed to give a similar account under oath to a court stenographer.

I took the stand in my own defense at the Miranda hearing, and I noticed two of my father's cousins were at the trial that day.

In my ninety minutes on the stand I testified that I was confused, bewildered, and tired when I confessed to the killings.

"I don't recall very much," I said. "By then I was getting pretty out of it."

In his summary at the hearing, John insisted the confession was the product of my physical and mental fatigue and that the police isolated me and weakened my resistance by denying me proper access to my relatives and pastor while I was being interrogated. He said I'd been psychologically beaten during the eight hours of intensive grilling and that, before admitting the murders, I had not knowingly or voluntarily surrendered my constitutional rights.

"Harry didn't know what rights he had," John explained. "There are many forms of torture in this world besides the iron boot or the thumb screw."

Richard Salkin, who often appeared fairly low key, argued that the authorities took great pains to make sure the rights were given.

"Miranda was not intended to dictate to police that they should do everything in their power not to get a confession," he declared. "The police treated this young man fairly. But this man never shut up. He kept talking all day."

After the summaries the court was recessed while Judge Madden made his decision, and during the fifteen minutes he said he would need for that the reporters and TV people passed the time of day by taking monetary bets on what the decision would be. At 3:10 Judge Madden announced that he would admit the confession into evidence, except for a reference to the polygraph examination which he ordered stricken from the confession to keep that information from the jury. Later he read his reason, based upon other rulings that would validate his. The following is an excerpt from his six-page ruling:

The State has met its burden, the totality of the circumstances lead the Court to believe that the police not only acted properly but showed sound investigatory practice. The defendant, although only 18 years of age, appeared to be coherent, intelligent, and aware of the situation which confronted him. Notwithstanding the fact he had been awake since 8:00 A.M. the previous day, he never asked for sleep, never asked for food, nor indicated at any time that he wanted questioning to stop. No argument is made that there was any physical coercion, and this Court is convinced that the totality of the circumstances do not support a conclusion that the defendant's will was overborne by psychological coercion. A point was made by the defendant that he was not allowed to see his Aunt and Uncle and his Pastor. This is not in and of itself conclusive. In the total picture, it appears that the defendant was of the age of majority, apparently coherent, and at the time, willing to cooperate, and therefore this is not a fatal flaw in the State's case. *State v. McKnight* 52 *N.J.* 35 (1968). *State v. Graham*, 59 *N.J.* 366 (1971).

The only apparent opportunity for the defendant to have been allowed to see his Aunt, Uncle, and Pastor was at the end of the sworn statement concluding at 12:45 P.M. By their own testimony Pastor Nilsen and John Greer were not present at the Police Department. They had gone to notify Harry, Jr.'s grandparents. Further, at this time, Harry had become a suspect and had agreed to take a lie detector test. Apparently his Aunt did not pressure anyone to see Harry after she saw him at a distance at the Montvale Police Station. The police did not act improperly. *State v. Smith*, 32 *N.J.* 501 (1960).

In conclusion, the State has met its burden in demonstrating beyond a reasonable doubt that the Miranda warnings were given and that the effectiveness of the defendant's waiver of these rights was not diminished by physical or psychological coercion.

The confession is admitted.

People in court kept saying I seemed too cool and calm. But when Judge Madden admitted that confession I reacted so strongly I wanted to throw the water pitcher that sat in front of me.

The admission was a triumph for the prosecution but devastating for the defense. As John said in an interview with Lucinda Fleeson, a reporter for *The Record*, "The apple has been baked. Now I've got to take it out of the oven and try to repolish it."

As soon as the judge gave his decision the jury was brought back in, and Frank Del Prete read the second sworn statement. I stared at the wall while he read it, and John, in an effort to be supportive, clasped me by the shoulder and said we'd do all we could.

On the following day John cross-examined Del Prete, and there was much discussion about whether ten or eleven bullets were fired the night of the shootings. I loaded the gun with ten bullets when I planned to go the range. But there was an extra bullet in the chamber, and we don't know who put it in. The state says ten bullets were fired. But John and I say eleven. In arguing for eleven John counted two in my mother; two in my father; one that missed my father and made a hole in the pillow, mattress, and a wooden part of the bed; one in Ronnie, two in Eric; one under Eric's bed; one inside Eric's tee shirt; and one under Eric's body on the floor. The prosecution's count is ten because the state believes that the second bullet that was fired at my father came out of his eye and made the hole in the pillow, mattress, and wood. But there was no blood by the bullet hole which seems to be extremely unusual.

After introducing more than one-hundred pieces of physical evidence—the color photographs of the bodies, the bullets, and the bloodstained bedding and clothing—the prosecution wrapped up its case with the second statement to police, the most incriminating piece of evidence against me. Twenty witnesses, most of them police officers, had testified for the prosecution.

35

Before the defense began Judge Madden turned down John's motion to dismiss the charges on the grounds that the prosecution had not presented enough evidence.

The judge also denied a motion for a mistrial when John brought out the point that the jurors had been permitted to visit their families in Camden the previous Saturday. At the time, the defense hadn't known the sequestered jurors had been bused to Camden County to visit with their families in a special room in the Ivystone Inn in Pennsauken while four members of the sheriff's department patrolled the tables where they sat. John contended that the jurors had not been properly supervised during the two-hour meeting and could have discussed the case. But Judge Madden denied the motion after each of the sixteen jurors polled said they hadn't discussed the case among them-

selves or with relatives. Personally I think common sense tells
you that of the twelve final jurors at least one had to talk to his or
her family about it. How could four sheriff's officers effectively
watch sixteen jurors and their families? I think it would have
been better if each juror had been polled in private rather than
in a full courtroom.

My defense began with three of my friends testifying for me.
Vinnie Trojan came in a three-piece suit and Jeff Fritts, by then a
security guard, arrived in uniform. Both said I had indicated to
them that I planned to return to The Citadel after Thanksgiving
vacation. Vinnie took it for granted that if I returned by car I was
taking my Mustang back, and Jeff recalled I told him I'd see him
on Christmas vacation. Jeff DeCausemaker followed them on the
stand and Jeff looked pretty much the same with his still-longish
hair, fine features, and bright-colored sport shirt.

Jeff said he had seen both Ronnie and me using marijuana.
Then he added he used to see Ronnie several times a week down
at the bowling alley.

"He would be looking for marijuana to sell at Pascack Hills
High School," Jeff testified. "He wanted to set up a dealing
business for the money, prestige, and friends he would make
from it."

Jeff said that Ronnie, though interested in acquiring harder
drugs to sell, because he could sell them readily, always turned
down anything but marijuana for his own use. Generally the
main point of Ronnie's conversation was getting some sort of
drug operation going, but he was concerned about money and
not having the financial means to set up the drug operation. Jeff
also stated that Ronnie had expressed a fear that my father would
discover the drugs and beat him.

The next day Steve Mahoney—wearing his good blue blazer
and sporting a small mustache—talked about our activities during Thanksgiving vacation and answered questions about Ronnie
and drugs. One of the things he talked about was Ronnie's
Saturday party the night I came home from The Citadel when
my parents went to Port Jervis. He told how he and I stopped at
the house and how he saw Ronnie with a box on his lap that held
rolling papers, rolling machine, a scale, and some other things.

We smiled at each other as he left the stand and mouthed the words "Nanuet Mall," I was thinking of the happy times when we acted like idiots up there.

Word had gone out that I would be on the witness stand that day, so there was a line outside of the courtroom as spectators waited to get in. When one person left, another would be admitted and that went on all day.

I testified for 2¼ hours and when I took the stand I noticed some jurors adjust their glasses and really start to stare. I told how I had killed Ronnie and one of the jurors started to cough and looked about ready to get sick.

John asked me several questions about my relations with my father. But Mr. Salkin objected to this questioning and Judge Madden ruled that such testimony was not relevant.

"Harry W. De La Roche, Sr., is not on trial," he stated.

"Maybe Harry De La Roche, Sr., is not legally on trial," John countered. "But maybe the jurors would like to know when they sit in judgment of his son what sort of person the father was."

On the following morning people woke up to what was called the blizzard of '78. It was the second worst storm in the county in the past thirty years, and driving was so treacherous schools, plants, and businesses were closed. The storm was a motorist's nightmare, so court was cancelled on Friday and, also, on Saturday when the jurors had asked to work, since Monday would start their fourth week in court.

To me, it was a personal loss, since it interrupted my testimony and delayed the trial longer. John was angered at the two-day halt because delay in my testimony detracted from its impact and was detrimental to us.

When we resumed the trial on January 23 I testified that my confession of the killings was only half true and admitted I had lied in several statements to police about how my family was slain. I said I could give details of the crime by using Ronnie's description, and I stated that when I told those lies my mental state was confused.

Prior to the cross-examination, which lasted for more than an hour, John patted me supportively on the shoulder. Then Mr. Salkin attacked my credibility by forcing me to continue admitting I'd lied several times. He hammered away at discrepancies and insisted—as he had the first day—that I was trying to frame my brother. It went against me—as John expected—that, as usual, I showed no emotion. But how can you help what you are?

During his cross examination on how I'd been treated and how I felt November 28 Mr. Salkin asked the following:

Q. When did you first begin to feel real tired that day, Mr. De La Roche?

A. I don't recall. Most of the—it wasn't tired. It was just actually a strange feeling, what had happened.

Q. Did you really want to go to sleep after what you had seen and what you had done?

A. Well, what I really wanted to do was to commit suicide, go to jail and commit suicide. That's why the statement was given.

Q. Mr. De La Roche—I'm sorry. Were you—

A. No, go ahead.

Q. Mr. De La Roche, when you put Ronald's body in the trunk, did you feel like commiting suicide?

A. I don't know what I felt.

Q. When you took your father's body and moved it to Ronald's bed did you feel like commiting suicide?

A. Mr. Salkin, I can't put in words how I felt and I don't think you've ever felt that way at my guess. I don't know how you can explain how a person would feel finding his family dead, finding the person who did it living—being a brother, someone who you love, shot him and then realize what you've done. Now, how are you supposed to feel?

When court recessed at 2:35 I went back to my cell. But before the night was over I was moved to a suicide watch cell. Nobody said so in so many words, but I knew what the authorities were thinking—that things were going so badly for me they weren't taking any chances. I didn't like the idea at all, and I was really mad. All of my things were moved in with me, so, in addition to a cot with rolled-up sheets for a pillow, the cell was a hodge podge of boxes with my books, tapes, and mail. There was a table in the center of the room for a small TV, and one wall had an ironic sign that asked "Are You In Control?" I was still mad the next morning when I went back to court—and Aunt Arden said she knew it the minute she saw my face.

The high spot of the trial that day was Dr. David Gallina, the psychiatrist for the defense who told the jury he'd had approximately thirty hours of direct talking with me and twenty-five hours of evaluating. He described me as a bright, nonviolent young man, and emphasized that my personality traits included denying a problem existed and excluding from my consciousness painful or unacceptable memories, desires, and impulses. Then he added that another trait was my compliance with authority figures all through childhood.

"From a psychiatric point of view I would say Harry's personality structure was not one of a youngster who was well-adjusted," he explained. "I would say that his growing up process was a very tumultuous and emotional one, and I suspect that he did better, and felt better when he was younger than he did as he approached adolescence."

When John asked for a fuller explanation of my personality structure he gave the following description:

"Everything is very black and white to this boy. He sees his growing up in only one of two ways, either he does what his parents want from him or he doesn't do what his parents want from him. There's no middle ground. There's no bending. There's a rigid, fixed kind of person. An analogy would be a sapling that can bend and find a middle ground to work out problems as against a pipe or stick of metal which doesn't bend hardly at all and when it does, and it finally does, it doesn't bend, it just snaps. This is the rigidity of this boy's basic personality structure. He's a very distrustful and guarded type of person. No one really knows what his feelings are until the feelings just explode and come out. Then they're apparent to everyone. But to look at him, by and large, he looks pretty much okay."

When Dr. Gallina began to talk about the night of the murders he said that at that time I was psychotic, emotionally trapped, and residing in a pressure cooker of fear. As he talked directly to the jury he described a personality conflict that developed between my father and me over my education at The Citadel. He testified that during Thanksgiving vacation I became obsessed with the thought that I couldn't return to school, but I was torn between my desire to leave and my desire to stay and please my father and work out what I was supposed to do. The conflict between these desires was intense, and the problem was I couldn't bring myself to confront my father because my personality structure would be devalued, my father would withdraw his love, I couldn't contend with the impulsive and violent reaction I anticipated, and I wasn't equipped to deal with this stress.

I knew from all of my reading that "psychotic" meant Dr. Gallina thought I was suffering from a mental disorder often involving disorganization of the total personality, with or without organic disease. And from the moment he used the word it became the basis of much argument between the defense and the state.

Before the arguments began, however, John asked Dr. Gallina to tell the jury what I'd told him had happened on November 28. In answer Dr. Gallina described how he'd gone over the confession I'd given at 4:00 P.M. in great detail with me. Then John asked if I had also discussed my statement that Ronnie shot the family. When he answered, "Yes, he did," you could sense confusion in the courtroom—enough confusion, as a matter of fact, to make the prosecutor ask, "Can we have clarification, your Honor?" The judge agreed he'd like that, too. Then John asked for a short recess since we'd been at it for an hour and a half.

Following the recess John showed Dr. Gallina a copy of the confession and asked if he'd actually gone over it line by line with me. Dr. Gallina answered, "Just about," so John's next question was, "Assuming that Harry had done the acts set forth in this document—and at the time he performed these acts—was his ability to do these acts or the awareness of the consequences psychologically impaired?" Mr. Salkin objected to the form of this question so the jurors were excused while John and the state argued about the direction of the questioning on a psychological impairment. The judge got into the middle and a bombshell that baffled the courtroom took place.

THE COURT: I would like to put this on the record. I would like to know what defense we are pursuing here and as to what counts of the indictment. Are we going to a general insanity defense here or are we going to diminished capacity just in connection with the alleged murder of Ronnie or the four individuals? Are you hitting me with something that might be an alternative situation. "I didn't do it, but if I did, I was of a diminished capacity at the time?"

I would like to know what we are doing at this time because you have got me confused. Where am I and where are we going?

MR. TAYLOR: I had set up at the beginning of this case, your Honor, a defense of insanity under the rules and I so notified the Prosecutor.

MR. SALKIN: Yes, I have a notice of insanity defense, your Honor. At one point Mr. Taylor indicated he was withdrawing the insanity defense.

MR. TAYLOR: I never indicated I was withdrawing the insanity defense.

THE COURT: I will tell you quite frankly I didn't know everything that went on during the pretrial but I thought that you were pursuing the defense of diminished capacity. That was my understanding. I could be wrong because I don't have the record here, but I will listen to that argument later.

What are we going on, a general defense or insanity now? Is that the—

MR. TAYLOR: We are going on a defense, your Honor, of general insanity to all four counts.

This took the courtroom by surprise, and Judge Madden asked my lawyer twice if he understood him correctly. Later people considered the abandonment of the earlier defense that I killed only Ronnie an admission that I'd killed everyone and was insane when I did it. They called it a sudden reversal or a switch in defense.

I wasn't surprised at this move, however, because on a previous evening John and Bob Kleinberg had met with Dr. Gallina and decided that the way the trial was going it would be wise to try to get me into a mental hospital rather than a state prison. Inasmuch as the confession had been admitted—and because the judge wouldn't allow testimony on my childhood and family life—they felt the jury would believe the confession. With this in mind they thought it would be better to ask the jury to find me not guilty because I was insane and unable to appreciate the quality of the act. If acquitted because of legal insanity I'd face commitment to a mental hospital until I was judged sane. If found guilty of first-degree murder I'd face a mandatory life sentence.

On the morning that Dr. Gallina was to testify John explained where we stood on this and asked if I wanted to go along with it or whether I'd rather take a chance on going down and doing time.

"I'll go along on the insanity plea," I told him immediately. "Maybe it won't be the right decision. But it's what I want to do. I'd rather go to a funny farm than be killed in a state prison."

After a short discussion about going to this defense the judge and prosecutor mentioned an August 1977 report in which Dr. Gallina had said I was mentally competent to stand trial and appeared to be legally sane by the common standards of McNaughton.

"Now tell me, how you are going to overcome that statement on cross-examination?" demanded Judge Madden.

John argued that the statement referred to my ability to cooperate in my defense. But before anything was really resolved the judge recessed the court for lunch. After lunch he ruled John could change his defense because he had found John had notified the Prosecutor's Office that the defense would be insanity. The document never specified how many murders the insanity defense would apply to.

When the jury returned to the courtroom Dr. Gallina continued to testify that at the moment of the deaths I was no longer in control and unable to make judgments. He said that emotions were running my life and that my mind was not registering such external facts as what's right, what's wrong, what the law is, what might happen to me, or even what the consequences were of what I was doing to the people involved.

"I don't think Harry would have available to him at that time of the killings the intellectual process to know what he was doing, or even to realize the concept of death," he pointed out. "Before his emotions exploded he was hopelessly trapped between two hopeless situations." Then he went on to explain to the jury that the acts after the murders might be the result of a person coming out of psychosis, a person who is frightened because of what had happened.

John asked again if Dr. Gallina had discussed the statement in which I'd related that Ronnie had shot the family and that I, in turn, shot Ronnie. When Dr. Gallina said, "Yes, I did," for a second time we had the following testimony:

> Q. In your opinion as a psychiatrist, does Harry believe this statement?
> A. Yes, I think that at this point he truly believes that this is the occurrence that happened on the evening in question to the point that the story almost verbatim now covers the same ground, uses the same words. He is totally undeviating in any suggestion that it may have happened in any other way.
>
> He out and out refuses at this point to even discuss that first statement which we went through this morning. He demonstrates the same flatness of emotion in his discussions now, and that has become more pronounced although he never discussed the incidents or the acts involved with much emotion.
>
> He is completely fixed in his story. I believe it is totally unyielding. I don't believe anyone will ever get him to change it or to say anything else to the contrary, and I believe he firmly is convinced and believes, himself, that that is what happened and this is true.

Mr. Salkin opened his cross-examination by referring again to the August report in which Dr. Gallina had said I was capable of standing trial and legally sane. He asked many questions about the report and stressed that Dr. Gallina had indicated there were no psychotic responses.

> Q. Will you indicate to me looking through this report where you use the language that Mr. De La Roche had a psychotic episode on this night (the night of the slayings). Will you show me where that is, Doctor?
> A. The report does not direct itself directly—let me put this a little differently. The report was written in an attempt to give a fair and complete appraisal of Harry De La Roche's character

structure and personality exactly along the lines I went through at some length this morning. The actual application of what happened on that evening or on what his mental status was at the time that he committed these acts is not specifically referred to in this report.

Dr. Gallina went on to re-emphasize that the report only dealt with my state of mind during the psychiatric examination and that at that time I did not suffer from a psychosis. He said the psychotic behavior was presently in remission but held it could be triggered by any stressful situation at any time.

"His prepsychotic personality has been with him for many years, and it could not be ruled out that he could be suicidal," he declared. "This is a person who under pressure such as prison is capable of doing harm to himself. He could reach such heights that he could again become psychotic as he did on that night. He needs long-term hospitalization, drugs, and psychotherapy."

After Mr. Salkin's cross-examination the defense rested our case. Next, we waited for forty-five minutes while Dr. Joseph Zigarelli, the psychiatrist for the state, was called. I thought he was patronizing on the stand and sometimes it seemed he talked as much about being a major in the Second World War as he did about my case. He said he'd examined me on three occasions and testified I was not psychotic when my family was slain. As he discussed my mental state—or mental malady—the prosecutor asked:

Q. Doctor, do you have an opinion with respect to Mr. De La Roche's ability to understand and be aware of the nature of his acts during the early morning hours of November 28, 1976?
A. He was capable.
Q. And, Doctor, with respect to his acts in the early morning hours of November 28, 1976, could he appreciate the nature and quality of those acts?
A. In my opinion, he could.
Q. With respect to those acts of the early morning hours of November 28, 1976, Doctor, was he able to—did he have the ability to distinguish right from wrong?
A. In my opinion he could.

When John cross-examined the state's psychiatrist and seemed to be probing for answers Dr. Zigarelli lost his cool and stated directly to the judge that he didn't like that type of probing. But the judge said John was within his bounds of cross-examination, so after that little interlude the cross-examining went on. As soon as John completed it the state rested in rebuttal, and I was returned to the suicide watch cell till court resumed the next morning for the lawyers' summations and the judge's charge.

36

Before the lawyers' summations the morning proceedings opened with a discussion of the items offered into evidence. Whatever was in that category would be sent into the jury room for the jury's deliberations. John objected strenuously to not having family letters admitted. But the judge ruled they couldn't go in.

At the final tally the state had a total of 144 items that were marked for identification or offered into evidence. Of this total, 112 were earmarked "Evidence" and available to the jury. The defense had a total of 67 items, 28 of which were offered into evidence.

John began his summation a little before 11:00 A.M. Both he and Mr. Salkin were wearing vested suits, and as they presented their summations both of them gave emotional pleas—John for aquittal on the grounds of insanity and Salkin for conviction for four counts of first-degree murder. I didn't look at the jury or the lawyers during the summations. Instead I either kept my head lowered or stared at the door behind the judge's bench. As I listened it seemed that my whole life was under a microscope.

John spoke for ninety-four minutes directly to the jury and, sometimes, his voice became so soft only the jury could hear it. He pictured me as a dazed psychotic who couldn't sense right from wrong on November 28, and, as he paced in front of the jury, he said I was sick and in need of help. He mentioned my life at The Citadel—and my desire to quit—and declared I had lived in two private hells, one, the hell at The Citadel and two, the hell of not being able to talk to my father.

"Then the clock ticks and it is almost time to return to his hell," said John. "The pressure cooker builds. Harry comes home, and he sat there with the gun. He walked back and forth in his parents' bedroom, and he finally screams out 'I can't go back' and then Harry starts firing the weapon, and his family is gone.

"A rational boy," he told the jury, "could have said 'Pop, I'm not going back.'

"The prosecution would have you believe the plan for the slayings started at The Citadel," he continued. "Can you reasonably believe Harry thought out the plans? The whole thing is bizarre. It should not have happened. I don't know how pressure builds up in a boy. But it did."

Later John asserted that when the police began to question me two-and-a-half hours after my parents and Eric were dead I was a sick boy—"a boy who we know had either shot and killed one person or four.

"He was psychotic," John stated. "You can't tell me that any one who killed his family is not mentally insane."

Next he went on to stress again that my initial confession to all four murders came only after the police had isolated me from my aunt, uncle, and minister and placed me under severe interrogation. When he talked about secreting the pistol, taking Ronnie to the attic, and dragging my father from his bed, he added, "Can you think of a more feeble, more stupid, more inconsistent and more insane act? This was deranged, psychotic.

"Dr. Gallina told you that Harry could shut out things to make believe it never happened. But the story Harry told you is one he truly believes. You must make a judgment as to which statement is correct or incorrect or whether you believe them at all."

Toward the end of his summation John said to the jury in a

voice that was close to a whisper, "Is anybody concerned for Harry at this time? He was mentally, medically, and legally insane.

"But he can be salvaged," he pleaded in almost inaudible tones. "While ill now there may be a future for Harry De La Roche, Jr.!"

When he finished John said he felt so much emotion he was close to tears, but, as usual, most people commented that I showed no emotion. They didn't know how I felt, though, while I listened to the summations on which so much depended.

Mr. Salkin began his thirty-minute summation by agreeing that I was sick and in need—but contending I'd weighed the four murders.

"Of course, he's sick," he stated. "You'd have to be sick to do what he did. You may think he needs hospitalization. You may think he's crazy. But that doesn't mean he's legally insane."

As he half-sat on the counsel table in front of the jury box, he told the jurors in a low voice, "This is a classic example of first-degree murder. The defense would have you put The Citadel on trial, the defense would have you put Harry, Sr., and Mrs. De La Roche on trial, the defense would have you put Ronald on trial. There is only one person the defense would keep you from trying and that person is the defendant."

He stood up and talked louder and angrier while waving the twenty-one-page confession and reading excerpts from it.

"If anything, Mr. De La Roche is not out of touch with reality," he declared. "If he was, he could not have given this statement. It tells us what he was thinking. That's the key word: What he was thinking. He knew what was going on when he was doing it. You don't come up with details like this unless you were there. What he did subsequent to the murders is indicative of knowing. He said he switched bodies and hid the gun twice. These are thought processes."

Next Mr. Salkin called the defense's position about psychosis a desperate gamble and likened it to watching a Charlie Chan movie and having someone turn abruptly to *Medical Center* on TV. He described it as an eleventh-hour psychosis that was right next to the eleventh bullet John was looking for.

"If there was a psychosis, was it a secret, an afterthought—an attempt to pull the chestnut out of the fire, an attempt to rally when all else has failed, when they couldn't prove it was Ronald?" he demanded.

"You're too intelligent, too sophisticated and have too much common sense to fall for an eleventh-hour psychosis," he asserted, charging again that if Dr. Gallina felt I was suffering from a psychosis he should have put statements to that effect in his August 1977 report. "You don't turn psychoses on and off like a water faucet."

By the time the prosecutor asked the jury to return four first-degree murder verdicts he had succeeded in portraying me as a cunning killer and an accomplished liar. But, despite its damaging effects on my case, Mr. Salkin's summation was good. His last line was powerful and dramatic.

"Don't let the truth become Harry De La Roche's fifth victim!" he shouted to the jurors.

Before the jurors got the case they listened to an hour-and-fifteen-minutes' charge in which Judge Madden spoke loudly, clearly and rapidly while explaining the law and the insanity defense. He kept his robe zipped as he started the charge. But ten minutes into the charge, he unzipped his robe for comfort as he so often did. He began the charge at 2:45 and announced that before a final jury of twelve people retired for deliberation all sixteen juror's cards would be put in the lottery barrel. The four jurors whose cards were pulled out would become the alternates and be excused from deliberating. They'd sit by the side of the jury box whenever court was in session. Outside of court they'd be sequestered in another room and not permitted to discuss the case. As he continued instructing the jurors he informed them that during deliberation they could only ask questions about the law. After they reached a verdict and returned to court the forelady, Mrs. Althouse, would rise and read the verdict.

While outlining the law the judge gave the jury a choice of four verdicts.

"Under the current law in New Jersey murder in the first degree is deliberate, wilful, and premeditated," he said. "It is murder with intent to kill and premeditation can be only a few seconds. It carries a mandatory life sentence.

"Murder in the second degree is without deliberation and includes all kinds that are not first degree. It carries a maximum thirty-year sentence."

The other two choices Judge Madden outlined were acquittal by reason of insanity (which was what we were going for) or complete innocence in three of the slayings. Because I admitted on the stand to shooting Ronnie, the jury in that slaying could acquit me only on insanity.

In explaining legal insanity and the insanity defense, Judge Madden pointed out—as he had said earlier—that to be acquitted for reason of insanity I must have been unaware of the quality of my acts and unable to perceive right from wrong. He told the jury and the crowded courtroom that if the verdict were "Not Guilty By Reason of Insanity" there would be a hearing on insanity to determine my present mental status and to see what should be done. The decision could range from a commitment to a mental hospital to unconditional release. He added that if the defense of insanity was sufficiently established the law allowed acquittal of all criminal responsibility.

When it was time to choose the alternates a sheriff's officer pulled out four names and handed them to the court clerk to read. We lost three women and one man. The alternates were: Sheryl Anyzek, the twenty-year-old girl with the long straight hair who was the youngest juror; Dorothy Krumm, the middle-aged housewife who had lost a son; Joyce Saye, the black-haired second-grade teacher; and Anthony Skokowski, a middle-aged supervisor from Camden.

The jurors went to the jury room at 4:45 P.M, and I was returned to my suicide watch cell. John was not optimistic. He said he expected a guilty verdict and that I should expect that, too.

"For all intents and purposes, the case was destroyed the day the confession was allowed into evidence," he told me, giving me another of his supportive pats.

I was aware that prospects were dim as I sat in my cell and waited. But some of the mail I got during the trial helped keep me going. I pulled out the two top letters from my paper bag full of mail. The first came from South Carolina from a stranger named Chris:

Dear Harry,

I felt I had to write. For many days I've had your situation on my mind. I seriously do believe your story even if no one else will, and I hope you will have a happier future than you've endured this past year. Best of luck. I'm thinking the best thoughts for you and take it easy.

The second was from another stranger:

Dear Harry,

You do not know me; we have never met. And yet there is a sense in which I know you: one human sensing and feeling and understanding another human in his suffering and confusion and deep hurt. In that sense I write, because feeling these things for you I had to let you know. There are many who feel deeply for you, and maybe that knowledge can help you just a little. You do not have to feel entirely alone. We can understand the pain a young person feels in reaching maturity in a cold and callous and seemingly indifferent world. We can understand the troubled teenager. We have once been young people ourselves, and we have children your own age who have known many of the confusions and hurts you have known.

You are so young, Harry. Life can be good again. There is hope in the world, even though there is little justice. You have still to know the quiet yet profound happiness life can bring. I pray for you, dear Harry.

A Friend

Pastor Immendorf came to see me while I was sitting alone, and I'll never forget his kindness in spending the evening with me. Together we sat in that cluttered cell and watched *The Newlywed Game* plus other TV programs till we were called to the courtroom at exactly 8:15.

I wondered if the verdict was in, as the pastor and I went to the courtroom where Aunt Arden and a few other people were waiting for a verdict. Uncle John had had to leave to go a company annual meeting.

Instead of a verdict the jurors had a question about the law, and they wanted Judge Madden to redefine first and second-degree murder and re-explain the meaning of legal insanity. They also wanted to see Dr. Gallina's report of August 1977. The judge said he'd redefine the laws promptly at 9:00 A.M. Then he recessed the court for the night and the seven-man, five-women jury was bused back to the motel.

When the jury came in Thursday morning Pastor Immendorf, Tink Thompson, Aunt Arden, Steve Madreperla, Jack Looney, and spectators were scattered in their seats. I noticed none of the jurors seemed able to look at me as Judge Madden gave them a redefinition of first and second-degree murder. For a verdict of legal insanity or "Not Guilty by Reason of Insanity" he said for the second time around that the defense must prove by a preponderance of evidence that I was laboring under such a disease of the mind that I did not know the nature and quality of the act I was doing or that, if I did know, I did not know the difference between right and wrong. Since Dr. Gallina's August 1977 report had not been offered into evidence the jurors could not take it into the jury room.

Before I went back to that suicide watch cell I asked John to try to arrange things so Aunt Arden, my godfather, and a few other people could come to the cell to see me while we waited for the jury's verdict. John spoke to Under-Sherriff Stasse who said I could see a few of the persons who visited me regularly. Aunt Arden was the first one to come and we talked about the trial. She also promised she'd see me after the verdict was in. Steve Madreperla came in next and our visit wasn't very much different from the other times we had talked.

I think the people who saw me while the jury was out hoped that they could get close to me and talk about how I felt. But I couldn't let go and do that and when they were ready to leave I avoided any kind of goodbye by saying they'd have to excuse me while I left to go to the bathroom. Pastor Immendorf was the last to come in since he planned to stay in the cell with me until I was called for the verdict.

While we waited he read the Bible to me—a few verses from "Ephesians"—and then he particularly discussed "For by grace are ye saved through faith; and that not of yourselves; it is the gift of God."

XIII

The Verdict—
and Aftermath

37

At 1:38 on January 26, 1978, we got the word that the jury—after six-and-a-half hours of deliberation—had arrived at a verdict. It was three weeks, practically to the minute, from the start of the trial. Pastor Immendorf went to the courtroom with me and sat down at the counsel table. John shook my hand when I came in—and then we made small talk and waited.

Now that the moment was actually here I felt really vulnerable and trapped, just as I'd felt so many times during my nineteen years. Two guards stood right behind me, and two others stood nearby, more than I'd had at any time during the weeks of the trial.

The courtroom was filled to capacity as people came in for the verdict, and many of the faces were new ones that I hadn't seen before. Finally the jury filed in, with Mrs. Althouse holding tight to the verdict. I looked at her and the rest of the jurors. But none of the twelve looked at me. One was chewing a piece of gum as I tried to search his face.

I felt John Taylor brace his arm on my back, and Pastor Immendorf took my left arm when Mrs. Althouse stood up with the paper and read those eight fateful words: *Guilty on four counts of first degree murder.*

I stared straight ahead and said nothing while the pastor tightened his hold on my arm, and John grasped my shoulders even more. Then each of the jurors was polled on each charge. This meant that along with hearing the original guilty verdict I heard the word "Guilty" dropped like a hatchet forty-eight additional times while each juror said "Guilty" four .times. Naturally, newspapers would say I sat with my chin resting in my hand and showed no emotion at all.

After the verdict and before the sentence Judge Madden asked the lawyers, Pastor Immendorf and me to stand. The newspapers said that I stood erectly, and when the judge asked if I wanted to speak I told him, "No, sir," very softly. Right after that he imposed the sentence: *Life imprisonment on four counts to be served concurrently in state prison.* That meant I'd be eligible for parole after 14 years and 8 months. If I had had consecutive life terms I would have had to serve 58 years before being considered for parole.

"At least the judge didn't screw me," I said in a whisper to John.

When everything was completed I heard the judge say, "That's it."

That's it! It seemed so casual when suddenly my life was nothing and the total of my past, present, and future was one big question mark. The judge excused the jurors, and they filed out one by one. I shook hands with John and Bob Kleinberg, and John said he'd see me in the morning to talk about appealing the verdict. Before I was led away in my handcuffs I saw Tink Thompson looking distraught and trying to control her sobs.

Pastor Immendorf came back to the cell and sat for a little while. Then a bit later Aunt Arden came in, as she'd promised she would. I'd already changed to my jail clothes and was lying on my cot.

"You're not going to cry, are you?" I asked.

"No," she said. "I won't cry."

She took my hand and then hugged me, and I thought back fourteen months when, as an aunt who scarcely knew me after I grew up, she'd said to John Taylor, "Hug him for me," on my first morning in jail.

"I don't care what that doctor said about me, Aunt Arden," I told her. "I didn't kill my mother, father, and Eric."

We talked about trying for an appeal and looking ahead to that. Then I told her I'd like to see Uncle John before I left for prison. I knew I'd be leaving in the morning, so she said he'd surely be there.

Ever since my family died I had told everyone that what I wanted to do the most when I got out of jail was to go to George Washington Cemetery to visit the four graves. Aunt Arden knew I was thinking of that as we sat in the suicide watch cell, so she wasn't surprised when I asked her if she could talk to Sheriff Job or Under-Sheriff Stasse and try to arrange this for me. I wasn't sure how I'd react. But I knew I wanted to go.

Aunt Arden left to see Mr. Stasse and—again—I got out of saying goodbye by taking off for the bathroom, as I had done throughout the day when visitors were ready to leave.

I wanted to be alone for a while after Aunt Arden left. But as one hour went into the next in my last night in the county I wished I could have a visit from Tink Thompson or Pastor Nilsen. I had a lot of things to say and I felt—if I'd had a chance that night—I could let down my defenses and open up to them. That wasn't to be, however, so I kept myself busy by packing my possessions into one large box. On Friday Aunt Arden repacked them into some smaller boxes and took them to her house. I was allowed to take nothing—not even a carton of cigarettes that hadn't been opened yet.

On Friday—after spending my last night in the county under a suicide alert only about six miles away from my first night in an incubator—I got up early and prepared myself for the trip to the prison. I dressed in my suit and yellow shirt, but I skipped the vest and tie. Uncle John came right after breakfast and told me—by special arrangement—Sheriff Job and Under-Sheriff Stasse were allowing me to go to the cemetery so I could pay my last respects as I'd wanted to for so long. He said when we were ready to leave Aunt Arden would be called and she and Pastor Immendorf would go along with us. John Taylor arrived soon after that to discuss an appeal and say he would seek a new trial on the grounds that my confession was obtained improperly, and, also, that Judge Madden erred by allowing it into evidence. When he left he said, "Keep your chin up. Everything will be all right."

Later Bob Kleinberg told reporters my spirits weren't very

good. "Harry feels he won't live—that he's a dead man and that he will be killed in prison," he said.

When we were ready to leave for the cemetery—and the ride to prison—one of the detectives gave me his coat since it was a frigid morning. Uncle John met Pastor Immendorf and took him in his car. Aunt Arden went with Under-Sheriff Stasse, and I went with the detectives in the back seat of an unmarked car. After I was belted and handcuffed the officers took me out of a door by the sheriff's office, since all of the reporters were waiting at another spot. It was just about eleven o'clock, and we made our exit so quickly, nobody saw us go. Outside the temperature was twenty degrees and snow was frozen on the ground.

When we got to George Washington Cemetery the officers and I stayed in our car while the rest of the people got out. I watched the group look for the snow-covered graves. Then after they kicked some snow around I saw Uncle John lean over and partially clear off a stone. While Pastor Immendorf and Uncle John stood there, the others moved to the background. Then the officers opened the car door and walked me to the grave, holding tightly to my arms. I could see the name "De La Roche." Then we all stood in silence. In a moment Uncle John said softly, "Pastor, would you say a prayer."

Pastor Immendorf said, "Harry, will you join me." Then he and I stood together while he read a prayer for my family, and then a prayer for me.

Heavenly Father, we know that you are all-powerful and all-knowing. We realize that you are the righteous God of Heaven before whom we all will stand and receive our judgments from which we have no appeal. We ask that you, through your Holy Spirit, continue to work in Harry's heart increasing his faith in you through your Son Jesus Christ. Let Harry be strengthened by the knowledge that you will give him the power to withstand all assaults on his life.

Dear Lord help him to live this day quietly, easily,
To lean upon thy great strength trustfully, restfully,
To wait for the unfolding of thy will patiently, serenely,

To meet others peacefully, joyfully,
To face tomorrow confidently, courageously.

Heavenly Father, we ask you to look over and care for Harry. We
commend his well-being into your hands. Please watch over him,
we ask in Jesus Name.

Amen.

I almost cried when he finished—and when I had had this
moment that I had wanted so much.

When the officers saw I was starting to cry they whisked me
back to the car. Then one officer sat in the front seat while I got
control of myself. Everyone felt at that point that if I had stayed
by the graves any longer I might really break—and the officers
didn't want that.

Aunt Arden came over to my car, and when the officer rolled
down the windows she said "May I say goodbye?"

The officer started to shake his head so she asked him to say it
for her. Then he had a change of heart when he saw me blowing
my nose because he told her to go ahead and say what she
wanted to.

"Are you all right?" she asked me. I nodded and shook my
head "Yes." I realized that I couldn't speak, and Aunt Arden
sensed that too.

"Let us know your address," she said. "We'll keep in
touch—and we love you."

I nodded "Okay"—and lowered my head. I was still having a
problem, and I didn't want to talk.

I watched her walk away to her car. Then the officer who was
driving me started up the car and the long trip to Yardville
Reception Center and life in state prison began.

38

The Prison Reception Center at Yardville receives all men who are sent to the New Jersey State Prison Complex from the courts, returned as Parole Violators, or transferred from another institution. Its stone buildings were built in the sixties and generally it is considered one of the most modern, professionally run institutions in the state. Besides the reception unit, there's a permanent housing area for approximately five hundred inmates.

When the officers and I arrived we had to wait for half an hour till someone came out to the gate to admit us. Then we waited another fifteen minutes before I was led through the door and put into a cell. After more waiting an officer took me out of the cell and told me to strip and shower and get into prison clothes. My own clothes were taken away from me to be shipped back to the Greers. All I could keep were my eyeglasses and cross.

At the end of that first afternoon I was taken to a cell block and told I would spend two or more weeks in the reception center while the Inter-Institutional Prison Classification Committee evaluated me and decided where to assign me. During that time I saw a psychiatrist, psychologist, social worker, and chaplain. I can't remember these visits well, except I recall the psychiatrist had about thirty Bic pens in his two shirt pockets. I guess that isn't important, but there's such a sameness to life in prison you notice things that are different.

I stayed in Yardville for about four weeks, and all the while I was waiting, I hoped that I could remain there. That wasn't to be, however, since I was told on my second session with classification that I would go to either Trenton or Rahway state prison. I hoped it would be Rahway since that would be easier for visitors from home. I also heard that at Rahway I could wear my own clothes and have my stereo and TV.

Since I couldn't have visitors in Yardville, mail from people who wrote to say they believed me and cared about me was the big thing I looked forward to. The first letter came from Aunt

271

Arden and she ended her news by saying, "I love you, and always remember I want to keep helping you. But you must keep in touch. I think of you all the time and wonder how you're adjusting."

The next letter came from Florida from Steve:

> I just found out the verdict, and I almost broke my hand when I put it through the headboard of my bed. I had to break something and that was the closest thing to me. Will the case go to trial again? If so, I want to help as much as possible—even more than last time—because I believe you! You're my friend and I'm yours and nobody can take it away from us. I don't care what they say we're still buddies. If there is anything I can do let me know. Please write back.
>
> Your brother,
> Steve

After three meetings with the classification board I was told I would go to Rahway on February 25. On that wintry day ten of us were taken there by bus. We were handcuffed and leg-shackled in pairs, and the main thing on my mind was "I'm only a number now."

All I can do is wait and hope for John Taylor's appeal.

39

While Harry was adjusting to life as a number there were many after-the-verdict views and a mixture of varying reactions. Primarily the comments people expressed came from family and friends; acquaintances and strangers; courtroom observers; law enforcement officers; and professionals who were involved with the case. There were also reflections from the jury.

Speaking for the maternal side of the family, John Greer confided that the whole situation had been an enormous emotional drain.

"It's going to take us awhile to get our lives together again," stated John. "But we wouldn't abandon any human being in a crisis such as Harry has experienced."

"As soon as this happened we gave a great deal of thought to what was right for us to do regarding Harry," said Arden. "We asked ourselves what Harry's parents would have wanted us to do, and, after weighing everything, we came to the conclusion that Mary Jane would have wanted us to do what we are doing. I hope she knows we are helping her son."

"Our feelings have always been very basic," added John. "We've said from the beginning that if Harry did something he should be punished. On the other hand, if he were innocent he needed our help during this ordeal, too. We've chosen to stick with him all along—and we'll continue to do so."

On the paternal side of the family, Ernest Ebneter spoke for his wife in a telephone conversation.

"When I asked Honey if she wanted to talk to you, she just lay on the couch and shook her head 'No, No, No,' " he said.

"She just don't want to talk about it all the time," he explained, "and whenever somebody wants to bring it up again she cries 'Why don't they leave me alone?' It's something that hurts her very much, and every time this thing comes up she gets upset all over again. It seems there's no end to it.

"You can't understand how it is with my wife," Ernie continued. "She just can't get over it. Harry, Sr., was the only one we had. Now everyone is wiped out except the guy who did it. We used to have him here a lot—and now look at what has happened. I'm just bitter about the whole thing."

Honey's sister-in-law, Ethel De La Roche (wife of John, Sr., and mother of John, Jr.,) agreed there was bitterness in the family about the tragedy.

"But we feel nothing can be gained by talking about it," she stressed. "In fact, some of us are upset and concerned that some members of our family consented to lengthy interviews with other people that might be used out of context.

"The whole thing was just terrible, and as soon as the incident happened my son put up a poster in his home that said, 'God Bless Them All In Heaven.' "

Harry's godfather, Steve Madreperla, summed up the verdict by saying, "There is no one culprit in this case.

"As I have said so many times Harry, Sr., thought the way you loved the most was to discipline your children," he pointed out. "In many ways he should be admired for his hopes and aspirations for his family.

"Probably Ronnie and Eric might have made out all right with his kind of discipline. For some reason, Harry, Jr., was different. He marched to a different drummer."

Harry's best friends from his area still supported him. "He's not a criminal, and he'll never be a criminal to me," said Rutgers student Bob Gantt.

"More than one thing led up to whatever happened that night," reiterated Vinnie Trojan. "When I heard about Ronnie and the drugs I accepted that version. The whole thing pieces together."

Other supporters who'd wanted to believe that Ronnie had held the gun were on the fence when they heard the verdict and learned Harry was in prison. Now they said the jury was still out, as far as they were concerned.

"I continue to find the Ronnie version feasible," stressed one of the on-the-fence persons.

"To me it's a more logical story that the brother was on drugs and his parents found out and wanted to turn him in to the police," added Tink Thompson. "I've heard similar stories from classmates who had the same experience and ended up running away. I can understand this a whole lot more than a boy coming home from college and killing to avoid going back. That's a stupid reason to kill, and I don't think Harry could do it."

"Personally, I think Harry was a victim of his own family life," a neighbor pointed out. "He's also his own worst enemy—and he doesn't know how to change this. But the family wouldn't have wanted to acknowledge any instability. This would have been an unwelcome smudge on their family picture.

"They were really good people who always meant well," he

went on to say. "But I sometimes wonder, looking back, whether they unknowingly were a self-destructive family. Did they contribute to their own demise by failing to be responsive enough to what was best for Harry? And in trying to do what they felt was right were they going by *their* plans for Harry instead of Harry's plans for himself?

"In fact, I even wonder whether Harry, in desperation, reached a point where he'd rather kill than hurt or disappoint his parents."

Many people who've spent a great deal of time weighing the Ronnie version continue to ask where Ronnie was that final Saturday night. But no interviews or investigations have yielded a clear-cut, credible answer, and if anyone knows his real whereabouts that person isn't talking as this book goes to press. Harry said that in all probability Ronnie went to one of his hangouts—the bowling alley or the railroad tracks—after collecting his paper money when Harry dropped him off. Andy Cannon, Ronnie's best friend from school, felt sure he spent the evening with friends and ended up at a pizza place. But he didn't think Ronnie had money.

"I wanted him to go out," he explained. "But he said he had no money and hadn't collected from his paper route."

A college student from another town said she had heard that Ronnie was partying with a drug pal that night, while a peer who worked at the 7-11 a few doors from the De La Roche home said Ronnie was in before 9:00 P.M. to buy candy and exchange some singles for some larger bills. He returned to 7-11 around 11:00 P.M. according to a neighbor who said she saw him there. But nobody knows what he did after that and it's the general belief that Ronnie probably returned to his house sometime after 11:00.

In an interview after the verdict Dr. Lawrence J. Denson, the county medical examiner, stated that toxicological examinations in his office indicated there were no drugs in Ronnie's body. When asked what drugs would show—and what drugs wouldn't show—in such an examination, he said, "At any time any drugs that a kid would use today would show. If Ronnie had had drugs in his system that night, they would have shown."

People who attended the trial offered a variety of opinions after the verdict was in.

Ida Libby Dengrove, a courtroom and news artist for NBC-TV News Center 4, who covered—among others—such trials as Son of Sam, Joseph Kallinger, Dr. Mario Jascalevich, Clifford Irving, Joan Chesimard, Mitchell-Stans, Rubin Hurricane Carter and John Lennon saw Harry as a very sick boy as she sat and sketched him.

"As an artist, mother, and wife of a psychiatrist he impressed me as being very sick," she said after the trial. "Could he be believed? And was his father the personality who taught him not to feel pain or remorse?

"It was incredible to watch and sketch him while he read his dead mother's letters and recounted the gory death of his younger brother without the slightest show of emotion.

"Whoever was responsible for creating what I felt was a zombie perhaps received the full penalty for the efforts. His sickness should have been spotted years ago. Help should have been given then."

A retired man expressed concern over the definition of premeditated murder. "I'm bothered that this boy—who really needs help—was convicted on premeditation because of the way he described in court walking up and down the hall while he was holding the gun.

"They call it premeditation," this man pointed out. "But no one ever mentions that maybe that young boy walked up and down fighting with himself. Then if he did what they said he did the weaker side won out. I kept looking at him all through the trial and thinking he looks like my son. I hope that somehow in this crazy world people who resort to harrassment learn where this can lead."

Under-Sheriff John Stasse, who was responsible for Harry in Bergen County Jail, is convinced there's more to the De La Roche story than anybody knows.

"It's locked inside of Harry," he said. "He has problems, and he's sick. He was also very decent and nice—but something went awry."

At the end of the trial Richard Salkin stated in a TV interview that the whole situation was a tragic plight and the conviction for four first-degree murders was a victory he couldn't be happy about.

In other interviews with the media he stated: "In a case like this any responsible person or attorney can't jump up and down for joy. You have to feel as a human being. You have to feel something for Harry De La Roche. I hope he can get in touch with himself. Maybe with a little treatment he will.

"The confession was devastating," he added. "You have a man and the man is saying what he did—and why."

John Taylor obviously agreed the confession was highly destructive. Moreover, his case was a difficult one from the very start.

"In summing it up, we had to keep one foot in two buckets," he said.

Aware that he was criticized for what some people considered a last-minute switch in his plea, Taylor contended that the subtleties of his defense were lost on the people who liked to say, "If only it had been the insanity defense for four counts from the beginning," or, "If only the Ronnie version had been left out of the courtroom completely."

"The original defense was not guilty, and we also pleaded insanity," he declared. "But if I had stood up before the court and pleaded not guilty by reason of insanity early in the trial the state wouldn't have had to prove anything. In effect, I would have been saying, 'He did it.' No matter how defective the evidence is we're saying, 'He did it.' Therefore, if the jury says we do not believe he was insane I would have no appeal at all.

"But if I say 'Prove your case,' which is what 'Not Guilty' means, then, if there is an error in the introduction of evidence and the verdict goes against us, we have an appeal. If in the strategy Judge Madden went in our direction the defense would have rested at the end of the state's case. But when the confession was admitted the state's case was made. Then it became the duty of the defense to meet the confession.

"But how do you meet the confession? We argued that it wasn't voluntary, but we couldn't say in our minds 'Nobody is going to believe it.' Harry's second statement was too detailed. We had to believe the jury would believe it.

"Since that's where we stood then we had to consider whether the jury would accept a defense of insanity on the whole thing. That's when we spoke with Dr. Gallina and discussed the insanity defense. As a psychiatrist, Dr. Gallina felt that Harry was a psychotic—and in a psychotic episode—on November 28.

"It's hard to understand a psychotic defense because psychotics walk among us every day of our lives. You don't have to come right off the wall in order to be psychotic. But the psychiatrist for the state said you do. Did the jurors really understand what Dr. Gallina said? Or did they believe Dr. Zigarelli, who was more flamboyant?"

Dr. Gallina discussed the case after the trial was over and pointed out that in the court the issue had to be that Harry was accused of pulling the trigger and had to stand trial for that.

"But delving deeper the real issue is not just Harry's role," he maintained. "It's the family pathology that's back of everything. If by any chance two brothers were murderers that night the focus on the family pathology is even more intense. But the fact that anyone pulled a trigger has to say something about that family.

"I believe that all five members had a very limited ability to communicate with each other and express and share their emotions and feelings. Harry is the perfect example of a psychological breakdown—of a person who says, 'I can't take any more.' But, still, he was tied to his family with bonds that kept him from running away."

Dr. Thomas Bellavia, the Bergen County Jail physician who examined Harry after the crime and who saw him periodically during his incarceration, said there had to be questions about the night and what the motives were. And in an interview with John Banaszewski of *The Record*, Dr. Alan Tuckman, an area psychiatrist who has had vast experience in criminal court cases, declared that the De La Roche case illustrates that people must be able to release pressures.

"I think the lesson to be learned from this case," he stated, "is that you cannot repress or oppress people in a family and not expect them to react with rage."

Pastor Roy Nilsen felt from the start that the period after the verdict would be a critical time for Harry.

"There's no way we can give up on him," he said. "Like everyone else, it has always concerned me that he hasn't shown more emotion. But I know the emotion is there. I've had insights and glimpses of it before he quickly changed a subject.

"Actually, I don't think anyone can really comprehend the tragedy of something so terrible happening, so for self-preservation you block out that terrible happening. One day I even said to Harry, 'I think you're trying desperately to preserve your sanity and not dwell on these things.' He answered, 'That's right. I am.' I'm convinced Harry believes Ronnie did it."

In in-depth interviews after the "Guilty" verdict the jurors spoke of many things. Most of them spoke freely, though a few preferred not to talk because their feelings were too personal or because they felt excessive stress from the experience of being on the jury.

"It's an experience we're putting into our past," said Vincent Squazzo.

In the jury room only one ballot was taken on each of the four counts. Each was unanimous. One or two of the jurors felt ready to render a decision in less than the six hours it took. But the others wanted to discuss all the points and not run too fast on a verdict.

"For me the turning point in the trial was when the confession was read," said Richard Kowlowski, the twenty-four-year-old tape librarian and computer operator. "Once that was read it was hard to pull yourself in any other direction. But I wondered how the officers got that out of Harry? What other circumstances were involved?

"I think that most of the jurors knew that there was more behind this case that we weren't hearing about. I know the 'why' isn't supposed to be an important part in a trial. But I think a lot of us felt in the dark about what had gone on before, who Harry was as a person, and all that sort of thing. We would have liked to know the 'why' and made some sort of decision from that. Harry wasn't a vicious person. He wasn't out to kill the world."

"It was hard for me sitting there all along, thinking Harry could have been my son," said Mary Flexon, the mother of five. "My own son, Harry's age, also hated the first college he attended and wanted to change the first year. He did change at the end of the year, and he loves where he's going now. As parents you sit and listen. You just don't state, 'Go back.' But once Judge Madden redefined first-degree murder and legal insanity the jurors didn't see how they could render anything except a first-degree verdict."

"I think anybody who goes as far as Harry did was unstable to some degree," revealed Michael Ronca, the twenty-four-year-old manager. "I also think he needs help. But as the judge described the law I didn't feel at the time—and I don't feel now—that he fit all the criteria to be legally insane."

"Moreover, when it was determined that it falls upon the defense to prove insanity the jury did not feel the defense had proved this," added Daniel McCarthy.

Some of the jurors felt that what they kept calling a switch in pleas hurt the case for the defense. They speculated it might have been better to have gone with an insanity plea right from the very beginning.

"Then the confession wouldn't have mattered so much," stated one juror. "Actually I didn't know how I was going to vote until the entire tactics were changed and the plea was for insanity. Then it appeared that both the defense psychiatrist and lawyer were admitting that Harry killed all four."

Other jurors didn't agree that the defense might have been different.

"I thought the defense attorney did everything he could in the boy's behalf," said Mary Flexon. "He had a hard case to work with, with that confession in black and white. When he went for insanity I'm sure he knew the jury was convinced the boy had committed the murders. And I'm sure, as a father, his heart went out to the boy he was defending."

As the jurors agreed on the verdict and prepared to announce it in court Vincent Squazzo said, "I must confess. There were some wet palms." Later in an interview with Tony Mauro of the *Camden Courier-Post* he declared, "We tried to maintain our composure, but I talked to the jurors afterward and we all had some anxiety feelings." The feelings were not feelings of doubt, Squazzo said, but they were a realization that "this was a critical set of circumstances. A man's life hung in the balance. Some of us called on divine resources for help."

Another juror also talked about the need for guidance.

"One Sunday during the trial eight or nine of us had a Bible study," said Michael Ronca. "As we sat together we prayed that the Lord would lead us and grant us the wisdom to make the right decision in the responsibility we have. The fact that we made the right decision, according to law, doesn't dispel the feeling and sympathy I have for Harry as a person. I hope he is able to get some help and that somehow, someway he finds what *Harry* needs and wants."

The bus trip home was a time of both gladness and sadness for the jurors—gladness that the trial was over and they were returning to their families and sadness because of the verdict they had had to give. For the first time they could talk freely and they talked of many things. Some said the Ronnie version had been too far-fetched to believe. Others said that at the start they'd considered it might be possible. Naturally Harry's lack of emotion came up for discussion, too. The fact that he was so calm and composed got to a lot of jurors and many were stunned that he was so cool when the verdict was read.

"When we got back to the jury room you heard things like, 'Oh, my God, I can't believe it,'" said Richard Kowlowski.

"But he had emotions he was hiding," Mary Flexon maintained. "Underneath the surface a very hurt kid was crying."

"I guess we weren't supposed to look at his emotions," pointed out Paul McGuire, the disabled bus driver who had four children. "But even though we were only supposed to go by the facts you had to observe him to give him a fair shake. Often he acted as though he was in another world. Nothing seemed to bother him. I really think if he had sat there and looked a little more concerned he might have helped his cause—though I don't know what he had to help him."

All of the jury members who consented to interviews said that they had a clear conscience that they made the right decision on the material that was given them. But most admitted to feeling sorry that they had had no alternative to the verdict the law said they must give.

"It shook me to think that this young boy was in such trouble and that his whole life would be affected by the verdict," said Mary Flexon. "But it was something that had to be done. As a jury it was our duty."

Dorothy Krumm, who'd lost her twenty-one-year-old son in a car accident, had the same reaction.

"I think everyone felt sorry for him, and I disliked some of the inefficiencies of the police and the way they treated him," she admitted. "But that can't alter your feelings if he did it. You have to go by the facts. I went home and said to all of my friends, 'Don't push your children too far.' I think we all had the feeling that you can push children too far."

"At one point while going home on the New Jersey Turnpike we could look in the direction of Yardville and see the prison buildings," Daniel McCarthy said. "Then one of the deputies commented, 'That's probably where he'll be placed.' You could feel a hush come over the bus. Everything quieted down."

"When you're as close in age to Harry as I am you put yourself in his shoes," said Sharyl Anyzak in summing up the jury's feelings. "Harry was old enough to make his own decisions, yet he was also aware of the teaching that you should respect your parents' decisions. They're older. They're supposed to know better. Maybe if they'd been more understanding of Harry's feelings this tragedy wouldn't have happened. I hope he can get the help he needs while he's young enough to still have a life."

As a final comment on how people felt after the verdict was in, a college student who had known Harry since they'd been confirmed in their church wrote the following to *the Record*:

"I have a confession to make. I think we all have to make a confession. Those who know Harry De La Roche, Jr., cannot blame him completely for his actions. How many of us perceived his loneliness yet continued to add to it. How many of us contributed to the mockeries? How many of us can honestly say that we have never harmed him? We forget what the word 'human being' means when it comes to others.

"Can you think of any Harrys that you know?"

XIV

Rahway State Prison

40

When we arrived at Rahway State Prison—still handcuffed and legshackled in pairs—we were taken inside to be stripped and searched. Then we were sized for clothes.

Outside, the prison didn't look too bad with its trees and low privet hedge, and somewhere I'd heard that once upon a time the slate-like dome that topped the sand-colored stone building had been the third largest dome in the world. Inside, I saw there were four cell blocks that extended from the circular structure underneath the dome. These cell blocks house inmates and offices, plus visiting and hospital facilities. The prison is overcrowded, though—so overcrowded, in fact, that a trailer park of eighteen trailers is used for specially screened minimum-custody inmates. Most of the time the inside is both dismal and damp, except for the overpowering heat we have to endure in the summer.

On the day of my arrival an officer conferred with me and asked me if I'd like to be placed in protective custody.

"You know this place better than I do," I said. "What would you advise?"

"Protective custody," he answered—so off I went to P.C., which was on the fourth floor.

Once up there I was put into a cell that measured approximately ten feet by six feet. This first cell—No. 210—consisted of two school desks, a bed, sink, and toilet. A little later I received the clothes for which I'd been measured, plus boots, a bowl, utensils, and a garbage pail. Again, I was in a windowless cell. But the corridor in front of the cells has windows on the other side, so during the time you're out of your cell you can look out and see the road that passes the front of the jail. Many of the P.C. inmates hang their laundry by these windows to dry.

The big thing on my mind in prison has been the pending appeal and the hope I have for this. While I was still in Yardville John filed a Notice of Motion for a new trial. This Notice—the first legal procedure for appealing the verdict—stated that John would make application to the Bergen County Court to grant me a new trial because of legal errors in my first one. According to law, John had to seek this new trial from the trial judge in the County Court before my conviction could be appealed to the Appellate Division of the Superior Court. The latter is a three-judge court, and this court can either overturn my four first-degree murder convictions or turn down the appeal. If the judges rule against me unanimously or two to one John will have to go to the State Supreme Court. If they rule in my favor the State will go to the Supreme Court.

By the time John submitted a brief in support of a Motion For a New Trial and asked Judge Madden to grant this trial on the grounds of the legal errors that were made we'd learned an interesting tidbit. This came in the form of an after-the-trial phone call to John's office from John Fitzpatrick, a Montvale teacher in the system I attended. In this call Fitzpatrick said he regretted he hadn't come forward and spoken up sooner. But after the verdict his conscience made him feel he must tell John that just about four days after the murders he had met Capt. John Hanna and Hanna told him I'd been a suspect right from the start on November 28, 1976. John got an affidavit from the teacher and presented it as new evidence and another argument that my cmnstitutional rights had been violated that day.

In his Motion For A New Trial John claimed that Judge Madden should not have permitted into evidence my two statements to police. He contended again that my constitutional rights were violated. He also said I was deprived of a fair trial because the statements to police were read into evidence by Detective O'Donovan and Inv. Frank Del Prete. John also contended he should have been allowed to introduce family letters because they would have supported an insanity defense. In addition, he stated the court should have declared a mistrial because members of the sequestered jury were permitted to have contacts with members of their family in an uncontrolled atmosphere.

After a hearing on this in March Judge Madden denied John's motion and rejected his contention that new evidence had been discovered and that legal errors were made during the trial. He said that Fitzpatrick's statement could have impeached Captain Hanna's testimony. But he felt the statement was not sufficient to warrant a new trial and he regarded the affidavit as rather weak. During the arguments, Richard Salkin pointed out that Captain Hanna was never involved in the investigation but was merely trying to locate Ronnie. Shortly after Judge Madden turned us down on a new trial John filed a Notice of Appeal on March 27, 1978, stating I was appealing to the Superior Court of New Jersey, Appellate Division. At this writing we're waiting on the appeal, and I'm hoping what I call an injustice will be rectified in this court.

There were other legal proceedings in March when the investigation into how the Long Island newspaper *Newsday* obtained and published details of my confession came to the front again. When that story, containing actual excerpts from the confession, appeared in December 1976, a Bergen County grand jury issued a presentment. I learned at the time that a presentment is a reprimand which does not involve criminal charges. After the presentment Judge Trautwein ordered the document sealed until the end of the trial. As a result, the "leak" was hushed up till March 1978, when Judge Trautwein met with Prosecutor Roger W. Breslin, Jr. and Montvale police officers, to consider police objections to the presentment. Supposedly the grand jury presentment was critical of the way the Montvale police handled the confession, and the cops objected to part of the presentment and reportedly wanted the document kept secret. Later, when the report was made public the grand jury recommended that the Montvale mayor and council discipline Det. Michael O'Donovan for allegedly allowing a reporter to copy the murder confession. The presentment called O'Donovan "grossly negligent" in permitting the reporter, Kenneth Gross of *Newsday*, to see and copy the statement I made. Thirteen latent fingerprints taken from O'Donovan's copy of the confession were identical to Gross's. Later the Montvale mayor and council defended O'Donovan and, after discussing the report, chose not to act. The mayor indicated the council would seek some type of light, disciplinary action at the regular council meeting. After that I understand the entire matter was completely hushed up with a token slap on the hand.

As those things go on in that other world beyond these prison bars I try to exist as well as I can while I wait for my appeal. I'm determined not to allow myself to become like some of the inmates, and I'm trying to maintain enough self-respect to remember the person I might have been if this whole thing hadn't happened. I still keep everything inside and show no emotions here. But the people who say I have no emotions weren't there when I went to the green room in Bergen County Jail. They weren't there at Montvale headquarters when I cried while I was alone. And they weren't by the graves in the cemetery when I said my goodbye to my family.

I'm not a cold, heartless bastard, and a lot of people know it—though here, as everywhere else in my life, people have mixed opinions about me. I've heard that some of the inmates say I'm very antisocial, and I guess it bothers some of them that I hardly come out of my cell. Sometimes I come out as little as only eight times a week. But I like to be alone in my cell, and I can't really help it if some people say I remind them of a bear in hibernation. I also get the word sometimes that some people think I'm arrogant and living in a fantasy world in order to forget my problems and cope with where I am.

Sometimes this place does get to me, and I feel alone and helpless. In fact, I wrote Tink Thompson one day that if I tend to sound flaky sometimes I may be getting terminal nerves. I often get down on being in here, knowing how few people believe me, and it really surprised and hurt me when one of my friends revealed he thought I was really guilty—but that he was still behind me. Lots of times it's a zoo in here, so it's easy to get depressed, especially with the racial bull and the homosexual advances. I still have a will to survive, so I try to hold my own.

My cell is drab and dreary and painted a neutral shade, and my bed with its sheet and blanket dominates one wall. A basin for washing and a toilet (with a cardboard box top for a cover) take care of another wall. The third has two foot lockers which hold most of my belongings. I use them as a table and for some of my stereo equipment. My stereo was sent down from the Greers, and I also have a TV. I have no chair or mirror and my rug is a piece of cloth. The only thing that looks like home is my familiar blue bathrobe that hangs in a corner of the cell.

While I'm locked in my cell I watch TV and listen to radio and stereo music that ranges from mellow to hard rock. I also read and write letters—and I think an awful lot. Sometimes—very occasionally—I go out of my cell to play cards. Most of the time it's boring as hell, and I'm unable to get a job while in the P.C. wing. In the future, I hope to take college courses that are given through Edison College. But until I can arrange this, I don' t know what I'll take.

By September 1978 there were occasional rumors I might be sent from Rahway to the Yardville Correction Center. But there were also ongoing rumors that I would be moved to general population—something that I dread very much because I fear for my life. One day I'd hear that a special committee was voting me out of P.C. Then the next day I'd get the message I wouldn't be moving right away. As I understand it, an inmate who is signed into P.C. is not supposed to leave it until he signs himself out. If this is the case, I won't sign a release, I feel a lot safer here.

In September I also turned twenty—and I got eight birthday cards. The first came from Roy Nilsen. Then, later, the Care Committee from my church sent me a birthday package from its voluntary "Love Collection." Tink Thompson sent me a food package, too. Tink also sent a *Nothing Book* in which she'd written an assortment of little sayings and poems. She's a friend, sister, and confidante, and her thoughtful gift meant so much to me I sat right down and wrote her.

Dear Tink:

Thank you for your words of friendship, love, and wisdom. I may not be able to write like that, but I'm sure you know how I feel toward you. Thank you for being there when I needed a friend and a shoulder to cry on. You are many things to me, and I'll never be able to put into words how special you are to me. But I think you know.

As I sit alone in my cell my thinking covers everything—from chocolate Oreo cookies and barbecued potato chips to how I can help my appeal. I know that I shot my brother—and there was a reason for it—and I also feel a sense of guilt for the three deaths I didn't cause since I didn't talk to Ronnie and try to do what I could. But whether there was a reason or not I'll never forget that night—and the days and nights ever since. I haven't grown bitter at the verdict. It wasn't the jury's fault. In fact, I don't hold anything against anyone connected with the trial.

But I do have unanswered questions about some things that happened. So when I'm thinking about them I ask again and again: What about the Montvale detective who leaked my confession to the press and then only had his hands slapped? How about the other two Montvale cops who told conflicting stories on the witness stand—and who got no charges or reprimands? Why did it take so many months for the state to start checking the evidence? Why were there contradictory statements by law officers on the evidence? Why didn't they check out the Type A and Type O blood in my brother's hands? Why didn't both Ronnie and I get a paraffin test? (Even though the police said at the trial they didn't want to give me the test I can describe the equipment because it was sitting in front of me before I was taken to the police station.) Why didn't the prosecutor's office check the body hair in the clothes they say I wore and the clothes they say Ronnie wore? They knew well in advance what I was going to say in court, and I believe they had hair samples from both Ronnie and me. But they didn't bring this up in court.

I'd also like to know why the doctors said my mother was never ill with cancer when the family doctor once said she had it, when she went through several operations, when she gave up smoking because of this scare, and when she mentioned her cancer in a letter to me? Why didn't the police follow up on the person I talked to at "Maximus" when they had the name and address in my wallet? Why didn't they check out my story with him? (The first time I saw the address again was when I saw my wallet in court.) Why were sequestered jurors allowed to go to an inn in South Jersey and talk to their families during the trial? And why didn't the defense know about it before the visit took place?

I get a respite from my thoughts through visitors and my mail, although the visitors who come here add up to a handful of people. John Taylor comes to confer with me, and I see him in a special cell reserved for visits with attorneys. The Greers, as my nearest relatives, have monthly contact visits, and I'm also permitted to telephone them on a weekly basis. Other visitors must come on weekends to a regular visiting area with the usual mesh between us. My church keeps me on its prayer chain, and I get its bulletins each week from a woman who has written to me from the time I went to jail. On the second Thanksgiving after the deaths I received a beautiful Thanksgiving card signed by many church members. I wrote a "Thank you" immediately that was read in church the next Sunday, and I told the people it was nice to know that there was someone out there, particularly at a time of year when it's always especially lonely.

I also telephoned the Greers—between Thanksgiving and November 28—and when we talked about my family and mentioned memories I said, "I don't know whether I've told you before, but I'm glad that you're both out there."

The people who write me letters help me tolerate prison life, and, though the mail keeps slowing up, those who continue to write me realize how lonely I get. I live through other people, so I always wish for more mail—especially from people my age who are busy doing the kind of things I'd normally be doing now. A lot of people ask me, "What should I write about?" and I answer "Write about yourself and what you do every week." I see the outside world through their eyes which is why I'm so grateful for mail.

Some of the very best letters I get are those that come from Chris Greene, one of the strangers who wrote me at the end of my trial. Chris is three months older than I, and through him I've been introduced to others who write me from South Carolina.

Chris has a sixth sense that comes to him in prophetic dreams, and even though some may scoff at this and wonder whether Chris is for real or a fantasy I've dreamed up, he is a very real person—and other persons in addition to Chris have vouched for the dreams he has. In one dream about a friend, he saw a car crash that happened four days later. In another he saw one of his friends standing, in black, by a tombstone inscribed "November 11." Two months later—on November 11—this woman's young son died. Chris described his dreams about me in the following letter.

Dear Harry,

How I came to believe in you and your story started a lot of years ago when a wise and loving black-haired woman who was old enough to be my grandmother made six predictions for my future when she came to me in a dream.

The third prediction was the most important. It was "Within four days following a major holiday, you'll hear a name. It won't mean anything at first. Then the name will stick in your mind. It will be the name of a northerner who will look guilty. But he'll be innocent. You should trust your first instinct."

Now let me go to November 28, 1976, when I heard a news report. That was the first time I heard your name. The report said you were from New Jersey and that fulfilled these predictions—the one about being a northerner and the one about four days following a holiday. I think then I said to myself, "Probably coincidence." But your name stuck in my mind, as I moved on to other things.

Later the dream that brought your name back into my conscious thoughts came in December 1977, when I had a dream about a young man on trial. Later I read in the papers that your trial was just starting in Hackensack, New Jersey.

As I followed the trial the same dream recurred several times, and it was always the same. It was like I was an observer in the court-room, but my presence seemed invisible. The jury came back in from deliberation, and the forewoman stood.

It was like I could see inside the young man's mind. He said over and over to himself, "I'm innocent, I'm innocent!" Then "Guilty! Guilty!" rang out in the courtroom. The young man was led away without showing any emotion.

Finally about three days before the end of the trial I decided to try and write you. I didn't know where to start except for your name and Hackensack, New Jersey. A little over a month later I got your reply. You said it felt good to know I believed you. Now that we correspond regularly I truly believe we're friends, and I know I believe in your innocence without doubts. I care about what happens to you, and I'm going to stand behind you.

Your friend,
Chris Greene

I'm sure I don't have to tell anyone how much this letter means—and how often I think of the circumstances that prompted Chris to write. My grandmother Greer loved the eerie and stories such as this, and I wonder about the coincidence of the woman who came to Chris—the wise, black-haired loving woman who was old enough to be his grandmother. It's a perfect description of Grandma Greer. But he couldn't have known about her since she died in 1970.

As I come to the end of this part of my story I wonder about the plan for my life and what will happen next. I believe in God and Jesus, and I think about getting out.

I still have faith in justice, too, so I'd like to say as my final statement—as I've said so often before—that I have no guilty memories of committing three of the murders. I have a picture in my mind of what happened November 28. To me that picture will always be there.

To me that's the way that it is.

Epilogue

Ever since the winter day when I first met Harry in jail, amid the clang of ringing bells behind a steel cell door, people have asked, "What is Harry like?" and, "Was he the guilty one?"

My obvious answer to the latter is, "A jury has stated 'Guilty,' while Harry continues to believe—and to say—he didn't commit four murders. But, as a person who sat with him for an uncalculated number of hours, I personally believe and will always feel that if he shot four people, only his body held the gun. "His mind and his heart—at that moment—didn't know what the body did."

As people discuss the unalterable mistake that happened November 28 many conclude that a great many persons were guilty contributors. In fact, some blame society as a whole for the De La Roche tragedy, for failing to see and to sense desperation before it was too late. But society is not—and can never be—an all-purpose guardian. Instead, it's a total of all of us, responsible on our own, for sensing and seeing troubles and needs in an individual way.

My answer to, "What is Harry like?" is summed up in the words, "He is the true fifth victim of a terrifying, fateful event." Thirteen months after the verdict he left Rahway to go back to Yardville. And as he sits in a prison cell with no way to get needed help, he's a fatality, in a sense, of a harrowing family disaster.

Yet given the same situation and same kind of breaking point, he's also the tall, lanky, hurt young man who might have been anyone's son instead of another number in the human dumping ground that's the prison population of arsonists, robbers, and rapists—and convicted murderers. I often think of his letter to me his third Christmas in confinement. It could have come from my own son—or any of his friends:

Dear Roberta,

Hi, how are you? Well, I hope. Hope you have a very Merry Christmas and a safe and happy New Year.

I got the Cream tape *Disraeli Gears* that you sent to me today. Thank you very much. Uncle John told me the trouble you had trying to find it and then finding it in 8-track and having to go out and look again for a cassette—when you learned that's what I needed. Thank you for going to all that trouble.

I'm playing the tape right now. There are two songs on it that I forgot were there, but I'm happy to have them.

Take care. I'll be waiting to hear from you.

Love,
Harry

Because of the contradictions and incongruities in this case—and the varying stories and viewpoints on the Harry De La Roche family—it has been a formidable task for the past two years to separate truths from untruths and determine which statements are right. Many nights I couldn't sleep as I tossed and turned till dawn searching for understanding and wrestling with assorted facts. Like everything else in Harry's young life there are—and always will be—conflicts that aren't quite resolved.

As of now the story isn't over. There are still loose pieces of the puzzle, and many of us who know Harry well (or as well as anyone can) wonder whether we'll ever know the whole story of November 28.

But still one truth stands before us: "It can—and did—happen here!"

So as we look for more answers and draw our own conclusions we're faced again with the question that will always be timely and timeless: Why do families go awry? What causes intrafamily breakdowns? How did this human tragedy start?

And where is it going to end?

R. R.